JUN 0 7 2019

P9-CRH-681

Why Superman Doesn't Take Over the World

Emily O'Roark

Why Superman Doesn't Take Over the World

What Superheroes Can Tell Us About Economics

J. Brian O'Roark

OXFORD
UNIVERSITY PRESS

OXFORD
UNIVERSITY PRESS

Great Clarendon Street, Oxford, OX2 6DP,
United Kingdom

Oxford University Press is a department of the University of Oxford.
It furthers the University's objective of excellence in research, scholarship,
and education by publishing worldwide. Oxford is a registered trade mark of
Oxford University Press in the UK and in certain other countries

First Edition published in 2019
Impression: 1

Published in the United States of America by Oxford University Press
198 Madison Avenue, New York, NY 10016, United States of America

British Library Cataloguing in Publication Data
Data available

Library of Congress Control Number: 2018954999

ISBN 978-0-19-882947-8

Printed and bound in Great Britain by
Clays Ltd, Elcograf S.p.A.

To Emily, Katie, and Maggie who still believe in superheroes, and to my mother who was one.

"Look up in the sky! Is it a bird? Is it a plane? No, it's Super-Econman, Brian O'Roark, the mild-mannered author of *Essentials of Economics* with his latest adventure, *What Superheroes Can Tell Us About Economics*. Brian uses the lens of economics to analyze the actions, reactions, and behaviors of dozens of superheroes. This light and breezy read will have your mind soaring as you learn to see your favorite heroes in an entirely new light. Up, up and away!"

Dirk Mateer
Author of *Principles of Economics* W.W. Norton,
and Professor, University of Arizona.

"Why doesn't Superman take over the world? This is just one of the many questions I didn't even know I needed answers to until I picked up this book. Whether you are a fan of comics, an economist, both, or neither, this book lets you dive into far-fetched worlds and realize that perhaps superheroes and villains aren't always so out of the ordinary. Using an economic perspective, Brian explores what drives superheroes to do the things they do, and be who they are. Why does Batman even need Robin if he can do everything Robin can and more? Why does someone like Spider-Man keep his true identity secret, while Reed Richards doesn't seem to mind if the world, and the villains out to get him, know who he really is? And of course, if Superman is so powerful on Earth, why doesn't he take over the world? With a fun and interesting take, it is revealed that superheroes alike, are faced with many of the same struggles as those they strive to protect, and aren't really that different from you and me."

Tahlia Murdoch
Host of the *Everything Economics* podcast.

"Economics and superhero stories seem worlds apart, but under the surface, they are very similar. Both build logically from premises to create convincing worlds, and our belief in those worlds depends on how well the models follow their own rules. Brian O'Roark cleverly applies the analytical tools of economics to questions that have stoked arguments among comic fans for decades, gently offering examples of economic reasoning and principles that today's students might find more entertaining than the typical textbook approach. With *Why Doesn't Superman Take Over the World?* O'Roark scores a trifecta, bringing social sciences, comics studies and pedagogy together in a unique and entertaining package."

Rob Salkowitz
Author of *Comic-Con and the Business of Pop Culture*,
FORBES contributor, and affiliate faculty, University of Washington.

"Brian crafts a captivating book that presents economic concepts through the lens of superheroes. This symbiotic relationship actually works! Just like the relationship between Batman and The Joker, or Superman and Lex Luther, Brian has managed to make superhero comics an integral part of the economics discipline. *Why Superman Doesn't Take Over the World* allows the reader to understand economics with ease while at the same time being entertained by the actionable stories of our favorite comic book superheroes. I'm convinced Brian goes to work incognito just like Clark Kent, so let this book be Brian's superhero gift to you in the pursuit of increasing your economics superpowers. I just wonder what color spandex he wears for his alter ego!"

Frank Conway
Lecturer, Waterford Institute of Technology
and host of the *Economics Rockstar* podcast.

Acknowledgments

As in the production of any book, there are many people who make the author look better than he really is. Even when the topic involves something as enjoyable as economics and superheroes, even when the early drafts are incredibly easy to write, there are people who bring you back to Earth and make the final product inestimably better.

First, Frank Conway deserves credit for making this book happen. Frank produces the *Economic Rockstar* podcast, and insisted, much to my dismay, that we talk about my nascent work on superheroes. Apparently, there is a larger audience for the pod than I imagined.

Christie McMahon and Jerry Isakoff were their wonderful selves. Thank you so much for the use of your place on the lake. Those four days made all the difference in completing the first draft.

To great friends who read early draft chapters for a variety of reasons. Jason Farone and Jarod Kettinger because they like economics; Ben and Janette Marnik because they couldn't believe comics and economics could go together; Matt Frey because he is curious; and Jeff Konzcal because he's my brother-in-law and an all-around great guy.

To the fantastic people at Oxford Press who made this endeavor possible, thank you. Even though the ink is dry, it seems impossible to think that this project happened. To, the amazing Katie Bishop who, in the comics is the new Hawkeye, but must have an alias as an editor, I can't believe you listened to Frank's podcast! Lydia Shinoj, who answered all of my questions and then some. Thank you so much for putting up with some rather odd requests. Elizabeth Stone for her expert editing work. Michael Janes for correcting the many grammatical errors and not making me feel too bad about it. Phil Henderson, Kim Behrens, and the marketing team, including the most amazing cover design artists in the publishing world. Alannah Santra, Catherine Owen, and all of the people at Oxford Press who made this a reality. You are a real life team of superheroes.

Finally, and most importantly, to my family, who allowed me to take time away from what they were involved with to write a book that mixes a very new interest with a much older one. Without their patience, and editorial and creative advice, there is no conceivable way this book would have become a reality. Now that it is complete, it is time to catch up on all those CW hero shows we got behind on. Thank you, and I love you.

Table of Contents

List of Figures

List of Tables

Introduction

For most, superhero stories and economics could not be more different. Superhero stories are entertainment, whilst economics is not generally seen as the most entertaining subject. Answering questions about what happens in the comics using economics may therefore at first glance appear to be a fool's errand—but economics isn't all theories and equations. It is a social science, born of the inquiries into human behavior that have fascinated us since the beginning of time. Economists—like sociologists, psychologists, political scientists, and historians—are trying to understand what makes people tick and, in discovering this, aim to make the world a better place. In that sense we're kind of like superheroes. Sure, we don't have the cachet of Superman, the ability to deliver a quip like Spider-Man, or the adoration of Wonder Woman. We're probably looked at more like the vigilante, dark and edgy. They get the job done but they're just on the border of legal, and the crowds are waiting to turn on them.

Who am I kidding? Economists are most definitely seen as the villains in comics are. A jumpy, twisted lot who revel in imagining we are the smartest people in the room, overlooked for the geniuses that we are, and lacking in social graces. As such we turn our powers to the misery of the world, creating diabolical torture devices such as profit maximizing formulas, Solow residuals, and Keynesian crosses, all while fomenting marginal revolutions. Considering the myriad of other tools at our disposal, the majority might have it right. Perhaps we are villains.

Before a conclusion can be drawn on that point though, I ask that you at least finish reading this introduction. Despite the possibility of diabolism, it is the purpose of this book to enlighten. Economists like to say that economics is everywhere, and I can think of no better testing grounds for that presumption than the world of comic book superheroes. If indeed the maxim is correct, these dreaded economic tools should be applicable even in the imaginary world of caped crusaders, masked marvels, and daring do-gooders. So, like a giddy tornado hunter, here is an economist running headlong into what is likely to be a chaotic and turbulent ride in the hope of answering some of the most perplexing comic book puzzles through the tricky tools of economics.

Most sections of this book revolve around peculiarities that have been raised by many comic fans, both casual and serious. As a more recent convert to comics, and an economist for longer than I'd like to admit, I bring a different perspective to these questions. Exploring why people pursue certain courses of action is part of the job of an economist, and with the tools of the trade at my disposal, this book provides a new angle on some of these questions. Issues such as why heroes fight each other (Chapter 4), who pays for all the destruction inflicted on innocent bystanders when heroes battle villains (Chapter 7), and how non-powered heroes can be part of the action (Chapter 8) are queries that are perfectly situated for economic analysis.

If you've never taken an economics course, don't be cowed. This book is for you. I have provided definitions of terms along with explanations of theories to guide you. If you have taken an economics course but it's been a while, then hopefully these applications will trigger some fond memories of an eloquent professor. If you are currently studying the dismal science,[1] this book will hopefully illustrate to you that economics can be found in places where you least expect it, and that by understanding the basics you will gain a deeper appreciation for the subject.

If you don't know anything about comics, this book is for you too! These days, comics are ubiquitous. Not only do superhero movies top the box office charts year after year in terms of attendance, and more importantly revenue, but they also form the premise for television shows, video games, and merchandise that are watched, played, or worn by hundreds of millions, if not billions, worldwide. An in-depth knowledge of comics is not necessary to read this book, however. If you have heard of characters like Black Panther, Captain America, the Flash, Spider-Man, or Wonder Woman, you've got all you need to know.

That being said, following comics can be a bit tricky. Story arcs are rarely straight. Continuity can be difficult to maintain and not every adventure written about a character makes it into the canon. There are many different types of stories and the links I will be making here are not always part of the accepted comic universe for particular characters. Some graphic novels provide excellent economic content but are stand-alone chronicles. What happens in those stories stays in those stories. For instance, if a character dies in a graphic novel, it doesn't mean they are dead in the rest of the comic world. To the avid comic readers, I apologize ahead of time for adopting this irreverent approach, but since this isn't a book about comic history I do not feel bound by the canonical limits of the stories.

Another issue that might irk some comic devotees is that I am openly and admittedly biased in my reading. I will chalk it up to watching cartoons in the 1980s but I have penchant for DC (although when it comes to movies, Marvel gets the nod). I have tried to temper that enthusiasm as much as possible but old prejudices are hard to squash entirely. You might think that my references to Batman, Superman, and Wonder Woman are too frequent, and that I have missed an opportunity to explain how the Hulk, Doctor Strange, or Ms. Marvel are equally impacted by economic circumstances. Believe me, I understand and would be more than happy to hear what you have to say about these characters. I came to comic books later in life and I admit there are lakes into which I have not dared to dip a toe.[2]

That's just to say that if I did not include your favorite hero, it was by no means intentional (at least it probably wasn't intentional, we all have biases against some characters, just as much as we have biases in favor of others). The most likely reason was because I just haven't had the time to read every comic out there. If you think there is something I missed, you are almost certainly correct, and I'd love to hear your insights.

A Brief Primer on Economics

Chapter 1 discusses what economics is in some detail, but I think it would be valuable to provide a quick introduction to economics for the non-economist at this point. Firstly, economics doesn't have to be mathematical, although it often is. It doesn't have to be dry and boring, although it often is. Economics doesn't need to be mystical, although it often is. According to one great economist, Alfred Marshall (1890/1920), economics is simply "a study of mankind in the ordinary business of life." That means that if you are human and engage at any level with other people, you are a walking model of economics. The reason we have to conduct such mundane business is due to scarcity, what some refer to as the economic problem. Humans are needy creatures, but even if we have all that we truly need to survive, there are many things we want. Whether it is due to wanton avarice or a vicissitude of fortune, there are always things we would like to have but cannot acquire. In this world there isn't enough of everything for everyone to have as much as they want, which means we all have to deal with scarcity, thus we all deal with economics.

The consequences of scarcity have led economists to split their discipline into two areas: micro and macro. Microeconomics is the study of how individuals, firms, and industries deal with scarcity in everyday life. It is a smaller analysis, but by no means unimportant. Macroeconomics explores larger scale events, data, and decisions. Things that happen at the national and international level are macroeconomic in nature. These terms are not meant to convey importance, rather they are descriptive. The distinction is made to better understand at which level of everyday life we are looking.

The economics of this book will lean much more heavily towards the micro. Characters in the stories make decisions that are driven by their own self-interest and will have relatively small-scale consequences. Why heroes wear costumes (Chapter 2), why a hero needs a day job (Chapter 5), and why criminals keep trying even in the face of constant defeat (Chapter 6) are questions focusing on the decisions characters make that impact their personal lives. Even when groups of heroes team up (Chapter 3), they are still confronting issues at a micro level as their choices will affect themselves and a smaller group of people. There are a couple of macro questions in the comics though, as sometimes hero work is geared toward the good of a nation, or the entire planet, as is the case in Chapter 9 "Why don't heroes take over the world?"

An Even Briefer Primer on Comics

Comics are made-up stories with made-up characters fighting made-up villains. It is pure, unadulterated fiction with pictures to help the story along. That does not mean they are for kids. Many comic stories are built around adult themes and some deal with particularly serious issues. Furthermore, comics are also not just a haunt for superheroes. Many comics and graphic novels skip the spandex and masks. While some stories are written to deliver a social commentary, most books are written and illustrated to tell stories and entertain readers. Despite the variety of comic formats, this book focuses on the fantastical world of heroes with exotic powers.

Within the world of hero comics there are two dominant producers: DC and Marvel. There are other, smaller publishers but the vast majority of characters find themselves in either the DC or the Marvel universe. As a comic fan, there is no need to swear allegiance to one set of heroes or another, although fans will often have a preference, perhaps tied to a favorite character. While there are some devotees who pledge their fealty, most readers are looking for well-developed characters and storylines. Beyond this, comics are written to indulge your imagination, and as such, there is nothing else more you need to know to follow the book in your hands.

Now, the Rest of the Story

This book is intended to help people appreciate two areas that are special to me: economics and comics. I have found that some of the most interesting developments in comics have economic undertones, whether the authors knew it or not. One of the reviewers of this book insinuated that comics are more morality play than real life and therefore aren't suitable for economic analysis. I couldn't agree and disagree more. We're dealing with people who possess extraordinary powers and who, more often than not, have to decide the best course of action to take with those powers. We can only hope that they make the right choices. In this context, comics are indeed morality tales; however, just because it is a morality play, doesn't mean the actors don't have to deal with economics. In fact, because they have to choose, they are, almost by definition, dealing with economics.

So, as we embark upon the adventure that awaits us in the coming pages, it is my hope that you find yourself reminiscing about the times when you fancied yourself a superhero. Those were carefree days when our imaginations were encouraged to run roughshod over anything that might get in our way. Hero stories have a way of making us dream of how the world should be. I remember, on frigid winter days when the teachers deemed it too cold to go outside for a break, playing an orderly game of some sort with the other kids. Unbeknownst to them, I was secretly a crime-fighting superhero who, without warning, would go flying through the kindergarten classroom in search of damsels in distress. Sadly, those days have passed me by. Perhaps I've become jaded, relegating the superheroes to the pages of comics where they occasionally provide some much-needed escapism.

This sad epitaph isn't the end of the story, though. There is a beam of light shining through the clouds offering a glimmer of hope for those brave enough to follow it. There are still powers to be discovered, they just come in different packages than our six-year-old selves might recognize. In the end, none of us have actual superpowers. Alas, there are no superheroes. However, we can employ a different set of powers, equally as mighty as the most over-powered character on the printed page, for at the end of the day, we are all economists.

Endnotes

1. It still baffles me that economics can be referred to as the dismal science. While the origin of this phrase is a bit fuzzy, good researchers have narrowed it down to Thomas Carlyle's critique of Thomas Malthus' prediction that the world was going to be devastated by a population time bomb, as described in Malthus' work *Principle of Population* (1798/1985). Very good researchers, namely David Levy (2002), explain that this view is entirely wrong. The phrase "dismal science" indeed originates with Carlyle, but comes from Carlyle's intense racism. While economists were arguing that the rule of law should be applied to all regardless of their skin color, Carlyle and his ilk were appalled that economists—the dismal scientists—couldn't see that slavery was the natural order of things.

2. One of the reasons I stayed on the sidelines for so long was that the internet helped me find out how many characters there are and how much I didn't know. That was intimidating and I had absolutely no idea where to begin. Eventually I just took the plunge by glomming on to a few childhood favorites.

References

Levy, D. (2002). *How the Dismal Science Got Its Name: Classical Economics and the Ur-Text of Racial Politics*. Ann Arbor, MI: University of Michigan Press.

Malthus, T. (1985). *An Essay on the Principle of Population*. New York: Penguin Books (Originally published in 1798).

Marshall, A. (1920). *Principles of Economics*. London: Macmillan and Co. (Originally published in 1890). Available at: http://www.econlib.org/library/Marshall/marP2.html#Bk.I,Ch.II [Accessed April 4, 2018].

1

Everyone Loves a Good Backstory, Even Economists

In Shakespeare's play *Twelfth Night* the protagonist Malvolio is told in a letter from Maria that he should not fear greatness. "Some are born great, some achieve greatness, and some have greatness thrust upon 'em" (Act 2, Scene 5) (Shakespeare, 1994). Comparing superheroes with Shakespeare might seem odd, but when exploring the origins of the characters who are stronger, faster, and tougher than the rest of us, this line of the Bard is particularly instructive. Heroes might be born with supernatural powers, but that does not guarantee greatness in the eyes of the world. There are, after all, plenty of villains who are graced with powers too. Instead, heroes "achieve greatness" on the mean streets of the cities they are trying to reclaim, in the dark vacuum of space, or somewhere in between. Heroes might also have "greatness thrust upon 'em." Not everyone is willing to assume the mantle of hero. Sometimes a life-threatening or civilization-ending situation is required for metamorphosis to occur and a hero to emerge. With apologies to Shakespeare, a reinterpretation of Maria's letter for superheroes might be that "None are born heroic, some achieve hero status because of the actions they take, others by the claims they stake, and still others because of the decisions they make."

While no one is born heroic, there are certainly some who are graced from birth with superpowers. These are typically heroes who are descended from gods—Wonder Woman and Thor are certainly destined for greatness. Like the titans of old, the destinies of these characters are wrapped up in their abilities to protect their homes and make the sacrifices necessary to stave off evil. Others achieve greatness by accident. The novel ways in which comic writers have attributed powers to ordinary guys and gals are legion. Superman would have been just another Kryptonian, but he was sent rocketing into space as his home planet of Krypton exploded. Fortunately for him, he landed on Earth, where environmental conditions spurred his powers. Captain America, Flash, Spider-Man, Wolverine, and myriad others accumulated their powers through experiments or coincidence. Others have indeed had greatness thrust upon them, sometimes through unusual occurrences—such as receiving a power ring from a dying alien (see the Green Lantern origin story) or through melancholy tales of woe such as the death of a parent at an early age. Such heroes experience a traumatic event that sets their lives on an unforeseen course.

All in all, heroes have unique starting points. The source of their powers is as much a part of the hero's identity as any of their famous escapades. These backstories set the tone for how each character views the question of what it means to be a superhero. Whether a hero's history is alien in nature, a reaction to the death of a loved one, a science experiment gone wrong, or derived from some hereditary capabilities, the recognition that they now possess powers and the discovery of what those powers can do forms an instrumental part of the story.

So, what does this have to do with economics? Actually, quite a lot. The transformation of a person from a civilian to a superhero, regardless of the process, not only alters them physically but also changes the way they live their lives. As Uncle Ben tells Peter Parker, "with great power, comes great responsibility."[1] Because they are endowed with super-human abilities, heroes can do things the rest of us cannot. This has direct consequences for many economic aspects of life.

Before we wade into the depths of economic analysis, let's begin by dipping our toes into the comic stream. This is a good way of testing the waters and warming up for what is to follow. Our first, most basic question is what does it take to become a superhero? The answers make superhero tales more engaging—and after all, who doesn't like a good origin story? As we explore their humble beginnings, we discover three fundamental economic ideas inherent in the genesis of a hero: incentives, utility, and productivity. Without at least one of these economic foundations, the extent to which we would have to suspend our disbelief of the tales to follow might be a bridge too far.

Why Do You Do What You Do?

If you asked an economist to define their area of study, you would likely get a wide array of answers. "The study of how we deal with scarcity" might be the most prevalent one. As humans we have insatiable wants. Unfortunately, we have limited resources to fulfill those wants. None of us have all the money or time to acquire or do everything we want in life. As a result, we have to make choices about which of our wants we will meet and which have to be given up. In reality, scarcity is a fact of life for every person in the world. For some it might mean that they do not have enough to eat or that they cannot afford a life-saving medicine; however, scarcity applies even to the wealthy among us. Jeff Bezos' fortune is vast, and he can buy pretty much any material goods he wants, but he still only has twenty-four hours in a day. How will he spend that time? As he has yet to invent a time machine (he isn't a superhero in the comic sense, after all), he must choose how to allocate this scarce resource. When he chooses to spend a given number of hours on the job, he must sacrifice time with his family. When he wants to relax, will he go on vacation to Monte Carlo or Courchevel? To try to do both would mean less time at each location or more time away from running his company. When you make choices, you give something up, and that is a signal of scarcity. As long as there are people who want things they cannot have, scarcity will exist, and it is left to economists to appraise how people and societies manage under this condition.

Not every economist sees economics as the study of scarcity. I had a professor in graduate school who was partial to the term catallactics. According to this view, the study of economics is essentially the disquisition of how we get what we want. Most of economic history has provided evidence that people accumulate things that make them happier by trading with each other. Alternatively, some have found war to be a way to acquire more without having to give up what they already possess (although the pesky threat of being killed or destroying the thing you want can limit this tactic). Throughout history, economic activity has been guided by exchange and it could be said that this is what catallactics really is: the study of exchange. While a segment of the economic community adheres to this definition, it is admittedly a very small segment.

Another, more popular response when you ask a room full of economists to define economics is that it is a study of how people respond to incentives. This seems far too easy an explanation for a subject that most people think of as falling between hieroglyphics and transdimensional physics, but it might be the most accurate of the lot. If we indeed live in a world of scarcity, where there isn't enough for us all to have everything that we want, then we must decide what we are going to acquire with our resources. Do you go to buy the newest edition of *Flash* when it hits the press, or do you wait and save that money, little by little, so you can fly to San Diego for Comic-Con? As a trip to the

Con can be expensive, you must be willing to give up other things to raise the funds to go. If attending the Con is what motivates you, that is your incentive to save for later rather than buying the new issue of *Flash* today.

What incentivizes us? Well, money is one thing. People do all kinds of outrageous things to make a buck. They work dangerous jobs, such as a deep-sea fisherman, underwater welder, or stunt double, for example. They make questionable ethical choices, such as dealing drugs, bribing officials, or stealing from their employers. Children take bets that they can jump their bikes over a couple of other kids lying on the sidewalk. We've all been lured by a quick payoff; if you need convincing then just look at how much money is spent on lottery tickets. You're more likely to be struck by lightning than to win.[2]

There are plenty of other things that provide incentives for us. Love makes us do crazy things. Listen to a country music station for long enough and you'll hear all about it. Some people use leisure as an incentive: If I just get through this week of work, I can do what I really want to do on the weekend! Once again, country music provides us with plenty of cases where the weekend motivates behavior. Retirement, buying a house, or sending our kids to college provide an incentive to save.

Incentives are what motivate us, and, not coincidentally, they can be found in the backstories of most superheroes. Understanding incentives allows us to see that heroes are like everyone else and they behave economically. In other words, they all respond to incentives. It's just that for heroes, incentives take them to extraordinary, sometimes other-worldly, places.

I'm a Hero Now

The most obvious example of an incentive leading to the creation of a superhero can be found in the backstory of Batman. Traumatized by witnessing the murder of his parents, Bruce Wayne's life is inexorably altered. The Waynes are murdered, young Bruce realizes the danger to the citizens of Gotham, and the Batman is born. This has been depicted in many ways since Batman's conception, but two of the more poignant tellings of the tale occur on the television show *Gotham* and in the comic arc *Batman: Year 1* (Miller and Mazzucchelli, 1987). In *Gotham*, we see the life of young Master Bruce in the years immediately after his parents' deaths. Raised and trained by the family butler, Alfred Pennyworth, Bruce is already thinking about the ways in which his life must change in order to protect himself and find his parents' killer. In *Batman: Year 1* we see an older and now trained Bruce Wayne returning to Gotham to begin his life as a vigilante. Although he isn't quite sure how to pursue this new vocation and makes some beginner's mistakes, he knows what is driving him; his incentives are clear. His motto says it all: "I made a promise on the grave of my parents that I would rid this city of the evil that took their lives. By day, I am Bruce Wayne, billionaire philanthropist. At night, criminals, a cowardly and superstitious lot, call me . . . Batman" (Loeb and Lee, 2002).

Batman isn't alone in being driven by revenge, yet not all heroes are compelled by such a disturbing cause. Sometimes, the incentive to be part of the hero world is to fight the bad guys; becoming a hero is a happy side-effect. Take Captain America's story (Kirby and Simon, 1941). Steve Rogers just wants to beat up some Nazis. Rogers' problem was that he was so weak and puny that the Army wouldn't take him, even during World War II. His intensity, however, attracts the attention of a scientist who is working on a super soldier serum. Unlike many heroes who take part in scientific experiments gone wrong, Rogers readily volunteers to be a guinea pig, despite the incredible risks that being injected with a foreign substance could present. Of course, the serum works and Rogers becomes the perfect physical specimen, a paragon of Nazi-fighting patriotism.

Othertimes, the incentive is more selfish. Doctor Steven Strange, world-famous surgeon (and super jerk), is in the medical field for all the right reasons, namely money and fame. However, his reflexes aren't quite what they need to be on the streets and, while racing his car on some back roads, he has a spectacular crash and badly damages his hands. Unable to perform the complicated surgeries he had before, Strange seeks a non-traditional solution for his injuries in the mountains of Asia. He may not have intended to learn the mystic arts, but in the pursuit of helping himself he first becomes the pupil of the Ancient One (think an Oriental Yoda), eventually becoming Dr Strange, the Sorcerer Supreme (Lee and Ditko, 1963a).

Still, at other times the incentive is to right a wrong that the hero has committed. In *The Rocketeer*, the titular character misses work when distracted by a rocket pack (Stevens, 1982). It just so happens that he works as a stunt pilot in an airshow. To give the crowd what it wants, the promoter presses a drunk pilot into service. Knowing that he should be in the plane and that the drunk and the spectators are in imminent danger, the Rocketeer dons the rocket pack and saves the day, thereby righting the wrong.

How Incentives Guide Our Actions

Economics addresses how people, communities, and nations determine how to best utilize their scarce resources in order to satisfy their unlimited wants. Incentives motivate economic actors to divert those scarce resources in a particular direction. Sometimes incentives are positive— for instance, if you do your homework, I will buy you ice cream. Positive incentives are the reward for doing something good. Incentives can also be negative. Consider how the student who won't do their homework might react if, instead of getting ice cream, they are threatened with the prospect of having their phone taken away from them if they do not finish their math assignment. Such a peril is a negative incentive: Do your homework or else!

The cases we have examined thus far may not seem as clear cut as to do or not to do your homework. No one is saying to any of these heroes that if you become the Flash, we'll give you candy. Nor is anyone saying that if you don't become Squirrel Girl, we'll send you to bed without supper. Rather, what is happening is that the events leading up to the transformation of a normal, everyday guy or girl have motivated them to choose a particular path. Steven Strange would never have pursued the mystic arts, even though it seems he has a particular aptitude for them, had it not been for the loss of his surgeon's touch. Without the evil of the Nazis, Steve Rogers would not have taken the super serum. He might have hit the weight room but he never would have become Captain America. Incentives change people's focus. However, there are two other kinds of incentives we have not yet discussed that may be more important to the superhero world.

Many incentives are direct, obvious. If Marvel starts a marketing plan offering you a $5 gift card if you buy the new *Jessica Jones* comic, sales of *Jessica Jones* are going to go up. It is a plain, old-fashioned incentive that leads to a predictable result. Direct incentives can be positive or negative. The case of the gift card is a direct, positive incentive. A direct, negative incentive might be, for example, if you are caught stealing a comic book from our store, we will paint you like Harley Quinn. Assuming such a threat is credible, it should stop most people from stealing. Direct incentives are easy to see. Where economists, the comic industry, everyday people, and even superheroes run into problems is when they face incentives that are not so straightforward.

Indirect incentives are the unforeseen results that arise when circumstances change. These are often referred to as unintended consequences. For example, as governments raise taxes on cigarettes, the direct incentive is that fewer cigarettes are sold. Even for a product as addictive as cigarettes, if you raise the price high enough, people will stop buying them. (If you don't believe this, go to New York to buy cigarettes. It may not get you to quit, but you will necessarily buy fewer of them. They are so expensive that buying a couple of packs could mean you don't eat for the week. Remember, limited resources prevent you from having everything you want). The unintended results of these high taxes include more home-produced cigarettes. More insidious, though, is that these high prices make the black market more attractive not just for sellers but also for buyers. If you can buy cigarettes in Virginia for a third of the price and drive them a few hours north, you can make a fortune by selling them to desperate New Yorkers for less than they would pay at the local bodega. This means sales drop in New York, which they were going to do anyway but, more importantly, tax revenue for the Empire State falls. That's not what was supposed to happen. With the combination of home growers and black market transactions, you may actually cause more smoking to take place in New York than before. Another possible side-effect of the high taxes is that people who want a chemically induced high, but find cigarette prices to be too prohibitive, switch to something else. Alcohol could be one thing but they might also move on to marijuana or some other illicit drug. At higher prices, the price differential between cigarettes and other drugs gets smaller. If they pack a bigger punch for each dollar spent, why not make the switch? The intention of raising cigarette prices is not to drive smokers from tobacco to cannabis, but that's the power of incentives.[3] People respond to them in predictable and unpredictable ways.

So, what are the unintended consequences in origin stories? Let's take another look at Bruce Wayne. He commits to fighting crime in Gotham to avenge his parents' deaths. This obsession leads to many problems for Wayne in the future. He is borderline neurotic, has no real friends, makes questionable decisions regarding romantic prospects, and in *Batman* #1 (King and Finch, 2016) we find him examining his life choices by talking to himself and his dead parents, wondering if his life was lived well enough to make them proud.[4] Bruce Wayne is a great crime fighter but he is a mess of a person. In fact, being a hero takes its toll on the people who have assumed the mantle. Personal relationships, if you have them, are at risk (see Chapter 2 on the burden of maintaining a secret identity). Physically, no matter what your healing factor, heroes take a pounding. Mentally too, there are scars. Deadpool, whose healing powers are so remarkable that he and Wolverine (who also possesses an overactive healing factor) regularly engage in gruesome battles where limbs are lost and more blood than a human could possibly possess is spilt, spends time walking through his own minefield of lost memories reminiscent of an Edvard Munch painting on LSD.

You might say that this is a part of the job and you would be correct, but when it comes to starting life as a hero, the possible downsides are rarely presented. Probably the most significant example of the unintended consequences of understanding one's new powers is Spider-Man (Lee and Ditko, 1963b). Bitten by a radioactive spider, Peter Parker wakes up with spider powers. He now has strength far out of proportion to his size and, in an underused technique for heroes, goes out to a local fight club to make some money. In the process, he allows a small-time criminal to escape. It turns out that this crook kills his Uncle Ben. The unintended consequence of doing nothing, when there was no real incentive to stop the thief other than it was the right thing to do, is the impetus for Spider-Man becoming the Web Slinger who protects New York City.

Fame is yet another motivator, but there is a problem for heroes who rely on it as their incentive: sometimes that fame results in significant problems for others. The siren song of celebrity instigates the Marvel narrative *Civil War* (Miller and McNiven, 2007). At the beginning of the comic, we see a group of low-level heroes setting up to raid a villain's safe house. These criminals have recently broken out of Ryker's Island Prison and are on the lam. The catch is that the raid is being taped by a superhero-based reality show film crew. In order to raise ratings for the show, this group of third-rate heroes decides to go after a more capable group of miscreants. The raid begins well. Three of the four escapees fall quickly but the fourth is determined to avoid capture. Tracked to a bustling elementary school, Nitro, who can explode himself and reform at will, does what villains do. To enact his escape, he detonates himself, killing at least one of the heroes and hundreds of school children. In the pursuit of fame, there can be consequences. In the hero world, the unfortunate side-effect of doing your job can be devastating, a topic that will be explored in more detail in Chapter 7.

What Makes You Happy?

While many protagonists get their start because of the incentives they face to do good, others get into the hero game because they are searching for a cause. They are inspired by existing heroes, or they want to be part of the excitement of fighting crime and cleaning up the streets. Maybe they're fed up with the bad guys running amok. Perhaps they are seeking adulation. Regardless, they want to be part of the pursuit of the criminal element because they think it will make their lives better.

Enhancing our happiness is the motivation for a lot of what we do in life. There are, of course, things we'd rather avoid: paying taxes, colonoscopies, holidays with the odd family member. We realize that in neglecting these things there are potential consequences, so, while they may not be the most fun, we swallow hard and do them. But we all know that if we could get out of these things, we would. In a world of limited resources, we want to utilize those resources to make our lives better, not worse. In economics, we use a somewhat abstruse term for happiness that derives from one of the more esoteric characters in economic history. The term is utility. The man was Jeremy Bentham.[5]

Utility is simply a measure of happiness. It is related to the idea of utilitarianism, which is probably most famous for the sop "the greatest good for the greatest number." This means that policy and life choices should be focused on making as many people better off as possible. According to such a theory, taking all my money and giving it to you and your brother is a righteous act because it would increase the good of society; after all, more people are better off. Utilitarianism is therefore fraught with moral concerns. How ethical is it to steal from one group of people and give it to a slightly larger group? In some places, that is referred to as mob rule. As a result, utilitarianism is not that popular among governmental philosophies.

Still, Bentham wanted to develop a way of making utilitarianism empirical so, being a good economist (well, maybe not a good economist, but at least a creative economist), he developed a unit of measure for happiness: the util. More utils means more happiness. According to Bentham's version of utilitarianism, people should pursue utils like a bloodhound on the trail of a rabbit and over time economists reasoned that such actions make sense. Under the assumption of acting rationally, people will try to gain as many utils as they can. At first blush, this may sound a little crazy but, then again, if you think of utils as Pokémon then perhaps it isn't so weird–you gotta catch 'em all.

The idea of utils forms the basis for determining how happy you are. The problem is, no one has ever seen a util, nor do we know how to compare utils between people. What is a util to you might not be anything to me. How many utils do you get by eating a box of donuts? What about the number of utils you get from watching *My Little Pony*? If Barry Allen returns from the Speed Force to reassume the mantle of the Flash does your util basket get bigger? It isn't going to be the same for each person and in some cases what increases your utils might decrease mine. After all, Wally West might be the best Flash in your mind and were he to disappear into the Speed Force you might be worse off. And then the question arises, how much worse off are you? Are my gains from seeing the real Flash reappear greater than your losses from seeing a second-rate Flash be sucked out of the storyline where he belongs?[6] This leaves economists in a bit of a conundrum: Are utils any good at telling us anything? In spite of this dilemma, the allure of being able to measure happiness remains. Economists say that rational people seek to increase their utility. We prefer to be happy than miserable; how we accomplish that is personal. In the case of costumed do-gooders, justice, revenge, power, and fun are all things that motivate heroes, but utility speaks to what satisfies them and, interestingly, some heroes realize that once their initial goals are met, they find that contributing to the good of all is more fulfilling than what was motivating them in the first place.

Nevertheless, there are some heroes whose origin stories are intertwined with the utility they receive from fighting crime. They look around and see that no one is doing anything, so they put on a cape and get to work. After the first few escapades they realize they like what they are doing and so they keep at it. Oliver Queen, who started out as a famous archaeologist,[7] had his origin story rewritten to make him a wealthy playboy who washes up on an island,[8] where he learns to survive using his bow (which he had conveniently grabbed before being swept off his boat into the sea), and defeats a drug-smuggling ring.[9] The action and adventure, coupled with a sense of doing the right thing, makes for quite a turn from his lecherous lifestyle.

Luke Cage, also known as Power Man, is subject to experiments while in prison for a crime he did not commit. In a spate of comic book karma, a corrupt guard who wants Cage dead disrupts the experiment, causing Cage to develop unbreakable skin and super strength (Goodwin and Tuska, 1972). He escapes prison and returns to Harlem, where he hangs his shingle as a "Hero for Hire." The comics depict Cage as hard-working but certainly not altruistic. He will help anyone as long as they can meet his price but, being a good guy at heart, he starts saving people gratis, which cuts into his income stream. Eventually he is put on the payroll of a group of heroes called the Defenders. Now with a regular paycheck, Cage can do something that helps others, thereby increasing his utility, and pay the bills.

Wonder Woman falls into the category of a hero who leaves her home because of a desire to do something more with her life. Wonder Woman, known as Princess Diana by her country women, lived on an island inhabited by a female warrior race, the Amazons, that was protected from the world of men by the goddess Aphrodite. When a man washes up on the shores of Paradise Island, Aphrodite commands that one of the Amazons must be chosen to return him to America and remain there to fight war and evil. Princess Diana's mother, the queen of the island, arranges a contest to find the worthiest Amazonian warrior, but prohibits the princess from participating. Diana dons a fairly transparent costume that amazingly befuddles the queen and wins the tournament. Her sense of honor intact, Diana heads to the world of men with the intention of helping America to win the war.[10]

As we will discuss later, this idea of utility is also something that keeps people engaged in the never-ending fight over who is the greatest superhero (Chapter 10). But before we close this chapter, let's take a look at one final issue that arises as ordinary people acquire superpowers.

How Are You Going to Use Those Superpowers?

Characters in hero comics are as often as not just people minding their own business when some seemingly random phenomenon transpires and sets them on a path to superpower stardom. Such accidents of fate are regular occurrences in the genesis of characters, be they scientific experiments gone wrong, acts of nature, or scientific experiments gone right. These accidents are kismet for some, a curse for others. Regardless of what the character thinks of their new reality, there is one inescapable and palpable certainty: their life is now entirely different.

Take the Green Lantern, for instance. Hal Jordan was an Air Force test pilot,[11] who as a child witnesses his father, also a test pilot, crash a plane and die (Broome and Kane, 1959). The brash, cocky, and at times entirely dislikable, Jordan follows in his father's footsteps despite protestations from his family. By most accounts, Jordan is an exemplary pilot, despite being prone to taking risks—from which he always makes an escape. One fateful night, a member of the Green Lantern Corps, an intergalactic, alien protection force, crash-lands not far from Jordan. The power of the dying alien's ring draws him to find his replacement on Earth. While the job of galactic policeman might have intrigued the risk-loving Jordan, he certainly did not seek it out. Instead, it sought him. Jordan had no inclination to become a superhero, yet once he puts on the ring and feels the power associated with it, there is no turning back. In fact, Jordan becomes one of the most powerful Lanterns in the galaxy.[12]

In the early Green Lantern comics, in spite of his newly acquired skills Jordan continues to work on Earth, being called away for various emergencies. Constantly off battling space villains and monsters in this early incarnation of the Green Lantern, the hero is rarely seen actually working, which begs the question: how does he keep his job? We'll return to a possible answer to this question later.

First, however, let's consider the events surrounding the origin of the Flash. Barry Allen is a gifted, if perpetually tardy, crime scene investigator.[13] In a fortuitous lab accident, Allen is doused with chemicals that are propitiously struck by lightning. When he wakes up he realizes that, yet again, he is going to be late for a date. He starts to run and discovers that he now has super speed. Already part of the police force, Allen announces that he will use his speed to help thwart crime (Broome and Infantino, 1959). As the story develops, we learn that not only can he run fast, but he can do everything fast, including collecting and processing evidence. Employing his speed, Allen continues to assist the police in fighting crime.

Let's also consider one more backstory before the economic lesson ensues. Wade Wilson was a troubled child. His mother died when he was young and his abusive father was murdered. The predictable course for Wade was that, after a very brief stint in the military, he ends up a mercenary (OK, that might not have been entirely predictable). At some point, he discovers he has cancer, the same disease that killed his mother. Desperate for a cure he agrees to participate in a study run by Department K, the Canadian government's version of top-secret, sci-fi weapons development. He is given an experimental dose of healing factor that enables his body to rapidly regenerate after suffering any injury, including gun shots, knife wounds, amputations, and, apparently, cancer (funnily, these healing factors haven't cured the horrible disfigurements he sustained while in the care of the Canadian government's weapons program). Nevertheless, the healing factor, along with a tremendous amount of training with heroes and villains, makes Wade Wilson, now known as Deadpool, a lethal assassin. Deadpool, the "Merc with the Mouth", may never shut up, but he gets the job done.

So You're a Hero Now? What Can You Do?

Green Lantern, Flash, and Deadpool come to the position of hero in very different ways, but they have one thing in common: they are now more adept at their jobs then they used to be. In economics, we recognize that in order to become more productive, businesses and societies can follow several paths. According to economists, productive means how effective an input is at producing output. If you want to make more things, you can hire more inputs; put more workers on the factory floor, hire more programmers, hire 1,000 monkeys and place them at

1,000 typewriters.[14] With more labor there will be greater output, but the quality may be questionable.

Another way to increase productivity would be to improve the quality of the inputs. Technological innovation happens pretty quickly these days but staying on top of the latest and greatest can be expensive. Investing in capital does not happen overnight, and even when it is accomplished it might be that, due to the rapidity of technological change, your new robots, factory, or machinery are already out of date. A better option than capital accumulation might be to spend some resources on developing your labor force.

Economists call this option human capital development and it is one of the most important avenues of economic advancement. Firms that want to get the most out of their employees cannot sit idly by, expecting their workforce to keep up with the pace of business. For productivity to continue, workers must improve their skill sets. Among other things, this is accomplished by achieving higher levels of education, job training, and on the job experience. Basic training for workers on how to utilize a computer can increase productivity in manifold ways. Think about how much more productive employees are when using the internet to communicate, or word processing software to type, as opposed to using fax machines and typewriters (and think about how much less work the monkeys would have to do if they had been trained to use Microsoft Word!). While important for blue-collar jobs, this is equally important for those who work in highly skilled areas. A doctor who doesn't learn about new procedures and treatments for patients puts them at risk.

This brings us to the punchline for Green Lantern, Flash, and Deadpool. Another way in which an individual can increase their human capital is by becoming a superhero. The powers that Hal Jordan, Barry Allen, and Wade Wilson are granted, regardless of how they were acquired, have made them vastly more capable of doing their jobs. Hal doesn't get fired because, thanks to his power ring, his productivity has increased so much that he can complete his work at Ferris Aviation while keeping Sector 2814 safe from marauding aliens. Barry Allen may still be late for a date but his speed at getting the job done, and his ability to do it well, keeps him fighting crime as the Flash while he remains employed with the police department. Wade Wilson can now execute his duties without fear of being shot, stabbed, or maimed. This means he can carry out his directives much more rapidly and effectively.

Because we know the backstories of heroes, we can see what they were like before. Some were successful and became more so. Others were floundering and became invaluable. By increasing their human capital, these ordinary men and women become extraordinarily productive.

It's Only the Beginning

Origin stories are part of the fabric of superheroes. While the initial issues of a hero's exploits provide minimal background on who they are and where they came from, those characters whose names are familiar to fandoms large and small have seen a history built up around them. Often those origins are retconned for one reason or another. For instance, Thor didn't start as the Norse god of Thunder. He was a handicapped doctor who stumbled upon a hammer with some magic words etched into it.[15] Aquaman's backstory also had a significant reboot from its incipient form where Arthur Curry's father used Atlantean science to imbue his son with powers. In this version of the story, Atlantis was a long-dead civilization. In the new version, Arthur's mother gets kicked out of the underwater kingdom for spending too much time with the surface dwellers. She marries a lighthouse keeper and gives birth to the future king of Atlantis. Hawkman's and Hawkgirl's backstories are so convoluted that it might take a Ph.D. in falconry to decipher them. Hawkman is either an archaeologist named Carter Hall who discovered a mystical metal out of which he built wings, a police officer from the planet Thanagar named Katar Hol, a combination of both characters, or a reincarnated Egyptian named Prince Khufu who finds an alien metal that transforms his soul. Hawkgirl is either a Thanagarian warrior and police officer who just really loves hanging out on Earth, a reincarnation of the Egyptian Chay-Ara (later Shiera after a few thousand years of reincarnation) who is linked to Prince Khufu for all time, or Kendra Saunders, the niece of Shiera who kills herself but is resuscitated by the soul of aunty Shiera Hall.[16] Even the great Spider-Man backstory has been tinkered with. In a 2001 story arc, it was explained that the radiated spider that bit Peter Parker was really a spider totem-spirit (Straczynski and Romita, 2001). The radiation did augment his powers, but it wasn't the radiation that was fully responsible for turning Peter into Spider-Man. The spider was going to bite him anyway. The radiation was just a coincidence.

The backstories of heroes are always complicated. Narratives are revamped, and new personas are introduced to keep up with the times and changing story arcs. Yet, behind nearly all accounts are three economic principles that whet reader's appetites for the source of these fictional characters. Incentives provide the foundation for why some people, powered or not, join the fray. There are a variety of motivations for putting on the tights, including revenge, fame, and fortune. These incentives are certainly not all pure, and sometimes there are unintended consequences for the decisions made, but that is part of making choices. It isn't any different for the non-heroes who live among us. We do not have a clairvoyant crystal ball that tells us how the future will unfold, and looking back on life, sometimes we make bad choices. Nevertheless, the incentives put in front of us guide our actions and might just lead us into a life of crime fighting.

Another economic force that drives the origin stories of superheroes is utility. It is clear that for some crime fighters the life they are living is a burden. The weight of keeping a city and its people safe sits like the world on their shoulders. Many other heroes take up the crime fighting mantle with joy. Their backstory essentially explains that "if I didn't fight crime, I would be nothing." The rush of adrenaline, the opportunity to save the day, and the adulation of the masses are more powerful than any drug. The brushes with death, the lack of a social life, and the bumps and bruises are all worth it. They are just happy to be fighting the bad guys.

Finally, origin stories illustrate how becoming a superhero makes someone more productive. As readers, we are amazed at how rapidly heroes can construct a hideout. We marvel at their record-breaking comprehension rates. Their strength lets them lift burdens that would take construction crews hours or days, their speed makes global travel an afterthought, and their stamina makes us ashamed that we can only work an eight-hour day. Because of their powers, these heroes can do so much more than us mortals. They are an employer's dream, although they prefer to be their own bosses.

Of course, the origin story is just the beginning. Once the transformation from ordinary Joe to superhero happens, expectations for your life change. It is a new day with a new job, and starting a new job usually means some new clothes. Superheroes might put their pants on one leg at a time, just like anybody else, but their pants are probably more colorful and form-fitting than yours. In the real world, people don't normally go to the office in spandex tights, a cape, and a mask. Honestly! Why do we as readers accept that these supermen and superwomen look as if they're on their way to a Halloween party? The answer is an economic one. When heroes don their masks, risks rise up like cockroaches in the Texas heat, not just for them, but for the people they care about. Protecting as many people as possible from those risks requires some innovative insurance, which means you are going to have to go to work incognito.

Endnotes

1. While this is traditionally attributed to Uncle Ben, the original line appeared in a caption at the end of *Amazing Fantasy* #15 (Lee and Ditko, 1962). In *The Ultimate Spider-Man* #1 (Bendis, Jemas, and Bagley, 2000), Ben delivers a speech to Peter saying something similar to this. The most famous recitation of these words of wisdom occurs in the movie *Spider-Man 2* (2002).
2. For instance, each Powerball lottery ticket has a one in 292 million chance of being the winner. According to the National Weather Service (n.d.), the odds of being struck by lightning are one in 1,083,000.
3. The argument that cigarettes and marijuana are substitutes for each other is an unsettled one. Goel's (2009) research suggests that they are. This would mean that as the price of cigarettes rise, the quantity of marijuana demanded would also rise.
4. This is the 2016 *Rebirth* series #1, not the original Batman comic.
5. For his time (1748–1832), Bentham was unique, an advocate for women's rights, separation of church and state, the right to divorce, and the decriminalization of homosexuality, which certainly set him apart; however, he is possibly most known for his will, in which he asked to have his body dissected and the remains dressed up and seated in a glass enclosed box. This, of course, was done. His skeleton, padded and dressed, along with a wax head (the original didn't really look so hot after a poor effort at mummification), naturally fitted with some of Bentham's own hair, can be viewed at the University College London. Interestingly, there have been a few occasions when the remains were wheeled out to attend a meeting of the College Council. At these meetings, Bentham is listed as present, but not voting.
6. Fans of the Flash comic usually have a favorite alias as there have been a few different speedsters to call themselves Flash. Jay Garrick was the first, then came Barry Allen. Barry was supposedly killed by a villain from an alternate dimension called the Anti-Monitor. This left the position of Flash to Wally West, who was the only Flash for a number of years until Barry was able to break out of the Speed Force, a field of energy from which all Speedsters derive their powers and to which Barry had been merged. As you might have guessed from the discussion, I prefer Barry Allen because he is the Flash I remember from my youth.
7. This is the original origin story from More Fun Comics (Samachson and Young, 1943).
8. This is the silver age re-write by Kirby and Herron (1959).
9. The comic origin story is a bit different than that of the television show, although both involved Oliver being stranded on an island where his skills are honed.
10. This is based on the origin story found in *Wonder Woman* #1 (Marston, 1942).
11. The first Green Lantern was named Alan Scott, who starred in 38 issues throughout the 1940s.

12. If you aren't intimately familiar with the Green Lantern saga, there are around 3,600 Green Lanterns, not to mention countless other Lanterns of different colors. Hal Jordan's responsibility is to space sector 2814, into which Earth falls.
13. The first Flash was actually Jay Garrick. He inhaled some gas while in the lab, which gave him his super speed. Garrick was the Flash from the inception of the comic in 1940 through the end of the decade. He still shows up now and then in stories with Barry Allen and other Flash characters.
14. Lest you think I jest, this is known as the infinite monkey theorem. The premise of which is that, given enough time and enough monkeys, primates pounding on typewriter keys could randomly reproduce a work of great importance, such as Shakespeare's *Twelfth Night*. Probabilistically, this could occur, but the odds are very, very long. You might as well start buying Powerball lottery tickets with the hope of winning four or five times in a row.
15. This gets explained away as Odin, Thor's father, reached the point where he was so sick of Thor that he transformed him into a mortal. This reveal happened years after the original story (Lee and Kirby, 1968).
16. If I've missed anything here, please forgive me, there are simply too many variations of Hawkman's and Hawkgirl's origin stories.

References

Bendis, B., Jemas, B., and Bagley, M. (2000). *Ultimate Spider-Man*, #1. Marvel Comics.

Broome, J. and Infantino, C. (1959). *The Flash*, #105. DC Comics.

Broome, J. and Kane, G. (1959). *Showcase*, #22. DC Comics.

Goel, R. (2009). Cigarette Prices and illicit Drug Use: Is There a Connection? *Applied Economics*, 41(7–9), 1071–6.

Goodwin, A. and Tuska, G. (1972). *Luke Cage: Hero for Hire*, #1. Marvel Comics.

King, T. and Finch, D. (2016). *Batman*, #1. DC Comics.

Kirby, J. and Herron, E. (1959). *Adventure Comics*, #256. DC Comics.

Kirby, J. and Simon, J. (1941). *Captain America*, #1. Captain America Comics.

Lee, S. and Ditko, S. (1962). *Amazing Fantasy*, #15. Marvel Comics.

Lee, S. and Ditko, S. (1963a). *Strange Tales*, #115. Marvel Comics.

Lee, S. and Ditko, S. (1963b). *The Amazing Spider-Man*, #1. Marvel Comics.

Lee, S. and Kirby, J. (1968). *Thor*, #159. Marvel Comics.

Loeb, J. and Lee, J. (2002). *Batman*, #608. DC Comics.

Marston, W. (1942). *Wonder Woman*, #1. Wonder Woman Publishing Company.

Miller, F. and Mazzucchelli, D. (1987). *Batman*, #404–407. DC Comics.

Miller, M. and McNiven, S. (2007). *Civil War*. Marvel Comics.

National Weather Service. (n.d.). How Dangerous is Lightning? [Online] National Weather Service. Available at: http://www.lightningsafety.noaa.gov/odds.shtml [Accessed April 4, 2018].

Samachson, J. and Young, C. (1943). *More Fun Comics*, #89. DC Comics.

Shakespeare, W. (1994). *William Shakespeare: The Complete Works*. New York: Barnes and Noble Books.

Spider-Man 2. (2002). [Film]. New York: Sam Raimi.

Stevens, D. (1982). *Starslayer*, #2. Pacific Comics.

Straczynski, J. and Romita, J. (2001). *The Amazing Spider-Man*, #32. Marvel Comics.

2

Who Is That Masked Man?

If you have ever considered becoming a superhero (and who among us hasn't?), you have probably also considered what superpower you would possess. Perhaps after missing the school bus you imagined running faster than the speed of sound (or at least faster than the bus). It would be incredibly convenient to have rapid healing powers after bashing your thumb with a hammer. Maybe there was a day that you forgot about a test—being able to read the teacher's mind would certainly come in handy.

Settling on a superpower is an imperative first step in any superhero reverie. Once you have established a power though, you are faced with two other related decisions that could make or break your career. The first is a credible name. Don't take this lightly. A solid hero name should describe who you are and what you do. Those unlucky enough to run up against The Hulk know to expect a huge and menacing opponent. If their adversary was called the Husky or the Jumbo, the message that you are better off avoiding this guy might not be quite so clear. Names not only establish identity but also reputation. Criminals tremble at the mention of Batman. Bats are kind of creepy and so is the man under the cowl. It is a curious juxtaposition that Batman's sidekick is Robin, a sign that spring is just around the corner after a long harsh winter. What's in a name? A hero by any other name might end up as the butt of many jokes, or in the dustbin of history.

Ruminate on some of the strange but true names of forgettable comic book rubes. Bouncing Boy and Matter Eater Lad were the inspiration of Jerry Siegel who, fortunately, had Superman to fall back on. 3-D Man was a result of Jack Kirby and Stan Lee hitting the wall of creativity (after so many successes they were bound to fail at some point). Negasonic Teenage Warhead is about as convoluted as a name gets and doesn't tell you much about this telepath who is connected to the X-Men.[1] Other names, in retrospect, should have been left on the cutting room floor.

Fruit Boy (he can grow fruit really quickly), The Whizzer (who can quickly run away from the bad guys who laugh at his name), Arm Fall Off Boy (guess what his power is), Lady Fairplay (infused with the spirit of justice), or Absorbing Man (who turns into the stuff he touches) are some of the ignominious names of heroes. In fact, the list of poorly-named characters is longer than the lines at Comic-Con. There is a reason you have probably never heard of these heroes, and why the powers they possess aren't featured in the most banal of superhero daydreams.

The other component of assuming a superhero persona is your costume. While you might not ever contemplate pulling on brightly colored spandex, the unforgiving tights are essential for most heroes. Part of this is marketing of course. As the world of heroes gets crowded you want to be able to distinguish your brand. A memorable logo and the right color combinations will help ensure some longevity. Getting the right look is important. The Green Lantern ought to be wearing green, and Deadpool wears red because it hides the blood better. Yet these choices aren't just aesthetic—the costume is the first line of defense in keeping the public and private lives of superheroes separate.

This chapter explores the economics behind maintaining a secret identity, and why heroes exert so much effort to obfuscate their enemies and preclude the press from outing them. At the most superficial level, costumes keep the bad guys guessing and close friends and family from becoming fodder for ruthless fiends. But there is an economic spin that can be put on the cosplay. By applying some basic cost tenets, and one of the most transcendental of economic powers, we can understand how rational it is to keep your face disguised and your real name confidential.[2]

What Do I Have to Lose?

To begin with, some heroes never adopt a secret identity. Powerman doesn't bother with a costume, even though his Heroes for Hire partner, Iron Fist, dons a green and yellow jumpsuit. Iron Fist's alter ego is Danny Rand, the child of a wealthy entrepreneur and heir to Rand Enterprises, so he has more to hide. Powerman's situation is very different. Due to his unbreakable skin, Powerman comes complete with a defense mechanism, so if a bad guy tries to hurt him, even in his sleep, they will need some serious weaponry to prevail.

Additionally, Powerman is married to Jessica Jones, a superhero significant other who can take care of herself, giving him one less thing to worry about. The Fantastic Four also share this characteristic; the people they hold most dear are each other. Reed Richards is married to Sue, whose brother, Johnny Storm, is also part of the crew, and Ben Grimm, the Thing, is Reed's best friend. Even if everyone knows their identities, the closest family and friends of the Fantastic Four can all defend themselves.

Most heroes, however, do try to keep their identities hidden. Their family members aren't super-powered and as a result can be liabilities. A common trope in comics is when the girlfriend, child, or parent of the hero is captured by the villain and threatened with harm. This means that a hidden identity has the advantage of ensuring that unscrupulous criminals don't know who to pursue. Sometimes, however, the rationale for remaining unknown is more self-interested.

Batman keeps his identity hidden not so much to protect others but to protect himself. Due to his obsessive vigilantism, Bruce Wayne doesn't form personal bonds very easily. Other than his association with Alfred, his relationships are often toxic. As a result, there are few people in his life who need protecting. Instead, his motivation for his undisclosed identity is his desire to continue his vigilantism—he is so successful at putting criminals behind bars that if anyone found out who he really is, the entirety of the criminal element would descend upon Wayne Manor like a swarm of locusts, breaking up the operation. For Bruce Wayne, his motivation for remaining secret is to continue his run as Batman.

Yet another reason to keep an identity under wraps is to maintain some privacy. Some heroes such as Tony Stark (Ironman), Johnny Storm (the Human Torch), and Crackerjack crave attention;[3] they really don't seem to care who knows who they are. Most other heroes need to be able to get away from it all on occasion and being anonymous promotes that goal.

For the comic fan, these revelations aren't new. Secret identities are part and parcel of the storylines of superheroes. Imparting an economic slant on this subject may seem superfluous. Surely the attempt to protect an identity is self-explanatory? After all, we've spent the last four pages doing just that. This is an economics book, though, and we have yet to touch on that aspect of identity preservation.

Every Choice Has a Cost

Economists are fond of saying there is no such thing as a free lunch. This means that no choice is costless, even if you do not have to pay money to acquire something. Think about a situation in which the boss comes into the office and offers to buy everyone lunch. Your co-workers are excited. The boss usually provides a pretty good spread when picking up the check. You start to think that whatever is served will certainly be better than the cold ham and cheese sandwich you have in the break-room. The office is eagerly anticipating lunch but to your surprise the boss says "everyone to the lobby, I've got a bus chartered. We are going out to eat!" Whoa! No one expected this. Three cheers for the boss! On the way to the restaurant everyone is chatting, the mood is high, the boss is nodding his thanks as everyone sings his praises. But you notice something odd. The boss has a sly look. Something doesn't seem quite right.

When you arrive at the restaurant, everyone disembarks and the wait staff ushers you to a reserved room. As soon as you step through the door you realize the trap. In the room there is a man in a suit, a man you recognize from the accounting department. He has a laptop and a projector set up and you can hear him quietly humming to himself. GASP! This isn't a free lunch at all! This offer was just a cover for the tedium that is the quarterly sales meeting!

No matter how good the food is, the cost of this meal just became exorbitantly high because of what is included as part of the process. The proposal that there is no such thing as a free lunch means that even if someone else is paying for it, there is some cost involved for the participants. Obviously these aren't monetary costs. Those are being picked up for you. The costs here are of a different nature.

When economists talk about costs we mean more than just what you pay for something. In fact, when you buy a movie ticket, a back issue of Nightwing, or the newest action figure, economists aren't talking about costs at all. When you make a purchase you are paying a price. Prices are determined by the interaction of demand—what the buyers want and how much they are willing to pay—and supply—what the sellers have produced and how much they are willing to accept to part with their goods. In a free-market economy these prices are not handed down from the price gods. There is no political body meeting in a smoke-filled room where the good of society is weighed before the price of baby spinach is graciously bestowed upon humanity. No, prices are much more of a mystery. Somehow, prices are determined without a centralized authority getting in the way. Adam Smith, still a force to be reckoned with in economics even though he died in 1790, referred to market competition channeling self-interest as occurring via the invisible hand[4]—a superpower that might best be analogized to Dr Manhattan, or Jean Grey on a Phoenix bender.[5] The invisible hand is an uncontrollable, fate-altering force that unifies opposing interests, interests that are brought into alignment through prices. The invisible hand is underestimated at every turn, and when evil miscreants try to thwart the invisible hand, their efforts are always met with disaster.

The Invisible Hand: Bringing Buyers and Sellers Together since 1776

The invisible hand is the impetus facilitating market activity, and before you dismiss the importance of this, consider that without markets it is unlikely you would have gas for your car, coffee for your commute, or even an affordable pencil. You see, markets provide the framework for bringing buyers and sellers together and it is the invisible hand that coordinates the price that is agreeable to both the buyer and the seller. Given that it is in the interest of the seller to charge as high a price as possible and it is in the buyer's interest to pay as low a price as possible, it might be the case that no transactions would take place, since each party is only interested in achieving what is in their own best interest. Put another way, both the buyer and the seller are really selfish. If no trades were to take place then the buyer and the seller would actually both be worse off!

Envisage this scenario. A comic book dealer has a new stack of X-Men comics. She knows that fans will be tromping down to her store after work to pick them up. The last issue ended with a tremendous cliff-hanger and Marvel has kept the conclusion to the story tightly under wraps. Because she knows all the X-Men fans must get their hands on this issue she decides to sell copies for $200 a piece. When the work day ends and the readers rush into the store, they are shocked by the obvious attempt at highway robbery. The store owner won't budge on the price and the fans file out of the store to get their X-Men fix elsewhere. The store owner has a stack of unsold comics and the readers are left having to go far afield to find the books. No one is happy.

Enter the invisible hand. While the store owner would like to sell lots of books at $200, she can't. Not even the most devoted fan will pay that. They have limited resources. So, the invisible hand whispers "lower the price." Bemused by the disembodied voice, the store owner rushes to the door of the shop and yells "Wait! Come back!" The disappointed fans lift their collective heads and turn them towards the shop owner's pleading cries. "How much do you want to pay?" she asks. A murmur runs through the crowd and they collectively call out "$1.00!" The shop keeper's shoulders slump. She knows that if she sold the books for $1.00 she would be out of business because at that *price* she would not be able to cover her *costs* of acquiring the books in the first place. Costs are what businesses pay to produce the things that consumers want. These include line items such as wages for workers, rent for buildings, your employee's cell phone plans, and what you have paid to acquire comic books for your store. In order to stay in business you must pay all of your costs, otherwise you are losing money, and at a price of $1.00 a book, the store will lose money because this price is not enough to cover operating costs.

So, the comic book store owner, knowing she can't stay in business if the price the buyers pay is too low, counters "How about $10?" Some in the crowd start to squirm. This is far less than the original $200 but still more than they would like to pay. While the members of the X-Men mob grumble, a voice, just loud enough for all of the horde to hear murmurs "Offer a higher price than $1.00." Wondering who made such an odd suggestion, someone in the crowd yells out "How about $2.00?" The seller is encouraged by this. $2.00 is much closer to her costs, but still not quite enough. The mysterious voice suggests she reduce her asking price to $5.00 and the buzz in the crowd is noticeable. Some of the rabble begin shoving, trying to get to the shop, but the stronger ones hold them back. "$2.99!" someone shouts, and the shopkeeper, knowing that at that price she can cover the costs of acquiring her inventory and make a little profit, agrees. The fans flood back into her store and buy up the available issues. All the customers are able to get the book and she has nothing left over. It was like an unseen force had shoved the seller and the buyers together and held them there until a mutually agreed upon price was reached. Sure, the seller would have preferred to charge $200 and the buyers would have been more satisfied at $1.00, but in a market both sides must receive a benefit from the transaction. Nevertheless, there is one reader who has remained outside the store, grumbling. When asked what is wrong, he says "In my day, comics only cost 99 cents. This cost is outrageous!" You walk away, silently correcting the old-timer. You know he is wrong. Comics never *cost* 99 cents. Comics were *priced* at 99 cents.

The use of the term "cost" is admittedly a bit confusing, and economists' insistence upon using the term correctly can make the non-economist worry about their sanity. Cost. Price. Who cares? Let's not debate that particular distinction too finely. Instead, let's examine a different aspect to costs, one that will bring us back to the point of this chapter which, of course, is to answer the question of why heroes work so hard to maintain their secret identities.

I Quit. Sincerely, Your Friendly Neighborhood Spider-Man

At the beginning of the chapter, we were thinking about what superpower you would have, what you might call yourself, and what your disguise would be. The dream of having superhuman abilities sounds great. Using that power to help yourself would make your life better, but could exercising this skill set to help others be equally beneficial? Helping people is inarguably a good thing—even if they don't know who you are, and even if you don't get paid for it, wouldn't it be a worthy goal? Your self-sacrifice to improve the lives of others, to protect them from harm, and to, in short, be a hero, is surely what having powers is about? Isn't it? Didn't someone once say "with great power, comes great..." Oh, rats, what does great power come with? Well, no matter. These new powers have been granted and you are determined to use those powers for good; not just your good, but for the good of all.

Time to review. Where did you get your powers? Was there anything that you did to acquire the ability to fly, the super strength, the x-ray vision? For most superheroes, power comes from an outside source. Regardless of whether they are born a mutant or if their powers come from Asgard, Atlantis, or the Weapon X Project, heroes don't pay for their powers. There is no hero superstore where a can of magnificence can be bought.[6] In essence, the price of powers is zero dollars and zero cents. Nevertheless, if we dissect the cost of being a superhero, not even the most over-zealous, impassioned, joyful hero would confess that the job is costless. When economists start talking about costs, you'd better watch out. Something bad is about to go down.

Consider Peter Parker. He gets bitten by a radioactive spider and voilà, he's got the strength to weight ratio of an arachnid! Not only that but he can leap amazing distances, cling to the sides of buildings, and sense when danger is coming. Now Peter, who happens to be a genius, has some physical aptitude to go along with his mental fortitude. Using his scientific acumen (and a sewing machine) he creates a high-tech, web-slinging device and one of the best costumes in comics. Overnight Peter has gone from being a nerd of the first order to being a supremely powerful nerd of the first order. He's going to have riches and fame. Except these things don't happen, at least not in the original storyline. Instead, Peter's uncle Ben is murdered and his Aunt May is left destitute, eventually developing some serious health problems. Peter wants to go to college, take care of his aunt, and live up to the legacy of his uncle, but being Spider-Man is increasingly becoming a full-time job and Peter realizes he may not be able to have it all.

Peter Parker can't do everything he wants in life for the same reason we non-super-powered people can't do all we want in life: Scarcity. In this case though, scarcity has nothing to do with money. Yes, Peter and his Aunt May are poor. Even with selling pictures to *The Daily Bugle* newspaper, Peter and May are just scraping by. He can't get a job as a researcher, for which he would be qualified, because his extracurricular spider activities get in the way. He could give up being the Web Slinger but he constantly feels the tug of that "great responsibility." Simply put, Peter doesn't have enough time to do all the things he wants to do. As a result, he has to choose—and here's where the costs come in.

A choice, by definition, means having to give something up. Think about going to your favorite ice cream shop. You look at the board that tells you what flavors are available that day. There are many good-looking options but you narrow it down to two. The rocky road looks tempting, but if you get that you know you won't be able to eat the coffee chocolate chip. Decisions, decisions! When you choose the coffee chocolate chip, you have given up the rocky road. This is what you would choose, your back-up choice so to speak, if the shop were to run out of coffee chocolate chip. Rocky road is your *next best* option, and since you didn't select it that makes it the sacrifice of choosing coffee chocolate chip. In other words, this is a cost of having to choose. In economics, we call this next best option, the option B, an opportunity cost. All choices entail costs, even if they aren't dollar costs, because choices necessitate giving something up.

At the beginning of this chapter I mentioned the idea that there is no such thing as a free lunch. The reason now has a name, because when you choose to go to lunch with someone, even if they are paying for it, you have chosen not to go to lunch with someone else, or not to do something else with your lunch break. Whatever your next best option is, that is your opportunity cost, and since there is a cost involved it means the lunch is not free. For example, Peter Parker might have the option of going to lunch with his long-time friend Mary Jane Watson. She has been out of town and really wants to get together. She even offers to pay. Peter, having no money, accepts. A free lunch, right? Wrong. Just after agreeing to Mary Jane's offer, Gwen Stacy, a girl Peter has had his eye on for quite some time, calls up. She too would like to see Peter and also offers to pay for the meal. Peter is now in a pickle. If he says yes to Mary Jane, he has to give up lunch with Gwen. That makes Gwen the opportunity cost. If he says yes to Gwen, he can't enjoy the meal with M.J. Now she's the opportunity cost. Either way, Peter doesn't spend any money, but there is still a cost to the decision he makes.

This issue becomes more pronounced as Peter continues his dual life as the indigent photo-journalist and friendly neighborhood Spider-Man. In *The Amazing Spider-Man* #17, an ill-fated encounter with the Green Goblin causes Spider-Man to run off, leaving many to wonder about his heroic status (Lee and Ditko, 1964a). In the next issue, we see Spider-Man calling the police to thwart a crime rather than taking care of it himself. Later, in issue #18, he is seen escaping from the villain Sandman (Lee and Ditko, 1964b). What's going on here? It transpires that Aunt May is sick, and Peter is worried that if anything happens to him, she won't be taken care of. For Peter, the cost of being Spider-Man just increased. Add to this the girl he likes, Betty Brant, won't talk to him because he skipped a date to do his webslinger thing and now she's seeing someone else. Determined to help his Aunt May and get a good job, he throws away all of his Spider-Man gear, super suit and all. The costs of being a hero are just too high. By the end of the issue, May is well on the road to recovery and Peter has once again donned his costume; but this won't be the last time he forfeits his role.

The most famous episode of Peter Parker quitting occurs in issue #50 of *The Amazing Spider-Man* (Lee and Romita, 1967). The storyline is similar to issue #18 but Peter is now in college. May is sick again, Gwen Stacy has asked him to a party, and he hasn't been on a date with Mary Jane for a while due to his late-night Spidey gig. He laments that "So long as I hang onto my Spider-Man identity I haven't time for anything... except new problems" (p. 5). Peter decides that it is time to grow up and, again, gives up the web shooters and the spider getup. The dramatic panel of him walking down an alley with his Spider-Man mask halfway out of a garbage bin is iconic. Despite the upturn in his studies, his job prospects, and his dating life, he is once again drawn back into the fray by saving an innocent who reminds him of his uncle Ben. The opportunity costs of not being Spider-Man turn out to be just too high.

Is It Better to Have Loved and Lost?

And then there's his erstwhile boss at *The Daily Bugle*, J. Jonah Jameson, who hates Spider-Man so much that he offers a reward for his capture. One of the causes of Jameson's outrage is the mask. To Jameson, there is nothing good that can come from someone wearing a mask. But without that mask, the risks to Peter and his family would be monumental. Peter goes to some of the greatest lengths in the comics to maintain his secret identity, and for good reason. The villains he faces are really nasty, and when they find out who he is they go to extremes to make him suffer. For Peter, the most emotional grief he experiences results directly from the revelation of his secret identity. In *The Amazing Spider-Man* #121, Norman Osborne, the Green Goblin, has lost his memories about the Web Slinger's true name (Conway and Kane, 1973). Overcome with grief due to his son Harry's illness, Norman Osbourne blames

Spider-Man for Harry's maladies, so when his memories are inevitably restored, Norman kidnaps Peter's girlfriend, Gwen Stacy, and flies her to the top of the George Washington Bridge. Before Spider-Man can enact a rescue, Osborne hurls Gwen towards the Hudson River below. Spider-Man grabs her just before she strikes the water, but in a rare instance when the laws of physics actually apply in comics, the abrupt arresting of the fall breaks her neck. Because his identity was revealed, Peter Parker lost the woman he loved.[7]

This trope is seen again in Marvel's *Civil War*. After a devastating explosion, Marvel's heroes gather together to discuss the possibility of being registered in a government program. Spider-Man shows up and warns that this could have the unintended consequence of causing heroes to retire from saving innocents. He notes that the identities of the Fantastic Four have been public knowledge for some time and they've never had a serious problem. In spite of this, he worries that the situation could be different for him. One day he could come home and find "my wife impaled on an octopus arm and the woman who raised me begging for her life" (Millar and McNiven, 2007, p. 20). This is the great concern for all heroes. By revealing who they are, the doors will be open for their enemies to come after their loved ones. Keeping their identities secret is one way to prevent that eventuality. Because evildoers are vengeful, the protection of their loved ones becomes an additional cost to heroes. The way to minimize that cost is to keep your identity secret.[8]

I Can't Believe You Didn't Tell Me. Now Get Out!

Yet another aspect of a secret identity that we should address involves an often-overlooked cost, the kind you can never recover. Consider a common governmental and business conundrum: When a business or government agency ploughs forward with a project that is well over-budget, but "so much time and effort has been put into it, we can't quit now", they are asking for problems. When cost overruns occur, the firm should stop and consider: If we keep going, will the future benefits outweigh the additional costs? If their focus is on the blood, sweat, and tears that have already been poured into a project then they are focusing on the sunk costs. This is a natural reaction. The more effort you put into something, the more intensely connected you are to it. When those emotional links override a rational response, you are succumbing to the sunk cost fallacy.

This fallacy applies to relationships as well. People often continue dating someone because they have invested so much time in that person that it would be a shame to break up with them now, despite the fact that they make you miserable. Other times, a bond of trust is broken and it may be irreparable. In either case, an economist would say "don't think about what has happened in the past, that's a sunk cost. Rather, consider whether the future holds more promise than the costs of continuing the relationship."

Those trust bonds are usually strained when a secret identity is not shared with someone close to the hero. Family and friends of superheroes who are not privy to the hero's secret are often left aghast when an identity is revealed. They are hurt that they weren't in on the secret. Human relationships are tricky. It is much more difficult to forget than to forgive, and while such resentments can poison relationships, it is more likely that a jilted lover will cling to the hurt of a sharp word than let the harm go. Sometimes it is the person on the delivering side of an argument who can't forget what they said. Taking back an insult isn't possible. A lie can't be undone.

This leads to the breakdown of relationships and introspection on the part of the hero contemplating any number of "what if?" scenarios. While this is a common refrain, economists look at such behavior and shrug. It's a sunk cost. You can't retroactively tell someone the truth. Salvaging the relationship will require forward-looking interactions.

The Flash provides a good example of this. In one of the earliest iterations of the Flash's origin story, *The Flash* #105, we see Barry Allen being hit by a combination of chemicals and lightning. Leaving the police crime lab late, he is worried about catching a cab before it pulls away and he starts running (Broome and Infantino, 1959). The rest, as they say, is history. In retrospect, he thinks to himself "I vowed that no one—not even Iris—must ever know that Flash and Barry Allen are the same person" (p. 6). This closely guarded secret becomes a sticking point for a future story arc. Flash forward (see what I did there?) to the *Flash Rebirth* series #25 (Williamson and Di Giandomenico, 2017). One of Barry's oldest foes, Eobard Thawne (aka the Reverse Flash, or sometimes Zoom),[9] reveals to Iris that Barry is the Flash. Thawne then takes Barry and Iris on a tour of what their life might be like, filled with scenes of Barry missing out on their children growing up. The kids turn rogue, a result that Thawne blames on Barry being an absentee father. As Iris processes the fact that Barry is the Flash, and Barry tries to apologize for not telling her, it seems as if their relationship is falling apart before the reader's eyes. Barry's response is that they can make a new life together now that everything is out in the open, but Iris isn't so sure and asks

Barry to leave. What both characters need to realize is that these costs have been incurred and cannot be undone. Iris understands that keeping his identity under wraps was to protect her, but she finds Barry's lack of faith in her disturbing.

Yet, in comics there are some relationships that readers root for. Iris and Barry are a long-running couple. It would be an injustice if these two didn't end up together, but the sunk costs could prevent it. Similarly, we see rocky roads for other couples due to past indiscretions. Jean Grey and Scott Summers overcome all sorts of skeletons in the closet— not least of which is Jean becoming a cosmic force of destruction. Green Arrow and Black Canary have a love-hate relationship that works because neither lets the other's past interfere with the present. A similar tale could be told for Luke Cage and Jessica Jones. The relationships that work are the ones in which the actors let the past remain in the past. Bygones are bygones. Sunk costs don't interfere with what the future holds.

I Can't Remember Who I Told About My Hero Work

This brings up one final cost concern. Once the initial shock of an identity reveal wears off, a hero and their love interest are more closely bound together. We might think it is because of the bond of trust but there might be another reason. David Friedman (1996) raises an interesting question in his book *The Hidden Order*. Why do people stay married? The answer, in typical economist fashion, has nothing to do with love but rather is based on a cost benefit calculation. Once you are in a relationship you develop what Friedman calls "firm-specific capital" (p. 318). In other words, the partners establish roles and specializations within the confines of their union that are worthless outside of it. Not only this, but there are shared experiences and secrets that are valuable as long as the couple remains together. If you ditch these and try to start over with someone else, you incur costs as you try to reestablish roles and memories with someone new. These transaction costs raise the costs of separating and lead people to conclude that changing partners isn't worth it. When you are in a superhero relationship that little secret identity thing raises the transaction costs of separating even more.

In the comics, there are some classic relationships that fans expect to last over time: Clark Kent and Lois Lane, Diana Prince (Wonder Woman) and Steve Trevor, Steve Rogers (Captain America) and Sharon Carter, Hal Jordan (Green Lantern) and Carol Ferris, Barry Allen and Iris West. The key here is that there is a hero and a normal, non-powered person and despite many ups and downs, these characters stay together. Even when someone dies they rarely stay dead and the relationship is revived. As a result, the hero remains true to a particular person. This may seem romantic, but by displaying a partiality to monogamy, the sharing of the secret identity is limited to one person and transaction costs of relationship building are kept under control. Unlike Nightwing, Peter Parker, or Starfire, the superhero versions of swingers who would have to keep their alter ego from (or share their alter ego with) a number of different people thereby raising the probability that they will be outed, the classic comic romances allow you to more easily keep your identity secret by minimizing transactions costs.

Like a Good Neighbor...

Secret identities are peculiar. Dressing up in tights and masks might be good for Halloween but doing so on a regular basis gets you some sideways looks. Yet there is one final, very practical reason why an otherwise normal person would don spandex before putting their life in danger. It's a low-cost insurance policy.

Insurance is a device that exists to protect people against unexpected events. Car insurance pays to repair the damage you incur in an automobile accident. If you are at fault, your insurance pays to fix your car and cover medical bills. If you hit someone else, you pay for the damage done to them as well. Presumably the incident was accidental, and because you don't expect automobile accidents to occur, you haven't prepared for that eventuality by setting aside a sum of money. You do, however, pay a monthly premium to your insurer to cover you if such a mishap occurs. Home owner's insurance is the same. If a fire ravishes your home, it would be catastrophic. The expense of repairing that structure is likely to be more than a family could bear. Thus, you have insurance to compensate you for such a calamity.

Costumes function in a very similar way. By fighting crime you place a target on your own back and on the backs of your loved ones. Since comic book prisons typically don't do a very good job of holding the criminals once they are captured (more on this in Chapter 6), it is important that the hero does something to ensure the safety of those in their sphere. Instead of paying a company a premium to protect those they hold dear, a hero dons a mask. Isn't it remarkable how a piece of black cloth over someone's eyes prevents a friend, family member, or co-worker from realizing who is behind it? Clark Kent removes his glasses and he might as well have green skin he is so unrecognizable. Oliver

Queen's goatee is identifiable from the moon, unless he has a green hood on. Deadpool and Spider-Man at least cover their entire faces, whereas Batgirl, Captain America, Huntress, and Iron Fist only have limited coverage. Still, these attempts to maintain anonymity do the job for the most part. In the hero world, managing risk is an everyday occurrence, one dealt with by protecting your identity.

Lex and Lois

Keeping a secret isn't the easiest thing in the world of comics, but the ignorance of some of the characters is astounding. How could you not know that Clark Kent is Superman? Lois Lane once reflects on the coincidence that when Clark Kent leaves town, Superman is nowhere to be seen. When she connects the dots she almost immediately dismisses the idea, chiding herself "Lois Lane, that's the stupidest idea in the world" (Loeb and Sale, 1999, p. 165).

Lest we treat Lois too harshly, sometimes the smartest man in the room can't see the evidence even when it is right in front of his nose. In an attempt to determine the secret identity of the Man of Steel, Lex Luthor runs a remarkably complex computer program, filled with data from a variety of sources. He is certain that the computer will be able to solve the mystery that has been plaguing him for years. When the results are spit out, Luthor is apoplectic. He can't imagine that, despite his great mind and complex algorithm, the computer could provide such an absurd pronouncement: "Clark Kent is Superman!" His incredulity is based on the premise that having such power would enable him to take over the world, but Superman does not pursue those ends. Instead, he uses his power for good. Luthor rants "I know that no man with the power of Superman would ever pretend to be a mere human! Such power is to be constantly exploited. Such power is to be used!" He then proceeds to fire the data analyst who reached the correct conclusion, saying "I have no place in my organization for people who cannot see the obvious!" (Byrne and Austin, 1987). This is, perhaps, the greatest protector of an identity: Acting in a way that is contrary to the expectations of the world.

Don't Violate the Code

Interestingly, heroes often know the truth. Revealing a secret identity to a fellow hero is a part of the code. As time goes on and the storylines of heroes begin to intertwine, we see an expansion of the characters' personalities and a deepening of their relationships. When partnerships are formed, they rely on trust, and the ultimate show of trust is revealing one's identity. Batman and Robin always know each other's alter ego. Working as closely as they do, it is essential. In stories of the Justice League we see, with some degree of surprise, the characters calling each other by their real names. Flash and Green Lantern are good friends. It would be weird to use those hero names all the time. Green Arrow and Black Canary almost never call each other by anything other than first names. In the *Authority*, Jenny uses code names despite knowing the names of her partners, simply because she doesn't want to slip and reveal the actual names of her teammates when they are in action (Ellis and Hitch, 1999). Barry divulges his identity to Wally West, the Kid Flash, after Wally accuses him of looking at their relationship as a one-way street where Wally should let Flash know everything without some reciprocation (Williamson and Merino, 2017).

Heroes are pretty good at keeping these secrets. Wally even keeps this secret from his Aunt Iris who, if you recall, happens to be dating Barry Allen. Exposing this most important of secrets is considered the ultimate betrayal of trust, which makes the actions of Superman in *Injustice: Gods Among Us* all the more baffling (Taylor and Raapack, 2013). In a battle between forces allied with Superman and those who have taken up with Batman, Superman announces to the world that Batman is Bruce Wayne. More than almost anything the maniacal Man of Steel does, this infuriates Batman the most. His sanctuary has been violated. No longer will he be able to use the Batcave as a respite.

The Answer Is . . .

Becoming a super-powered person sounds great but maintaining the balance between a public and a private life requires significant sacrifice. Being a superhero involves giving up part of the life you know. This means fewer parties, fewer friends, less sleep, and quite possibly a lonely personal life. Doing good is not free. Being imbued with powers, whether you must directly give up something to get those powers or not, is not costless. To protect the people you care about, you might have to keep a really big secret from them. You might have to stay away from them. Even if you do reveal the truth, there are potentially hurt feelings that you will have to deal with. The costs of being a hero are not typically monetary. They are made up of opportunities lost and things you can never get back. To protect the ones you love, mitigating the risks to them can carry a heavy burden indeed.

Endnotes

1. Nevertheless, good ole Negasonic found her way into the Deadpool movie.
2. SPOILER ALERT: Identities will be revealed in this chapter. If you do not want to know the true identities of Superman, Batman, Spider-Man, or other heroes, you may want to skip this chapter. Of course, if you do not know the true guise of these characters, I am not sure you should be reading this book. But I want you to read this book, so keep reading and ignore the spoiler alert.
3. Crackerjack is from the comic *Astro City* published by Vertigo, an imprint of DC Comics. Crackerjack's alias is not mentioned in the comic.
4. Actually, Smith never referred to market forces as an invisible hand, that is an application of the idea to markets in the years since Smith's death. In his most famous work, *The Wealth of Nations* (1776/1994), Smith mentions the invisible hand only once, in Chapter 4, Book 2, in the context of someone pursuing his own self-interest. That person "intends only his own gain, and he is in this, as in many other cases, led by an *invisible hand* [emphasis added] to promote an end which was no part of his intention. Nor is it always the worse for the society that it was not part of it. By pursuing his own interest, he frequently promotes that of the society more effectually than when he really intends to promote it. I have never known much good done by those who affected to trade for the public good" (p. 485).
5. These are some of the most supremely over-powered heroes in the comics. Dr Manhattan can be found in DC's *Watchmen*. He can pretty much do whatever he wants, whenever he wants to, and he knows everything about everything. His cosmic awareness is off the charts, he can teleport, emit radiation as a weapon, grow or shrink to any size, and is invulnerable to any attack. Add to that a touch of apathy towards humans and you've got a real force to be reckoned with. Jean Grey is a member of the X-Men. In some stories she is also known as, or is part of, the Phoenix force. This otherworldly power enhanced her already formidable telekinesis abilities to the point where she could destroy the universe with just a thought. Now that's some serious cosmic juju.
6. Although, there is a really cool store in Brooklyn called the *Brooklyn Superhero Supply Co.* where you can buy facsimiles of "Free Range Magnificence", "100% Pure Chutzpah", "Immortality", "Omnipotence", "Doom" and "Gloom", and a number of other hero-related elixirs.
7. Other than some alternative universe plot lines where Gwen becomes Spider-Gwen, the character of Gwen Stacy has never returned to the Spider-Man universe. The shock of her death still rankles some old-time comic fans.
8. Curiously, Peter chooses to side with Iron Man in the debate over registration and voluntarily reveals his true identity at a press conference. J. Jonah Jameson passes out from shock.

9. Without getting too far into the weeds on this, Thawne has been called by both names. Thawne has been around a long time in the Flash stories, being most closely affiliated with the Reverse Flash, who first appeared in 1963. He was called Zoom on occasion, but a new baddie speedster, Hunter Zoloman, who came on the scene as a foil to Wally West's Flash in 2001, is a little more closely associated with the name Zoom.

References

Broome, J. and Infantino, C. (1959). *The Flash*, #105. DC Comics.

Byrne, J. and Austin, T. (1987). *Superman: The Secret Revealed* #2. DC Comics.

Conway, G. and Kane, G. (1973). *The Amazing Spider-Man*, #121. Marvel Comics.

Ellis, W. and Hitch, B. (1999). *The Authority*, #1. DC Comics.

Friedman, D. (1996). *The Hidden Order*. New York: Harper Business.

Lee, S. and Ditko, S. (1964a). *The Amazing Spider-Man*, #17. Marvel Comics.

Lee, S. and Ditko, S. (1964b). *The Amazing Spider-Man*, #18. Marvel Comics.

Lee, S. and Romita, J. (1967). *The Amazing Spider-Man*, #50. Marvel Comics.

Loeb, J. and Sale, T. (1999). *Superman: For All Seasons*. Burbank, CA: DC Comics.

Millar, M. and McNiven, S. (2007). *Civil War*. New York: Marvel Comics.

Smith, A. (1994). *An Inquiry into the Nature and Causes of the Wealth of Nations*. New York: Random House (Originally published in 1776).

Taylor, T. and Raapack, J. (2013). *Injustice: Gods Among Us: Year 1*, #28. DC Comics.

Williamson, J. and Di Giandomenico, C. (2017). *The Flash*, #25. DC Comics.

Williamson, J. and Merino, J. (2017). *The Flash*, #19. DC Comics.

3

Keep Your Friends Close, Or Why Do Superheroes Team Up?

Batman and Robin: One of the greatest duos of all time. They are up there with the likes of Gene and Roy,[1] Bert and Ernie, Laverne and Shirley, Kirk and Spock, or Ren and Stimpy. You can never think of one without the other. In the cases of these television pairings, it was the interaction between the characters that made them great. In comedy partnerships such as Laurel and Hardy, Abbot and Costello, or Cheech and Chong, the two individuals are inseparable. The same can be said for some musical acts, although there are certainly instances when one member breaks away and achieves solo superstardom. Michael Jackson was the King of Pop, but he did have four older brothers, none of whom achieved anything after the Jackson 5 broke up. Beyoncé was a member of the group Destiny's Child. The other former members have had middling success afterwards, but nothing close to what they achieved as members of the group. Cher was once part of the duo Sonny and Cher—one of the more unlikely pairings in entertainment history. Sonny was so distraught after the pair split (they were also married for a time) that he entered politics.[2]

The point here is that partnerships often have multiplicative effects. They enhance the status and success of individual actors. For a while at least, the whole is greater than the sum of its parts, to an extent that even if individual members despise each other they will continue to perform together because they know the alternative is to flounder alone.[3] We can look at the service entertainers provide and be thankful for what we get, all the while wondering what makes such talented people resent each other, or we can consider the way those partnerships work and what makes them successful. This being a study of economics, we will do the latter. Reflecting on some of the pairings or groups we have thus far mentioned, it is relatively easy to pull them apart and see what each participant in the group has to offer. Let's instead dissect the Beatles. The Fab Four; John Lennon, Paul McCartney, George Harrison, and Ringo Starr formed what is arguably the most famous rock and roll band ever. They have sold billions of records, hundreds of millions of albums, and spent over a thousand weeks at the top of the *Billboard* charts. Despite the dysfunction in the group by the end of their run, and the sad ending of John Lennon who was murdered in 1980, this was an incredibly talented group of musicians. While Lennon got the band together, it was McCartney who was probably the most gifted. He composed music, wrote lyrics, sang lead, played electric, acoustic, and bass guitar, piano, drums, and a variety of other instruments. He sat in on songs for Ringo, who himself was an accomplished drummer. Which leaves us to consider, why did McCartney need the Beatles? He wrote most of the successful songs the group performed and could play all of the instruments. The answer is the focus of this chapter, a mysterious concept (though not quite as mysterious as the Beatle's relatively bizarre song *Revolution 9*) called comparative advantage.

How I Learned to Stop Brooding and Love the Sidekick

To answer the question about the Beatles and put that to rest, we simply need to consider the logistics of a band on stage. McCartney might have been better at everything, a more competent musician, singer, and songwriter, but to go on tour as a solo act would have been a problem. He couldn't physically perform all of the instrumentals to back himself up as a singer so he has a band. He finds competent musicians to help him out and the Beatles sell out stadiums and concert halls around the world. But how does this explain Batman and Robin?

Robin was added to the Batman storyline in an attempt to make the protagonist more accessible and to buoy sales by appealing to teenage boys who might see themselves participating in the adventures of the Caped Crusader. Robin's first appearance was in *Detective Comics* #38 (Finger and Kane, 1940). The readers liked the new character and sales rose significantly. The original Robin, Dick Grayson, was a member of a circus family. His parents were training him in the family business. As an acrobat on the flying trapeze, Dick was unknowingly developing the skills he would use to fight alongside Batman. Dick's parents were killed in a trapeze accident, coordinated by a mobster, during a performance. It so happened that Bruce Wayne was in the audience at the time. Seeing a bit of himself in the now orphaned boy, Bruce took the lad on as his ward. Dick spent the next forty years as Robin in the comics, eventually growing up and adopting the persona of Nightwing. Interestingly, Batman found that he liked having a Robin around, so when Grayson left another soon took his place.

Jason Todd, another circus acrobat, assumed the mantle of Robin in the mid-1980s. His character was quickly rebooted as a rebellious, teen-age street kid who tried to steal the tires off the Batmobile. Todd was more impetuous than Dick Grayson and many fans found him to be loathsome, so much so that when offered the chance to kill off a member of the Bat Family, fans voted to kill off Robin. As a legacy to this, the writers of Batman have used the death of Jason Todd to drive Batman's plot line. Todd's murder scarred the Caped Crusader almost as much as the death of his parents.

The next man up was Tim Drake, who used his powers of deduction in a way very few had. Drake was in the audience when Dick Grayson's parents were killed. He noticed the way in which Wayne consoled Grayson and put the pieces together, figuring out the identities of Batman and Robin. While Bruce was falling into a depression over the death of Jason Todd, Drake approached him with the offer to become the next Robin. The proposal was accepted, but not until Drake's mother was killed and his father crippled by a villain. While physically skilled, Drake became the hard-working, techy sidekick who used his brain as much as his brawn to help defeat crime in Gotham. He retired early, essentially fired by Dick Grayson who briefly took over as Batman,[4] opening the door for a new version of the boy wonder.

The next Robin wasn't a boy at all. Stephanie Brown, daughter of the criminal Cluemaster, stepped into the red and green tights for a brief stint (Willingham and Scott, 2004a). While somewhat helpful on the detective side of crime-fighting, Stephanie lacked the physical skills required for the job, and while she briefly dated Tim Drake, it wasn't enough for the demands of her employer and Batman fired her. The first female Robin was relegated to the unemployment line (Willingham and Scott, 2004b).[5]

The current Robin is perhaps the most alienating of all. Damian Wayne made his first appearance in the graphic novel *Batman: Son of the Demon* (Barr and Bingham, 1987). He is the son of Bruce Wayne and Talia al Ghul of the League of Assassins. Damian is a problem child *par excellence*. While undeniably skilled physically, his attitude toward the position of Robin is one of privilege and his disdain for the rules that Batman plays by is evident. The relationship between father and son is rocky at the best of times, and downright hostile in the *Injustice* series, where Damian accidentally kills Dick Grayson and actively fights against his father.[6]

So that's the background on the most famous sidekick in comic history, but again, what about this mysterious economic concept, the one that explains why Paul McCartney tolerates Ringo? How does that idea explain why Batman endures Robin? The marketers may want a new character to sell comics but would Batman really adopt someone to help him with his work? Bruce Wayne is a distant, introverted, conspiratorialist, paranoid hot mess. Accepting the help of a teenager, no matter how tragic the kid's backstory, seems entirely out of character. How is this going to work? It's time to reveal the mystery—it is called comparative advantage.

Anything You Can Do I Can Do Better, But That Doesn't Mean I Should

Comparative advantage is one of the most important, yet misunderstood, concepts in economics. Any confusion with the concept typically stems from the somewhat tedious exercises economics professors force upon unsuspecting students. The mathematical calisthenics, while fun in their own right to those perverse enough to enjoy that kind of thing, wear out the less numerically inclined. Beyond that mild torture, comparative advantage reveals something that even the dearly departed Adam Smith couldn't recognize.[7] Comparative advantage explains why the Scottish produce whisky, not wine; why the French make wine, not whiskey; and why, unbeknownst to Smith or anyone else at the time, Batman continues to hire Robins.

So, what is this great insight? To start off, let's give credit where credit is due. David Ricardo developed this idea in the early 1800s in his influential book *Principles of Political Economy and Taxation* (1817/1996). He was interested in the question of why a country like his, England, didn't produce all the things it needed and wanted. To him, the answer presented itself as an issue of resource allocation. If one country can produce a good, say battle maces, with fewer workers, or fewer machines, or if the production process itself was less expensive than the same process in another country, then it was clear that the maces should be produced by the country that can do it most cheaply. But it wasn't just a financial issue to Ricardo. The other costs involved in production were just as important. What if producing a mace meant you had to give up the production of something else? In other words, what is the opportunity cost of producing a mace? Let's say that in order to produce a mace you have to give up a Mjolnir—you know, a Thor-sized hammer. Thus, not only do you have the expenses involved in producing a battle mace but you also have an opportunity cost because you have to give up something you could have made with the resources used to make the mace. These opportunity costs are the basis for comparative advantage. According to Ricardo, if you can make a mace at a lower opportunity cost than someone else, then you have a comparative advantage.

How does that fit into the Batman and Robin narrative? Well, think about it this way: Batman is really good at a lot of things. He's considered by some the greatest detective since Sherlock Holmes. He's so skilled in fighting that he probably has a double kung fu, black belt in taekwondo and Brazilian ju-jitsu.[8] He can invent weapons that make the military industrial complex drool. He has the technical acumen of a Massachusetts Institute of Technology engineer and he knows how to use it. Batman is really great at just about everything related to crime-fighting. The question is, if he's so good at what he does, why would he need a sidekick? Superman doesn't have a helper, neither does Wonder Woman. Maybe Batman isn't such a great hero after all. Or maybe he has a little economic superpower up his sleeve called comparative advantage.

Yes, Batman can prosecute a criminal investigation like no other, but even he has limits. One of the significant restraints he has to deal with is that, like anyone making choices, he has opportunity costs. If Batman is chasing the Joker, it means he can't be hanging out in the Batcave working on an antidote for the Joker's laughing gas. If he is trying to deduce the answer to one of the Riddler's puzzles, he has to give up the chance to pursue some illicit activity being undertaken by the Penguin. Here's where a sidekick comes in handy. By picking up some of the tasks Batman would try to complete on his own, Robin can be of immeasurable assistance, and this is the magic of comparative advantage: Robin can help, even if he is worse at everything than Batman is.

Think about it. All of the Robins are much younger than Batman and far less experienced in all walks of life. This is one of the things that makes the angst-ridden Robins, Jason Todd and Damian, all the more detestable. Do they really think they are better than Batman at anything? As readers, we know this will never be the case. Usually, being the misunderstood, rebellious punks that they are means only that these Robins get themselves into trouble, from which Batman must inevitably save them (except in that one case where Jason gets himself killed—and there was much rejoicing!). Shut up young Robins! You know nothing!

But I digress. Batman puts up with the insolence, nonsense, and flagrant disrespect because he knows that, despite these hang-ups, he can get more done with help. Batman is great at everything, but even so there are things that Robin can do for him at a lower opportunity cost. Suppose at one end of Gotham there is a series of suspicious break-ins that Batman wants to investigate. Meanwhile, back at the Batcave, the Batcomputer can be used to hack into the networks of crime syndicates. This would be important for halting the flow of drugs into Gotham. What should he do? The answer is simple: Put Robin to work. But which task should he assign the Boy Wonder? The answer to that depends on where Robin's comparative advantage lies.

This is found by considering, at the time the decision must be made, how many causes of the break-ins Robin can determine relative to hacking the crime syndicates. Batman's computer skills are highly advanced. During the course of the night Batman can hack into five of the crime syndicate's networks and scuttle their plans. In the same time, he could investigate ten break-ins. Robin is also pretty good on a computer. He can hack four networks but, because it takes him a lot longer to put the pieces together, he can only determine the cause of four break-ins. This means that Batman must give up solving two break-ins for every hack he attempts, while Robin only gives up solving one break-in for each hack. Since one is less than two, we say that Robin has the comparative advantage in hacking. He doesn't have to give up as much of some other crime-solving activity to conduct a covert cyber war on the bad guys. That's why Batman leaves Robin in the Batcave to spend a lonely evening with the Batcomputer while he heads out onto the rooftops of Gotham to conduct his investigations. It's elementary, my dear Robin. Comparative advantage explains why you stay employed.

What About My Friends?

Sidekicks are just one example of how heroes employ the concept of comparative advantage in the story arcs. As even casual fans of the comics are aware, there are other ways that teaming up manifests itself, and these teams are almost always more capable because of the way in which they use comparative advantage.

Rarely does a comic hero remain stuck in the vortex of isolation. Word gets out that some new super-powered person is roaming the streets or the skies and the old-timers swing by to take a look. In the X-Men, Professor Xavier is constantly on patrol for new mutants. His intentions are, of course, benign. He wants to help them understand and control their powers, to protect the mutant and those around him or her. There is no direct intention of making the newbie a part of the X-Men, but if they happen to have powers that would be of service, all the better. There are certainly skill sets for which the X-Men have a need. Keeping the new mutant on the straight and narrow path, out of the clutches of some evil force that might bend the malleable youngster, is an added bonus.

In *Justice League of America* #9 (Fox and Sekowsky, 1962), we learn the origin of the Justice League. An alien that threatened to capture the heroes was only defeated through the power of teamwork. The 2011 version of the Justice League indicates that the heroes meet up with each other, trying to stop an alien invasion coordinated by the supervillain Darkseid (Johns and Lee, 2011). The group bands together in solidarity as they are being condemned on all sides as vigilantes, despite their intention to save the planet. The Avengers first get together to fight the Hulk, who has been framed by Loki. Ant-Man notes that "each of us has a different power! If we combined forces, we could be almost unbeatable!" (Lee and Kirby, 1963, p. 22). He's right—mainly. Whether they are unstoppable depends on how they divvy up the responsibilities of a mission.

In most cases, the formation of a team of superheroes is inspired by the success the group finds through the power of teamwork. Whether teaming up for an issue or two, or creating a full-time partnership, when heroes work together the message is that they will almost always come out on top. When they fight amongst themselves, really bad things happen. Of course, this is the message that cartoons and kindergarten have sent for decades. To quote that seldom remembered group of paladin, pre-school animals, the Wonder Pets, "What's going to work? Teamwork!" To quote the vastly more important, yet far less read, Adam Smith (1776/1994), "The division of labor, however, so far as it can be introduced, occasions, in every art, a proportionable increase of the productive powers of labor" (p. 5).

Now that's some serious eighteenth-century English! What does this gobbledygook mean? Smith is saying that by dividing up a task among teammates, each worker becomes more productive. Ant-Man must have been channeling his inner Adam Smith (or his inner Wonder Pet, if you prefer). Each member of a superhero team has a different set of skills. In the Justice League, if you want some help from the sea, you ask Aquaman. If you need something done really quickly, call the Flash. If you were to ask Aquaman to run off and get the team some coffee, you might be waiting a while, whereas Flash will be back before you can get the words "double espresso latte" out of your mouth. Batman organizes things and works as the brain, whereas Superman out-muscles the bad guys. Wonder Woman gets the truth out of the villains with her magic lasso. Each has a role to play, and by completing the tasks, they get the job done.[9]

The specialization of labor is made more evident in the Justice League stories when Cyborg joins the team. Now there is a tech specialist to help navigate the increasingly complex technological systems the Justice League needs in order to keep track of world events. This is a common practice in the comics when putting teams together. Because of a character's skill set, they are added to a team, maybe for one story arc, or even one episode, to help complete a mission. While the Avengers begin with a handful of heroes, the team variously expands and contracts depending on the operation at hand. The earliest addition is Captain America, once he is freed from the ice floe into which he was frozen (Lee and Kirby, 1964). Even Cap notices the variety of skills the members of the Avengers possess as he positions himself for an invitation to become part of the team. In *The Avengers* #9 (Lee and Heck, 1964), Hawkeye, an accomplished archer, demonstrates his skills and joins the team, which is later augmented by Quicksilver, a speedster, and Scarlet Witch, who has magical powers. These three begin their shifts as Avengers and provide proficiencies that were not previously represented in the group. This allows the Avengers to complete missions that would have been more difficult with only the original members.

This foundation of specialization is what makes comparative advantage so propitious. For instance, Brazil has a comparative advantage over Germany in the production of coffee. The climate for growing coffee beans is far more suitable on the hills of the rain forests than the rocky crags of the Alps. Correspondingly, Germany has a comparative advantage over Brazil in the production of cars. Even if we don't know much about how coffee beans move from a plantation in the Sul Minas region of Brazil to the bottom of the cup in a bistro in Stuttgart, we know that Brazil produces coffee at a lower opportunity cost because, well, if it didn't, Brazil wouldn't be in the coffee business. Markets determine who has the comparative advantage through the price mechanism. If you are able to produce something at a lower opportunity cost, that information will be reflected in the price consumers pay. It isn't that Germany can't produce coffee beans, it's just that if they did, it would be really expensive. That might be OK for coffee snobs who delight in drinking an exotic cup of java, but for the majority of people looking for a caffeine fix in the morning, the Brazilian blend is just fine.

As we noted earlier, Robin has a comparative advantage in hacking computers. Coincidentally, Batman has a comparative advantage over Robin in halting break-ins. If he were to give up hacking to turn detective, he would only have to give up half of a hacking job for each break-in he investigates. Robin gives up one hack for each investigation. Since one half is less than one, Batman has a comparative advantage in investigations.[10] This isn't determined by the market per se, rather it is an observation by the participants that leads to a more effective crime-fighting process; however, this can only happen if Batman gives up performing one of the actions. If he insists that he can do it all himself, thereby keeping Robin on the sideline, he will not only be eschewing the benefits of specialization, he'll also get a sullen Robin. More to the point, comparative advantage works when each party produces only what they have a comparative advantage in. This means that to experience the value of teamwork, the players have to be willing to do what they do well, and only what they do well. If Batman tries to do some hacking on the side, this will lead to greater productivity on the hacking front but less on the investigative front, especially if Robin gets annoyed and tries to investigate a break-in or two himself.

This is a danger of having a young sidekick. They are often too impulsive. They don't want to take instruction and consequently end up getting kidnapped, or worse.[11] It is when the helper deviates from the plan that things go sideways. There is a method to the training, and usually that means the impetuous accomplice has to wait their turn. Stay in your lane and all will be right with the world. That may not make for a great story but it certainly makes more economic sense. All sidekicks at some point want to be the main attraction, but as readers know, this impulsiveness almost always leads to the sidekick being captured.

Trade You My Apple for Your Cookie

This brings us to the final point about comparative advantage. Once it is determined who has it and specialization occurs, how do you make the most out of it? This is obvious in the situation where Brazil is growing coffee and Germany is making cars. The citizens of each country are better off when they are able to buy both cars and coffee, but if each country specializes in the production of one good, they should produce none of the other good. This would seem to be a problem for consumers. In Brazil, they have lots of coffee, and maybe the excessive caffeine will provide enough nervous energy that people can just walk everywhere. Germans have beer, so why would they even want coffee? Well, consumers are weird that way. They like options, preferring to have multiple goods available. The problem is that if both countries try and produce coffee and cars, they are producing a good that involves a high opportunity cost. Consequently, while consumers may have both goods available to them, the price tag will be higher. What a quandary!

The recommendation of economists, therefore, is to specialize, then take some of what you are producing and simply trade it to the other country in exchange for what you want. Economists illustrate the value that results from trade with a tool they call a production possibilities curve. This line shows the combinations of output that a country or an individual can produce given certain constraints. What you are about to see may seem like a trick Zatanna would perform, but it is real. By utilizing comparative advantage, trading partners can produce a combined amount of goods that is within their production limits—as noted by the production possibilities curve—but by specializing and then trading what you do well for what someone else does well, it results in a consumption bundle—the combination of goods consumers can enjoy—that goes well beyond the production capabilities of either. This means more things for everyone!

To see how this works let's examine the crime-fighting capabilities of Batman and Robin more closely still. Batman is ready to go to work and wants to get as many crimes solved as quickly as possible. As before, he can stop ten break-ins in a night or he can hack into five crime syndicates' computer systems. However, he also has opportunities that lie between these extremes. Batman not only wants to stop the local crimes, he also wants to stop those naughty syndicates from bringing drugs into Gotham. Thus, he might mix up his crime-fighting activity. One of his other options would be to stop six break-ins and hack into two computer networks. So the Caped Crusader has options. Which one should he choose? Before answering that, let's review Robin's alternatives. He can stop four break-ins or he could hack into four networks. If he wants to do a little of both, one option would be to thwart three break-ins and worm his way into one computer system. The full range of options are shown in Tables 3.1a and 3.1b.

With these options, a couple of patterns emerge. First, Batman is better at both tasks than Robin. That should be no surprise, he is Batman after all. Also, he is the teacher. Robin is learning detective work at the feet of a legend. For Robin to be better than Batman would be like an elementary student showing up at a painting class led by Degas and outshining the master. That is not going to happen. It isn't that he has no skill, it's just that he's, well, Robin. When someone is able to produce more of something than someone else, economists say that the production leader has an absolute advantage. When we discuss absolute advantages, how efficiently you produce things is irrelevant, as is whether you have a comparative advantage. This is a numbers game, pure and simple.

Table 3.1a. Batman's Production Possibilities

Option	Break-ins stopped	Hacks
A	0	5
B	2	4
C	6	2
D	10	0

Table 3.1b. Robin's Production Possibilities

Option	Break-ins stopped	Hacks
A	0	4
B	1	3
C	3	1
D	4	0

Absolute advantage doesn't matter when it comes to having a side-kick. As we have seen, Robin's role in the Batman universe is based on his comparative advantage. While Batman has an absolute advantage in both aspects of crime-fighting, he only has a comparative advantage in one and that is what matters. Batman can stop two break-ins for every hack while Robin can only stop one break-in for every hack. Again, as we determined previously, because Batman has to give up more crimes than Robin to engage in cyberwar against these firms, it is Batman, not the Boy Wonder, who should be out pounding the pavement in search of the baddies. Now, before we get to the punchline, let's present a picture of this analysis.

Economists are fond of using graphs to illustrate what we are talking about. We often refer to these graphs as models. Like a model boat, car, or rocket, an economic model is a picture of reality simplified on a grand scale. If you were to put together a model of an aircraft carrier, it should be considerably smaller than the real thing. Other than size, the really noticeable difference is that it is missing the nuclear reactor that powers it. The model is made up of molded plastic parts that you fit together to represent the real thing, but no kit in the world is going to provide the plutonium to power it, let alone the radar, military hardware, or aircraft that are components of a real aircraft carrier.

Similarly, economic models are much simpler versions of reality. The world is too complicated a place to boil it down to a graph, or even a set of graphs. Due to its complexity, perfectly modeling the world would require the computing power of about 10,000 Googles. We don't have the resources to buy that number of programmers or that number of gigawatts so we reduce the intricacy by making assumptions about our models. Essentially we shrug and say "hey, the world is complicated, and economics is complicated, and we're not really smart enough to put all the pieces into the model, but if you take a look at what we have, it's close enough to reality that you should trust our results." Sometimes that combination of pleading ignorance and self-confidence provides reliable models, and by reliable I mean models that help us understand reality enough of the time that we start to have faith in them and teach them to others. A good economic model is going to show you the way in which some parts of the overall economy fit together to achieve a result, despite its imperfections.

The model of why Batman should keep hiring a Robin even when they grow up or are killed is the production possibilities model. It incorporates the concepts of comparative advantage and specialization to illustrate that if you do what you do best, the outcome is greater than the sum of the parts. Lo and behold, I give you the production possibilities of the Dynamic Duo in Figure 3.1.

What is going on in these graphs? Let's start with some ground rules. Since this is a model, we need to lay out our assumptions. In order to focus on how comparative advantage leads to a better outcome, we have to make sure that there aren't too many outside influences impacting production decisions. Thus, we put constraints on our heroes. First, we have limited them to only two crime-fighting activities. There are no rescues of kidnapped hostages or saving children from burning school busses. Of course, we could lump those actions in with the break-ins stopped, but we want to keep things simple. Another approach would be to divide misdeeds into domestic and alien invasions. How the model is set up is the prerogative of the researcher, but if we are to rely upon the model it should be generalizable to multiple situations. The next assumption is that Batman and Robin are stuck with whatever resources they possess right now. This means they cannot enlist help from Batgirl, Batwoman, Red Hood, Ace the Bathound, or any other member of the Batman family. Neither can new gadgets be introduced into the fight. Whatever is in your utility belt at the beginning of the night is what you can use. This also applies to the current technology and computing power available in the Batcave, which would constrain the cyber warriors. In short, no new resources, no new tech, and importantly, no more time. This curve of production possibilities applies to a night's worth of work.

Now some basics about the curves themselves. The downward-sloping lines of the production possibilities curve reflect that both Batman and

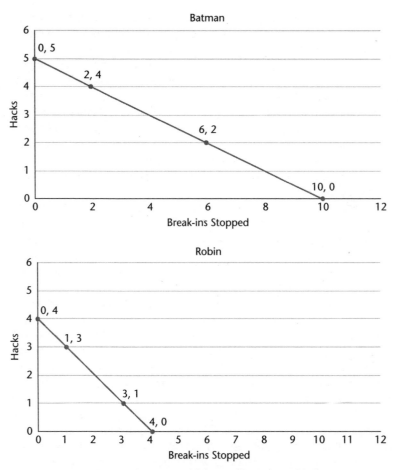

Figure 3.1. Production Possibilities of Batman and Robin.

Robin face scarcity. Starting from the point along the y-axis (the hacking axis), if you want to be able to fight more crime, you have to give up your time in the Batcave and hit the hard streets of Gotham. For Batman, he can hack into five firms when he isn't searching for criminals, but if he wants to solve even one of the mysterious break-ins he has to cut back on hacking. To stop two crimes, he would move down and to the right along the curve from a combination of (0,5) to the combination of (2,4), which corresponds to two break-ins stopped and four hacks. Thus, to stop crime on the street he has to sacrifice hacking. He cannot have more of both activities. This is the notion of opportunity cost at play. Batman is giving up one thing to get something else. His next best option for fighting the crime syndicates is to stop the small-time criminals on the street. For Robin, the production possibility curve is downward sloping because, although he can't do either task as well as Batman, he still faces scarcity. To stop crime, he has to give up some hacking as well. To stop just one break-in, going from zero to one along the x-axis (the break-in axis), he has to move down the y-axis (the hacking axis) from four hacks to three. This moves him along his curve from (0,4) to (1,3). So, point number one: Because we live in a world of scarcity, to produce more of one thing, we have to produce less of something else.

Production is limited by the production possibilities curve. Think of it as a boundary beyond which it is impossible to produce more because, as we have already noted, you are not able to increase your resources or your technology. However, it is possible to produce some combination within the boundary. Batman might decide to order pizza and while he waits, time ticks away, preventing him from getting to the scoundrels on the street. Similarly, Robin starts rocking out to some tunes he downloaded onto the Bat-phone and loses focus on his hacking activity. As a result, there is the very real possibility that the Caped Crusaders do not produce up to their potential. Thus, point number two is that while you are limited by how much you can produce, you can easily produce less than your potential. Such action would probably lead to some angst-filled regret monologue where the heroes lament not doing more. What they are saying is that they were producing inside their production possibility curve.

Prepared with the background and the basics, and knowing that Batman has the comparative advantage in pursuing criminals and Robin, while not as productive as Batman, has the comparative advantage on the computer infiltration side, we can now use the model to show the magical benefits of comparative advantage for crime-fighting.

Holy Comparative Advantage Batman!

We've noted that Batman and Robin should specialize in production. Now for the *coup de grâce*. By specializing, even though they cannot produce beyond the production possibilities curves, they can actually *consume* beyond those curves. To see this, take a look at the two tables below. In Table 3.2, we have a situation where both heroes engage in a little bit of street level crime-fighting and some digital skulking. In other words, there is no specialization.

The choice of activities for both heroes places them along their production possibilities curves. By summing the amount of each undertaking, we end up with nine crimes stopped and three hacks completed in total. That's a pretty good night's work. But they could do better. Table 3.3 shows the amount of criminal activity that is stopped when each hero performs the task for which they have a comparative advantage.

By specializing, the Dynamic Duo has increased the hacks by one and the number of crimes stopped by one. They can "consume" ten investigations and four hacks. So, how does this compare with the total production of the Caped Crusaders? Figure 3.2 shows the combined production of Batman and Robin, found by summing the two production possibilities curves. There is still a barrier beyond which the

Table 3.2. Heroes Do Not Specialize

Batman	Robin	Total
6 break-ins stopped	3 break-ins	9 break-ins
2 hacks	1 hacks	3 hacks

Table 3.3. Heroes Specializing

Batman	Robin	Total
10 break-ins	0 break-ins	10 break-ins
0 hacks	4 hacks	4 hacks

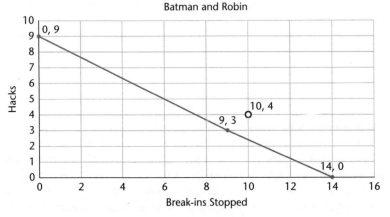

Figure 3.2. Combined Production of Batman and Robin.

two cannot produce, but notice one very, very important detail: If Batman and Robin team up and each specializes in production, the amount of activity they can generate puts them at the white dot in the graph above. That dot is beyond the production possibilities curve! What strange witchery is this? Has the Enchantress befuddled our heroes?[12] No! It is the power of specialization at work!

When Batman and Robin each specialize and provide those skills in the context of a team, the result is that more crimes are thwarted than if they had worked individually. This is why Batman keeps Robin around. Sure, he's a bit of a pain sometimes. His zany cracks in the 1960s television series (including Holy Hamlet, Holy alter ego, Holy haberdashery, Holy ravioli and many, many more[13]), his propensity for overstating his abilities, his later moodiness, and inclination to try and prove his worth, which leads to Batman having to bail him out of diabolical situations, are all worth putting up with because they accomplish greater things as a team.

There is one final component to teaming up. It isn't enough just to perform the task for which you have a comparative advantage. Batman could investigate break-ins and Robin could hack networks till the cows come home, but on their own they find that their crime-fighting efforts lack something. Robin never finds out what the word is on the street and Batman remains perpetually in the dark about the corporations' inner workings. In order to make sure that they get the most out of specialization, each character does what they do best and, in effect, trades that skill to the other. Such gains from trade can be found any time economic actors specialize, and this is the real reason why people engage in trade. You want something someone else has. Rather than beat them and take what you want, civilized societies have developed plans to trade. When trades are entered into voluntarily, both sides are made better off. Specialization makes those trades more profitable because even though you don't have more inputs to produce, both parties can consume more than they could on their own.

And the Answer Is...

This chapter has covered a lot of fundamental economic topics but they have all revolved around the idea of teaming up to get more accomplished. While our focus has been on heroes, these ideas apply to all production. Countries specialize in certain things because they can do them better and at a lower cost than other countries. Textiles come from southeast Asia, technology from the United States, Japan and South Korea, metals are mined in South America and Australia, oil comes from the Middle East. Sometimes countries have natural resources that allow them to produce in a lower cost fashion. Other times countries develop specialties over decades. Companies take advantage of the same processes. You call a law firm for legal help and head to the grocer to get food for dinner. Businesses do not provide one-stop shopping for all your needs. They specialize in production because by doing so they can become incredibly competent in a specific area, thereby reducing the costs of production and passing those savings onto consumers. We as individuals do this as well. We call the plumber instead of trying to fix a leaky pipe, or we head to the doctor rather than trying to diagnose our own ailments. Why? Because it is too costly for us to become experts in everything. We rely on others' specialized skills to make our lives better.

Heroes do the same things. They make the world safer, reduce crime, and use their powers to protect those who can't protect themselves. In order to make these things happen they sometimes find that a teammate is necessary.

Many heroes have sidekicks. Others join teams of supers to accomplish a larger task. Even the most super of characters is paired with others at times. Some heroes prefer working alone but realize the value of a team now and then. Just because Batman, Green Lantern, Jessica Jones, or Wolverine can be successful on their own, doesn't mean that they should remain that way. Comparative advantage explains why no person, country, or hero is better off doing everything for themselves. It is more beneficial to find what you can do at a relatively lower cost than anyone else and concentrate your efforts on that.[14]

Once you figure this out, specializing in what you do well means work is done more efficiently. Tasks are broken down into smaller bits and someone, or some group, focuses their attention on completing that single task. As a result, they get really good at that task and then take advantage of the gains by trading that specially-developed talent to the team. It's the teamwork that gets the job done because each hero is a cog in the bigger machine. Recall that Batman made a pledge on the grave of his parents to "rid this city of the evil that took their lives" (Loeb and Lee, 2002). Teaming up with Robin helps him fulfill that promise. But as the old saying goes, you should keep your friends close and your enemies closer. In the next chapter we are going to see how heroes sometimes have to deal with dissention in the ranks.

Endnotes

1. Gene Kelly and Roy Rogers were the pinnacle of singing cowboy stardom from the mid-1930s through to the mid-1950s.
2. This is a bit of an exaggeration. Sonny ran for mayor of Palm Springs in 1988, thirteen years and two marriages after his divorce from Cher. He won a seat to the U.S. Congress in 1995.
3. This, too, is the case with many musical groups. According to most accounts, Simon and Garfunkel couldn't stand each other, neither could the members of Guns and Roses, Pink Floyd, Brian Wilson and Mike Love of the Beach Boys, Mick Jagger and Keith Richards of the Rolling Stones, or Don and Phil Everly of the Everly Brothers—and yes, they really were brothers. The brothers broke up when Phil stopped playing and walked off stage in the middle of a concert!
4. It was presumed that Batman was killed in a battle with Darkseid in *Final Crisis* #6 (Morrison and Jones, 2009).
5. There was one other female Robin. Carrie Kelley appeared as Robin in the graphic novel *The Dark Knight Returns* (Miller, 2016) but is not considered part of the actual DC continuity. Her only appearance as Robin was in this graphic novel by Frank Miller, although she did appear as Catgirl in *Batman: The Dark Knight Strikes Again* (Miller, 2001–2002).
6. The source material for all things Robin comes from Beedle, 2015.
7. If you recall from Chapter 2, Adam Smith is the spiritual godfather of economics. Sadly, he left this world in 1790.
8. Such a thing does not even exist but Batman probably has it!
9. In the *Justice League of America* #9 backstory issue, the team is cleaning the secret cave hideout and Aquaman notes that they all take their cues from Wonder Woman. She distributes the resources and everyone has a task. While it is certainly efficient to divide up the tasks, it is also extraordinarily sexist to presume Wonder Woman knows the best way to clean, especially as she is regularly left at home during missions.
10. This is determined by taking what you give up and dividing it by what you get. Batman has to give up five hacks if he focuses on the break-ins but he can investigate ten of those. Thus, if you take five hacks divided by ten break-ins you get a ratio of one hack to two break-ins, or one half of a hack to one break-in.
11. Possibly the most disturbing sidekick scenario involves Roy Harper, aka Speedy, the ally of Green Arrow. At one point, Roy gets hooked on heroine. Green Arrow walks in on him as he is shooting up, smacks him around, and kicks him to the curb. Roy's rationale for the drugs is that he needs them to keep up with Arrow. Of course, Arrow immediately questions his own actions but then absolves himself by thinking that Roy is old enough to know better (O'Neil, Adams, and Giordano, 1971).
12. The Enchantress is June Moone, a freelance artist and psychology teacher who was given magical powers after falling into a secret chamber in a haunted

castle. After Supergirl kept her from gaining omnipotent powers, she turned to a life of villainy.

13. The entire preposterous list of Robin's holy this or that can be found at https://www.66batmania.com/trivia/robins-holy/.

14. That being said, while groups almost always get things done more quickly and efficiently, it is possible that if the players don't see it this way then their ability to stop the ne'er-do-wells will be curtailed. Some heroes just can't work well with others and it makes them somewhat less successful. For instance, the Punisher is too willing to kill people and the Hulk is too often out of control. He might defeat the bad guy and then turn on you.

References

Barr, M. and Bingham, J. (1987). *Batman: Son of the Demon*. DC Comics.

Bat-Mania. (n.d.) *Robin's "Holy"*. [Online] Available at https://www.66batmania.com/trivia/robins-holy/ [Accessed August 14, 2018].

Beedle, T. (2015). *Robin 101: One Name, Many Heroes*. [Online] DC Comics. Available at: http://www.dccomics.com/blog/2015/06/24/robin-101-one-name-many-heroes [Accessed April 4, 2018].

Finger, B. and Kane, B. (1940). *Detective Comics*, #38. DC Comics.

Fox, G. and Sekowsky, M. (1962). *Justice League of America*, #9. DC Comics.

Johns, J. and Lee, J. (2011). *Justice League*, #1–6. DC Comics.

Lee, S. and Heck, D. (1964). *The Avengers*, #9. Marvel Comics.

Lee, S. and Kirby, J. (1963). *The Avengers*, #1. Marvel Comics.

Lee, S. and Kirby, J. (1964). *The Avengers*, #4. Marvel Comics.

Loeb, J. and Lee, J. (2002). *Batman*, #608. DC Comics.

Miller, F. (2001–2002). *Batman: The Dark Knight Strikes Again*. DC Comics.

Miller, F. (2016). *Batman: The Dark Knight Returns, 30th Anniversary Edition*. Burbank, CA: DC Comics.

Morrison, G. and Jones, J. (2009). *Final Crisis*, #6. DC Comics.

O'Neil, D., Adams, N., and Giordano, D. (1971). *Green Lantern*, #86. DC Comics.

Ricardo, D. (1996). *Principles of Political Economy and Taxation*. New York: Prometheus Books (Originally published in 1817).

Smith, A. (1994). *An Inquiry into the Nature and Causes of the Wealth of Nations*. New York: Random House (Originally published in 1776).

Willingham, B. and Scott, D. (2004a). *Robin*, #126. DC Comics.

Willingham, B. and Scott, D. (2004b). *Robin*, #128. DC Comics.

4

But Your Enemies Closer...Why Do Superheroes Fight Each Other?

Heroes are typically thought of as the good guys. Superman is out to protect "truth, justice and the American way." Surely he wouldn't do anything to hurt the people around him? Spider-Man is friendly and he's from the neighborhood. His webs evaporate after a few hours so he isn't leaving a mess behind as he swings from building to building. Even the X-Men are sworn to protect a world that hates and fears them (Claremont and Cockrum, 1975). Nevertheless, what makes a hero isn't easy to identify. It's similar to the United States Supreme Court's definition of pornography...you know it when you see it.[1] Heroes have evolved over time as consumer tastes have changed, but even the anti-heroes, Deadpool, Wolverine, Elecktra, Rorschach, and The Punisher, among others, are battling for good, even if their methods might be less than savory.

The expectations we have for heroes makes this chapter a bit more difficult to compose. The good guys fighting the bad guys is an easy trope. It's what all the hero stories from the *Epic of Gilgamesh* to *Harry Potter* portray. At some point along the line, authors decided that audiences preferred the versions where the good guys win, and the more improbable the win, the better. Underdog stories fill us with hope. Redemption stories similarly lift our spirits. The little guy outsmarts the big corporation. The small-town team pulls off the inconceivable victory. The hero wins while the villain fails. All is right with the world.

These are the stories we expect but that theme can wear out its welcome. Even the villains get tired of the repetition. In *Injustice: Gods Among Us* (Taylor et al., 2016), the story is launched by the Joker leaving his normal haunt of Gotham for Metropolis because "every time you [Batman] and I play, I lose. I was getting a bit bored of always losing" (p. 34). Other characters have switched sides entirely. Lex Luthor and Catwoman are two of the more iconic criminals to turn over a new leaf, but there are others. Rogue and Magneto in the X-Men universe were once evildoers. Hawkeye, Sandman, Quicksilver, and Scarlet Witch are off-again on-again members of the Avengers, despite battling them in the past. Plastic Man was a petty criminal prior to gaining his powers.[2]

So, heroes battling villains gets old at some point. What about heroes fighting heroes? Curiously, superheroes, despite their attitudes of being above the fray and notwithstanding their attempts to maintain peace, don't always play well with others. Maybe it is the power going to their head, or an alpha dog mentality, or just general frustration with the poor efforts on the part of criminals, but sometimes heroes need to release their frustrations and other heroes can just end up getting in the way. For readers, such stories are incredibly intriguing. They help address questions of supremacy in the hero world and engage fantasies about who might be more powerful than whom. That all aside, there is actually an economic explanation for this behavior as well. It is found in a set of tools known as game theory. Game theory is an extremely powerful assortment of kit that can explain a range of behaviors and outcomes beyond the scope of normal economic models. Game theory can help us answer one of the most perplexing questions in all the comics: Why do heroes fight each other?

Heroes Fighting Heroes

One of the more significant instances of heroes fighting appears in the graphic novel *The Dark Knight Returns*.[3] Batman and Superman battle over a philosophical difference regarding how to prosecute the war on crime. The President of the United States calls on Superman to take out Batman and, ever the company man, Supes complies, or at least tries to. This epic storyline of its most fabled characters battling each other isn't unique to DC Comics. It also appears in the Marvel universe, in *Civil War* in particular, where heroes of all stripes sign up to fight other heroes on teams led by Iron Man and Captain America. For those who haven't grown up reading comics, this is downright weird. Weren't they the *Super Friends* on Saturday morning cartoons? Spider-Man's witticisms were on display as he and his *Amazing Friends* were embroiled with all manner of villainous chicanery.[4] What has changed that prevents heroes from getting along these days? Is it just a symptom of the vitriolic mood in America and the divisions that run deep? The answer to that is no. It's actually been that way for a long time, it's just that those stories are now making their way to the big screen.

It is amazing that that these characters who are so devoted to protecting the public good can so often go off the rails. Weldon (2016) provides a nice synopsis of the reasons why heroes often come to blows. His nine "conflict catalysts" provide some contextual rationale for why heroes forego their own advice of talking it out and resort to letting their fists speak for them. It is worth mentioning a few of the things on the list to set the stage for the economic angle to this chapter.

One reason to fight is called "the elaborate ruse". In the silver age of comics (1950s and 60s), putting characters into bizarre scenarios out of which they had to escape was commonplace. The story ended with a predictably zany explanation of why there was conflict between the paragons of virtue. These stories put the "ugh" in skullduggery.[5] Heroes might fight but it was all to trick some villain into thinking he had a chance to defeat the Super Friends who would never turn on each other.

Another explanation for why heroes fight is the doppelganger. This is perhaps the easiest explanatory tool available to writers, in part because there are so many duplicates, clones, and robots, as well as other universes, floating around in the world of comics. Nearly every major character has at some point been impersonated by a calumniator who is trying to besmirch the name of the good guy. For example, in 2017 Marvel put Captain America in the incredibly awkward position of being a Hydra agent (Spencer and McNiven, 2017).[6] After decades of anti-Nazi activity, Cap was shown as a member of the cabal he most hated. Immediately readers began posing theories of why. Turns out, it wasn't Captain America at all—just a duplicate.

Of course, sometimes the reason heroes fight each other is because they aren't in their right minds. Maybe even easier than the duplicitous duplicate is the hero who is under the power of mind control. With aliens, villains, and mystics possessing the ability to telepathically control others, it isn't a surprise that they often put heroes under a spell to get them to do their bidding. An example of this occurred when Jessica Jones was basically bewitched by the heinous villain Killgrave. He sent her on a mission to kill Daredevil, which almost cost Jessica her life (Bendis and Gaydos, 2003).

Then there is the old green-eyed monster, jealousy. Heroes are not immune to resentfulness and it can lead to famously tension-filled conflict. Mr Fantastic, aka Reed Richards, is married to Sue, but Namor the Sub-Mariner has the hots for her. If Mr Fantastic and Namor are in the same room it is almost certain that there will be a fight in the next panel.

These are just some of the ways in which heroes end up at each other's throats. While you might be familiar with the Batman versus Superman story, or the movie *Avengers: Civil War*, the stimuli for hero on hero violence has led to a number of other altercations throughout the years. Wolverine and Cyclops have never liked each other, based on a mutual attraction to Jean Grey, and have fought innumerable times. Similarly, Wolverine hates Deadpool. The problem with their fights is that both have incredible healing powers. A winner can be declared but no lasting damage will occur. These guys just like to fight. Superman and Wonder Woman have had their titanic clashes as well. The typical reason is mind control (see Englehart and Dillin, 1977; Rucka et al., 2005; and Tomasi, Mahnke, and Benes, 2015), although in *Injustice* there is some trickery involved (Buccellato and Miller, 2015). The Hulk and the Thing have battled multiple times for supremacy as the strongest of the strong. Their first bout was in 1964 (Lee and Kirby, 1964).

All of this adds to the point that heroes fighting each other isn't a new phenomenon. It's been going on for a long, long time. Here, however, let's put away the more mundane reasons heroes don't get along and examine a more encompassing and palpable set of disagreements. Sometimes heroes fight because they don't see any other way around a conflict. Just because heroes are always fighting for good, doesn't mean that they will agree on what good means or looks like. Heroes often have to deal with issues of extreme significance. Defending the world or making it safe for everyone often involves making choices on a grand scale, a scale that would have more universal ramifications than deciding what color socks to wear. The battle in Marvel's *Civil War* is a fight over how much government oversight to accept. Similarly, Batman and Superman fight over whether Batman should have free reign to conduct his war on crime. In *Injustice*, tensions escalate in the DC Universe over whether Superman should be allowed to become the ruler of Earth, and super-powered people are forced to take sides. These are momentous issues of social and political import. It is understandable why the heroes do not come to an easy agreement. There are enough people involved in debating the issues at hand that the elaborate ruse, doppelgangers, mind control, and jealousy do not explain the strife. Hero discord is a result of a more fundamental contention. It is the stuff of geopolitics. In these cases, there are vastly different worldviews on how heroes should do their jobs and what the job description looks like. If we want to understand why they fight, we need a different set of tools. It is now time to introduce ourselves to game theory.

Game Theory: The Basics

Game theory is actually a branch of mathematics. That means there are numbers and computations and, at times, remarkably complicated sets of equations that need to be solved simultaneously. It's like looking at the calculations movie scientists use when they are determining how to land a rocket on the moon, or the quantum physics necessary for time travel. With dramatic music setting the tone, mathematicians work their numerical wizardry until they fill chalk boards, or better yet glass panes so you can see not only the numbers but the concentration upon the face of the actors, and when they finally put down their writing instrument you release your breath and silently rejoice that you stopped studying math after high school.

That being said, some game theory is quite manageable for those who do not possess the superpower of computing integrals in their heads. It does require some concentration to work through games but the results can be rewarding, and helpful in understanding certain outcomes. While game theory is math, it has been co-opted by economists to analyze behavior in certain kinds of settings. To understand this better, think about the different types of games in the world. There are certainly games that rely upon chance, such as playing the slots. A slot machine, if calibrated correctly, will take your money a vast majority of the time. Occasionally you will win, but those occasions are purely random. Slots are a mindless game.[7] Put money in, pull the handle (or press the button), watch the wheels spin, see the one-armed bandit take your money. Over at the poker table, however, there are people playing hands of cards who are considering all kinds of facets of probability and manipulation. Yes, there is an element of chance in poker—the dealer needs to get you the best cards and that is supposed to be a random occurrence—however, there are strategies that players adopt to affect the way their competitors behave. For example, how much do you bet if you are dealt a full house? You want to draw out the betting to extract as much as possible from your competitors because you believe no one will have a higher hand than you. If you go all-in right away, everyone at the table folds and your take will be small. To be a good poker player it helps to be lucky, but you need to know the odds and you need to have a strategy when you bet. Game theory is like poker in that regard. It involves using mathematics to explain strategic actions taken by economic agents.

On a relatively basic level, game theory can be used to explain a lot of seemingly irrational behavior. For instance, why do firms advertise? Advertising is very expensive. Wouldn't two large, well-established firms in a market be better off not doing it? This would allow the two firms to increase their profits and they wouldn't lose customers because their competitor isn't advertising to try and take them away. Coke and Pepsi, Budweiser and Miller, DC and Marvel, advertising for these firms is not only a money-loser, it is also a peculiarity. Why do they do it? A seemingly unrelated question is why do so many professional cyclists and track sprinters take drugs? They have to know the side-effects by now. There are risks of being discredited as a fraud (right, Lance Armstrong?) and all kinds of health issues (right, all you studio wrestlers?). Yet they do it with impunity, paying significant sums to keep their behavior under wraps.

Of all the games in the game theory world, perhaps the most classic is called the prisoner's dilemma. The name insinuates that the actions of bad guys might pose a predicament once they are apprehended. That is true but the quandary doesn't just apply to criminals. It is this dilemma that explains why firms advertise and athletes cheat, and will finally help us answer the question of why heroes fight each other. Before we get to that answer though, we need to set up the rules of the game.

Please Read All the Rules Before Playing

All games have parts and game theory is no different. To begin, you must have players. An interesting game will have at least two players trying to use their mental prowess to best each other. The players also need to have a couple of options for how they are going to go about winning the game. These are called the strategies. What course of action will you take as the game progresses? Here is where game theory diverts from other types of economic analysis. The outcome of the game depends not just upon what strategy you adopt, but also on that of the other player or players. You need to incorporate the plans of the players you are up against into your strategy because your success depends upon not only your choices, but also the choices of your competitors. In other words, your actions are interdependent.

You also need a set of rules so that the game is played fairly. To understand the rules, it is important to realize that there are lots of different games that can be played and, as a result, not all games are the same. In fact, the rules will often dictate the outcome of a game and a little tweak to those rules results in a different predicted outcome entirely. There are a few things that must be firmly established prior to the playing of a game. One of those is to know whether you are playing a one-shot game or a game that has multiple, or perhaps infinite, stages.

A one-shot game, as the name implies, occurs only once. As a result, you do not have an opportunity to respond to the actions of another player. This would be like playing a single game of rock-paper-scissors to determine who gets the last piece of cake. It's a one-time, winner-take-all, type of game, and what strategy you adopt is based on what you know of your competitor. A game that is played multiple times allows you to react to what has happened in the past. If cake goes to the player who wins the best three out of five times the game is played, then there is an opportunity to react to the prior strategy of your competitor. So, if you are playing against someone who throws rock twice in a row, you might see a pattern and try to exploit it.[8] If the game was only played once and you had no information about your opponent, you would essentially be playing the game blind.

A second rule that needs to be established is whether the game is to be played simultaneously or sequentially. This rule deals with when you make your move. Do both players go at the same time, or does one player go first and the other react to them? In a game of rock-paper-scissors the game must be played simultaneously. Both players must throw at the same time, otherwise it isn't much of a game. If I could wait to decide what to do until after you had revealed your strategy, I would win every time and you would find the game pointless. Many games allow the participants to react to what their competitors do. If we are playing poker and you bid, I can call, raise, or fold. Because I have the opportunity to react to what you have done, the game is sequential.

These basic rules are enough for the game we will examine in this chapter because our focus is on trying to explain why heroes fight each other, that seemingly unnatural result of good guys failing to talk things out. Before applying game theory to comics though, there is one other important detail to consider. When the outcome of a contest depends in part on the behavior of others, it would make sense to gather as much information about the strategies of your opponents as possible. Sports teams do this all the time by studying film. Of course, teams know that their opponents are also watching past events so they need to switch up strategies every so often to keep their rivals on their toes. As research suggests, in some sporting events, randomization is the best approach for success.[9] This means that you try to vary your strategies to prevent your opponent from determining a pattern in your actions that they could exploit.

This could be true of the comic universe as well. The players are the professionals of the crime-fighting and criminal worlds and they repeatedly engage with each other. As a result, both sides have data on the others' reactions to particular situations. If you want to avoid always being caught by the hero, the criminal needs to vary their approach. Early in the graphic novel *The Killing Joke,* Batman admits to his butler-cum-confidant, Alfred, that "I've been trying to figure out what he intends to do. It's almost impossible. I don't know him, Alfred. All these years and I don't know who he is any more than he knows who I am" (Moore, Bolland, and Higgins, 1988, p.17). Batman's inability to predict the Joker's next move is the perfect example of the randomness that can affect outcomes in comics. Batman wants to apprehend the Joker, but determining Joker's strategy is impossible due to the arbitrary nature of his actions. Joker will engage in some kind of crazy connivance, but what will it be? When the Joker is at work there is no way to tell.

He'd Never Rat Me Out . . . Would He?

Late one night the fine men in blue of the Central City Police Department drag two staggering, bewildered hooligans into the precinct. The disheveled pair are thrown into separate holding cells to await processing and, perhaps, a visit from a public defender. Before that can happen though, the cops want to get some information out of the alleged perpetrators. In one cell the stoic figure of Leonard Snart sits peacefully. He's been here before and knows the routine. Snart has a list of aliases, but to most people he is known as Captain Cold.

Snart has been picked up for a relatively petty offense, especially considering his rap sheet. He was arrested for vandalism. Nevertheless, Snart has kept his nose clean over the past few years and appears to be on the straight and narrow, eschewing his former life of crime. Still, around Central City, fake bills have been appearing. A counterfeiting ring is afoot and the quality of the bills makes them nearly indistinguishable from the real thing. There is no evidence and there are no suspects, but word around town is that Snart is off the wagon. While he waits for what he expects to be the normal line of questions, Snart isn't worried about the outcome. He knows the other guy and there is no way he'll talk, even if Snart was part of the counterfeiting ring (maybe he is, and maybe he isn't, he'll never tell), the other guy is his best buddy, at least as far as criminals have best buddies.

Without warning, the door opens and in walks a young woman in a tailored suit. She sits down across from Snart and lays a folder on the table between them. She begins to ask the normal questions but abruptly stops when she sees the look in Snart's eyes. This isn't getting her anywhere, so she decides to lay all her cards on the table.

"Look Snart," she begins, "we've got you on the graffiti rap, and with your priors you're going away for two years, minimum."

No surprise, Snart thinks. He was expecting this.

"But, you better help us out with the counterfeiting stuff," the woman continues.

Not likely, Snart says to himself. That's a serious crime.

"If we find you guilty on that charge you're looking at twenty years with no possibility of parole," the detective informs him. She stands up and moves toward the door.

"Leaving already?" Snart snickers.

"Oh yes. You see, even if you don't help us, your pal next door is ready to talk. We've made him a nice deal if he turns state's evidence and he's willing to take it. One year. He knows you'll be gone for twenty so that's enough time for him to make a new life for himself far away. We'd offer you that deal too, but it doesn't seem like you're interested. Maybe you'll change your mind in a few minutes. I've got to go take a statement."

Snart's mouth drops open.

"He won't talk," he gapes. "Mick would never do that!"

But as the door closes, Snart's confidence is more than a little shaken.

Out in the hall, the officer smiles. Turning to the next interrogation room, she takes a breath and, without knocking, walks boldly in. Sitting there is Mick Rory, alias Heat Wave. He and Snart have been thick as thieves, literally, for a long time. Both members of the criminal group the Rogues, a team of DC-based criminals who frequently match wits with the Flash, they have been suspiciously quiet for some time now.

"Look Rory," she begins, "I'm not here to waste your time. We've got you on the graffiti rap, and with your priors you're going away for a couple of years."

No surprise, Rory thinks. He was expecting this.

"But, you better help us out with the counterfeiting stuff," the woman continues.

Not likely, Rory says to himself. That's a serious crime.

"If we find you guilty on that charge you're looking at twenty years with no possibility of parole," the detective informs him. She stands up and moves toward the door.

"Leaving already?" Rory snickers.

"Oh yes. You see, even if you don't help us, your pal next door is ready to talk. We've made him a nice deal if he turns state's evidence and he's willing to take it. One year. He knows you'll be gone for twenty so that's enough time for him to make a new life for himself far away. We'd offer you that deal too, but it doesn't seem like you're interested. Maybe you'll change your mind in a few minutes. I've got to go take a statement."

Rory's mouth drops open.

"He won't talk," he gapes. "Snart would never do that!"

But as the door closes, Rory's confidence is more than a little shaken. Out in the hall, the officer smiles.

This is the prisoner's dilemma. If both criminals keep quiet they will both get two years. Despite the officer's claims, she doesn't have enough evidence to convict them of counterfeiting. By the way, Snart and Rory are in cahoots. They are indeed running the counterfeiting ring, so if either wants to provide evidence for the prosecution, they could do so. The deal that has been offered is only good if one of the crooks talks and the other does not. If they both confess, they both get ten years. So, can Rory trust Snart to keep his mouth shut? Can Snart trust Rory? The answer is, they probably can, but they're thieves and as the saying goes, there is no honor among thieves, even friends like Rory and Snart. As a result, each criminal has a dominant strategy to confess, which results in an outcome that leaves them worse off than if they had kept quiet.

A dominant strategy is a choice a player would make no matter what the other player did. To see this more clearly, let's look at how the prisoner's dilemma game is illustrated in a game theory matrix like that of Figure 4.1. Each criminal is labeled along one edge of the matrix. In this case, Snart along the side and Rory at the top. There are only two strategies here: Confess or don't confess. Each cell within the matrix provides the number of years for each player. Those are the payoffs. To limit confusion, Snart's payoffs are underlined.

Notice a few things about this game. Because it is shown in a matrix, the game is considered to be simultaneous. Players make their choice of strategy at the same time. If Snart goes first then Rory can easily choose the best thing for him given Snart's decision. The question of whether he should toe the criminal line is an easier one. Since neither knows what the other will do with certainty before they make their choice however, it leaves them in a bit of a quandary. Additionally, this is a

		Rory	
		Confess	Don't Confess
Snart	Confess	10, 10	1, 20
	Don't Confess	20, 1	2, 2

Figure 4.1. The Rogue's Dilemma.

one-shot game. You do not have a chance to alter your strategy once you find out what your co-conspirator has done.

To find the dominant strategy let's examine the potential outcomes. If neither Snart nor Rory confess, that puts the hooligans in the southeast box where each goes to jail for two years. This box yields the smallest joint number of years in prison and that is good for them, but individually they could be better off. If Snart changes his mind and confesses while Rory stays silent, the outcome for the game moves to the northeast box where Snart receives the underlined value of one year in jail, while Rory's term goes from two to twenty! Thus, for Snart, if Rory is going to keep quiet and not confess, he is better off confessing because one year in the slammer is less than two. If, however, Rory decides he will confess, and perhaps he has told this to Snart ahead of time, Snart needs to incorporate this into his strategy. If he doesn't confess, the dastardly duo is in the southwest box. Here Snart gets twenty years while Rory only gets one. Snart would be better off turning informant and confessing because he would cut his sentence to ten years. Ten years is a lot of time in prison but it's far less than twenty years. So if Rory confesses, the best thing for Snart to do, in order to keep his jail time low, would be to also confess. Therefore, no matter what Rory does, Snart is better off by confessing, so that is what he will do, and that is what makes confessing a dominant strategy.

Rory's logic should follow similar reasoning. Again, starting in the southeast box where neither criminal confesses, Rory sees an opportunity. If Snart isn't going to confess then he should. That would cut his penalty from two years to only one. Thus, if Snart is not going to confess, Rory would be best served, in terms of less jail time, to confess. On the other hand, if Snart tells Rory that he will snitch no matter what Rory does then it is in Rory's self-interest to also confess. If Snart confesses and Rory does not, the scoundrels would be in the northeast box. There Snart serves a year, but Rory gets twenty. By likewise confessing, Rory gets ten years, again, not an insignificant amount of time, but far better than twenty years. So, no matter what Snart does, Rory is better off by confessing.

Not all games have dominant strategies but the prisoner's dilemma does. That's part of what makes it a dilemma. There is a path that the criminals can take that results in less jail time no matter what the other criminal does, but that path leads to more *combined* jail time than one of the alternatives. This puts the crooks in a real pickle. They end up with a joint sentence of twenty years, rather than the aggregated four they could have had, because the dominant strategy leads to this suboptimal outcome.

In real life there are ways to avoid the prisoner's dilemma. If you've ever watched a mob movie you've probably seen such a tactic. The mob uses the threat of bodily harm to you or those you care about to keep potential witnesses in line. If you confess, someone will either whack you, whack your kids, or torture your grandmother and your pets. It's a grizzly business, but it is actually an attempt to get out of the prisoner's dilemma. In the comics, the prisoner's dilemma is often gotten around by the plain fact that supervillains break out of jail with relative ease.

That's the prisoner's dilemma in the case of jail time; but we're not here to talk about criminals. We're supposed to explain why heroes engage in non-hero-like behavior. It just so happens that if we take the prisoner's dilemma and apply it to hero on hero crime, we have our answer.

What Heroes and Prisoners Have in Common

The dilemma we have just reviewed between two criminals can be explained by a lack of trust, but that doesn't preclude it from impacting heroes. Situations such as *Batman v Superman* or Marvel's *Civil War* or *Injustice: Gods Among Us* all have climactic, unexpected, punishing fights where we readers hold our collective breath as we wonder how they will play out. Yet, underlying the tensions between groups of heroes who had recently been on the same side is the question "why?" The implications of the prisoner's dilemma can provide insight into these cataclysmic battles among heroes, not to mention some of the more minor skirmishes that we discussed earlier in this chapter.

Since *Batman v Superman: Dawn of Justice* was such a bad movie, let's instead focus our analysis on Marvel's *Civil War*.[10] The movie and the comic take slightly different approaches in setting up the conflict. I am going to follow the comic storyline as it strikes a more tragic tone, but either way, the impetus for the disagreement is that a hero escapade results in unacceptable collateral damage.

In *Civil War* we find the organization of heroes called the Avengers at odds over how to react to a tragedy where a band of third-tier superheroes filming a reality television show try to capture an escaped cadre of villains above their pay grade. In order to avoid capture, the villain Nitro blows himself up (he can put himself back together so for him this is no big deal). The collateral damage was an elementary school where 800–900 people may have been killed.[11] This begins a serious discussion of whether to register superheroes with the government. After being confronted at a funeral by the mother of one of the children killed, Tony

Stark begins to rally the troops to the side of registration. Meanwhile, Captain America is ordered to help handle any supers who refuse to adhere to government orders to register. Believing that such governmental interference would lead to politicians holding puppet strings over heroes, Captain America goes underground, rallying troops to his cause.[12] A few attempts are made at civil discourse but they fail spectacularly. What we're dealing with here is a failure to communicate.

So, let's set up the teams. In one corner, we have Captain America, who doesn't want to be told how to defend people. In the other corner, Iron Man thinks it's a good idea to install a system of accountability. Each hero believes he is in the right and is ready to fight the other to prove it. In one climactic scene, a fight breaks out and the hero Goliath is killed. This ends any chance of reconciliation between the two sides. However, prior to this event, readers expect some diplomatic solution that never comes. The fighting is suboptimal. Not only is Goliath dead but a great fissure runs through the hero community. Because they are fighting each other, as Spider-Man correctly notes, it is only the bad guys who win. The fighting makes no one better off and actually makes a lot of people worse off. This sounds like a similar situation to that of the two guys sitting in separate jail cells trying to decide if they should become snitches for the cops.

In the game matrix shown in Figure 4.2, we can see what happens as the two groups make war. The two rows are Captain America's two strategic options, fight or talk it out, and the two columns are Iron Man's alternatives, fight or talk it out. In the payoff cells, Cap's payoffs are underlined. If they sit down and hash things out peaceably, assuming each side negotiates in good faith, it is reasonable to presume that both sides get something they want and no one gets hurt. It isn't a perfect solution for either side but that's what happens in a compromise. In this case, we find the heroes in the southeast box where both Captain America and Iron Man receive payoffs of 10.

If they go to war, they both get a payoff of 2 as shown in the northwest box. Call it comic book machismo but engaging in a fight yields

		Iron Man	
		Fight	Talk it out
Captain	Fight	2, 2	15, 0
America	Talk it out	0, 15	10, 10

Figure 4.2. The Avenger's Dilemma.

some positive benefit for the combatants (except Goliath of course, because he's dead). Where the dilemma comes into play, just like for the two jailbirds, is in the northeast and southwest boxes. These "off diagonals" show that by backing down in the face of a fight, the loser gets nothing. The principles they stand for are lost and they don't even get to throw a punch! This occurs for Cap if he chooses to talk it out while Iron Man fights, as demonstrated in the southwest box. Here Cap gets 0 while Iron Man gets 15. It occurs for Iron Man if he chooses to talk it out while Captain America fights, as demonstrated in the northeast box, where Iron Man gets 0 and Cap gets 15. Following the logic of the prisoner's dilemma, each party has a dominant strategy. No matter what the other hero chooses, the largest payoff for both heroes individually is to fight. If both heroes follow their dominant strategy, that puts the game in the northwest box, with a payoff of 2 for each. In other words, the Avengers (and other heroes in the Marvel universe) end up in a civil war rather than détente. The joint payoff could have been 20 (each side receives a payoff of 10 if they negotiate), but instead the joint payoff is 4 (each gets 2 for fighting). What we have here is not only a failure to communicate, but also a prisoner's dilemma, not between thieves but between heroes.

As fans of these characters, we are used to seeing them fight. It happens a lot, but the extent to which *Civil War* and other large-scale hero against hero battles lead to what can only be considered bloodletting is shocking. But that's what you get with a prisoner's dilemma. In the comic, it is only when Captain America realizes the damage the civil war is causing to the civilians he had sworn to protect that he surrenders to authorities and the war ends. Otherwise, the two sides might still be following their dominant strategies.

And the Answer Is...

Curiously, superheroes, despite their attitudes of being above the fray and their attempts to maintain peace, will often fight each other. Sometimes this is conducted within the scope of group rivalries. The Avengers and the X-Men battle occasionally but the more familiar fights occur within teams or between famous heroes. Any fighting amongst themselves seems oddly out of character, but employing game theory in general, and the prisoner's dilemma in particular, helps us to explain these uncharacteristically personal battles.[13]

People often engage in actions that are harmful. Only in hindsight do they realize that their strategies were poor, and comic book heroes are no different. Game theory can explain seemingly irrational behavior because it allows us to consider multiple strategies and how the players will react to each other. This interdependence isn't part and parcel of most economic models, but that doesn't mean that every scenario we face is a candidate for a game theoretic explanation. In fact, most of the time basic economic theory works quite well at predicting outcomes of events, but in some cases we need to dig deeper into the economic tool bag to understand hero behavior.

Endnotes

1. Supreme Court Justice Potter Stewart used this as a threshold for obscenity in *Jacobellis v. Ohio* in 1964. The case revolved around the question of whether the state of Ohio had the right to ban a movie called *The Lovers* and remain in compliance with the First Amendment to the U.S. Constitution. Justice Stewart said that the First Amendment allowed all pornography except the hardcore variety. When asked to explain what constitutes hardcore porn, he replied "I shall not today attempt further to define the kinds of material I understand to be embraced within that shorthand description; and perhaps I could never succeed in intelligibly doing so. But I know it when I see it, and the motion picture involved in this case is not that" (*Jacobellis v. Ohio*, 1964).
2. Plastic Man's powers were gained in a hardscrabble way however, as he had to fall into a vat of experimental acid and lived with monks in the mountains for a few months while he recovered.
3. If this sounds familiar, it is because this material forms the basis for the movie *Batman v Superman: Dawn of Justice*.
4. In the good ole days before cable television, cartoons would appear on network television for a few hours after school and for a few hours on Saturday morning.
5. Yes, I know there is no "ugh" in skullduggery, but there is an "ugh" sound so if you read it aloud this sentence works rather well.
6. Pervading the Marvel universe, Hydra is the ultra-secretive terrorist organization with Nazi roots against which Captain America has fought nearly his entire existence.
7. Walk through a casino some time and look at the slots players. Most of them are zombies. No, really. The mindlessness of what they are doing has sucked out their brains, their souls, and everything that makes them human.
8. As an example of this, Lisa and Bart Simpson play rock-paper-scissors to determine which of their names will go first on a script they have written. Lisa knows she will win because "poor predictable Bart. Always takes rock." While Bart is thinking "Good ole rock. Nothing beats that!" (*Simpsons*, 1993).
9. After studying the moves of goal tenders and players in soccer, Chiappori et al. (2002) show that the actions of these competitors, who study each other's moves and upon whom there are hundreds, if not thousands, of instances of taking and trying to block kicks, are closer to a randomized strategy than

almost any academic exercise. Similarly, Walker and Wooders (2001) demonstrate that tennis players must have some randomness to their strategy on the serve. If they continue to serve to their opponents forehand, no matter how good the serve is the opponent will beat them. These studies, along with one conducted by Palacios-Huerta (2003), demonstrate that randomness in adopting strategies is important in sports, primarily because of the many, many repeated interactions amongst players. At the professional level of sport, it is the expected randomness that allows economists to predict strategy—a random strategy. That may sound odd but all that means is that rather than focus on a strategy over and over again, in sports you must mix things up. In professional baseball, the pitcher who throws nothing but fastballs will not be a pro for long because the hitter always knows what is coming. If you take your penalty kicks low and to the left every time, goalies will stop you enough that you won't get a chance to take penalties often.

10. To support my contention, critics on the website Rotten Tomatoes (n.d.) ranked the film at 27%, while audiences gave it a barely passing grade of 63%.

11. In the movie the events that lead to the attempt to register superheroes is the devastation of the fictional country Sokovia in a battle with the villain Ultron, and the death of some Wakandian aid workers in an attempt to avert a biological weapon attack.

12. In the movie, the main combatants include Captain America, Hawkeye, Falcon, Bucky Barnes, Scarlet Witch, and Ant-Man squaring off against Iron Man, War Machine, Black Widow, Black Panther, The Vision, and Spider-Man. The comic book version of this story involves many other heroes and different alliances.

13. For more on heroes and game theory see O'Roark and Grant (2018).

References

Bendis, B. and Gaydos, M. (2003). *Alias*, #25. Marvel Comics.

Buccellato, B. and Miller, M. (2015). *Injustice: Gods Among Us: Year Four*, #9. DC Comics.

Chiappori, P., Levitt, S., and Groseclose, T. (2002). Testing Mixed-Strategy Equilibrium When Players Are Heterogeneous: The Case of Penalty Kicks in Soccer. *American Economic Review*, 92(4), pp. 1138–51.

Claremont, C. and Cockrum, D. (1975). *X-Men*, #96. Marvel Comics.

Englehart, S. and Dillin, D. (1977). *Justice League*, #143. DC Comics.

Jacobellis v. Ohio. [1964]. 378 U.S. 184 (Supreme Court of the United States); 1.

Lee, S. and Kirby, J. (1964). *Fantastic Four*, #25. Marvel Comics.

Miller, F. (2016). *Batman: The Dark Knight Returns, 30th Anniversary Edition*. Burbank, CA: DC Comics.

Moore, A., Bolland, B., and Higgins, J. (1988). *The Killing Joke*. DC Comics.

O'Roark, B. and Grant, B. (2018). Games Superheroes Play: Teaching Game Theory with Comic Book Favorites. *Journal of Economic Education*, 49(2), pp. 180–93.

Palacios-Huerta, I. (2003). Professionals Play Minimax. *Review of Economic Studies*, 70(2), pp. 395–415.

Rucka, G., Derenick, T., Jeanty, G., Kershl, K., Lopez, D., and Morales, R. (2005). *Wonder Woman*, #219. DC Comics.

Simpsons. (1993). [Television series episode]. The Front. Culver City, CA: Rich Moore.

Spencer, N. and McNiven, S. (2017). *Secret Empire*, #1. Marvel Comics.

Rotten Tomatoes. (n.d.). Batman v Superman: Dawn of Justice. [Online] Available at https://www.rottentomatoes.com/m/batman_v_superman_dawn_of_justice# audience_reviews [Accessed August 20, 2018].

Taylor, R., Raapack, J., and Miller, M. (2016). *Injustice: Gods Among Us: Year One, The Complete Collection*. Burbank, CA: DC Comics.

Tomasi, P., Mahnke, D., and Benes, E. (2015). *Superman/Wonder Woman*, #17. DC Comics.

Walker, M. and Wooders, J. (2001). Minimax Play at Wimbledon. *American Economic Review*, 91(5), pp. 1521–38.

Weldon, G. (2016). Superheroes are fighting each other because they always have. Here's Why. [Online] Mashable. Available at: http://mashable.com/2016/06/ 21/superhero-fights/#Xs2D339kUOqo [Accessed April 4, 2018].

5

Don't Give Up Your Day Job. Why Do Superheroes Go to Work?

Since the advent of money, people have wondered how they can transform what they have into something spendable. Economists investigate how the skill, education, experience, or other non-tangible attributes a person brings to a task, what we call human capital, can improve one's earning potential. They also pay close attention to income disparities. They debate such things as whether raising the minimum wage might help lift people out of poverty and whether cycles of poverty can be overcome. Despite their cold-hearted reputations, economists really do care about the well-being of all people, not just the rich. This means our deep-seated concern must extend to superheroes because, despite their varied talents, there isn't one of them called Money Man. Money Man's power would be shooting money out of his fingers. He would never be short of cash. He'd always pick up the bill for the team and he would almost certainly be an excellent tipper. Alas, he doesn't exist.

It is possible to imagine that if Aquaman walked into the corner tavern for chowder and fries or if Dr. Strange floated into a diner and asked for a milkshake, someone might offer to pick up the tab. After a while however, perhaps in one of those dark times where the general populace doesn't trust the hero world, Aquaman is going to have to pay for his own dinner. If he can't find a bank to convert the currency of Atlantis to dollars, he's going to end up doing dishes. Dr Strange burned through all of his money trying to fix his hands. If Aquaman asks him for a loan, he isn't going to get much help. What's a hero down on his luck to do? Well, they could behave like the rest of us and get a job.

In economics we talk about improving human capital to raise your earning potential so that you can not only afford rent and meals, but also start paying back that mountain of student debt you acquired while building the human capital. Heroes have had human capital bestowed on them in spades. Other than Squirrel Girl and Firestar, both of whom are or were attending college and probably paying tuition, there aren't any significant heroes who built their human capital through the traditional, expensive higher education system. Squirrel Girl isn't adding to her superpowers by attending classes, she just wants to learn about a lot of things. Firestar studied physics and got a job at the Jean Grey School.[1]

With superheroes, we have a segment of the population who possess a unique set of skills that should be able to make them enormously wealthy. If nothing else, they could become professional athletes. A team of baseball players with Flash leading off, Black Panther at shortstop, and She-Hulk batting cleanup would make the 1927 New York Yankees look like a little league team,[2] and those same Yankees would pay hundreds of millions, if not billions, of dollars to acquire that talent. Superman would be the first billion-dollar player. It isn't like heroes can't play sports. The X-Men regularly get together for a baseball game. Victor Stone, prior to becoming Cyborg, was a division one football prospect who now literally has a rocket for an arm. There are certainly ways that these heroes could employ their skills, even below the radar, to become rich beyond the dreams of avarice.

Yes, there are some characters who seem to be unburdened by the mundane concerns of subsistence. Bruce Wayne and Oliver Queen are famously trust fund babies. Danny Rand is the heir to Rand Enterprises, a multi-billion-dollar company. Professor Xavier is sitting on a pile of cash as a result of a financially successful father. How else can he afford to keep his School for the Gifted open and provide an SRS Blackbird for them to fly around in?[3] Black Panther, being the king of the nation of Wakanda which holds the world's only known reserves of a metal called vibranium, is a multi-trillionaire.[4] Those in the god category presumably have stocks of wealth—Thor, for instance, doesn't seem to be hurting for a little spending money now and then. Other characters are self-starters and were making a name for themselves even without powers. Tony Stark, Reed Richards, Emma Frost, and Adrian Veidt have made vast fortunes on their own.[5] This wealth was all created without the aid of superpowers.

What is curious about the hero world isn't how many rich people inhabit it, but rather how many poor ones do. Sure, it is expected that prior to attaining their status as defender of the weak, some of these people were weak and powerless themselves. Some were barely scraping by. After Peter Parker's uncle died, his Aunt May had to go into debt to pay the rent. Luke Cage was in jail preceding his elevation to Power Man. Silver Surfer was a slave for centuries so he's got no savings account to fall back on.

Others were doing OK but then their powers caused them to lose it all. The best example of this is Bruce Banner who, after becoming the Hulk, decided to give up his career as a scientist for fear of destroying everything and everyone with whom he came into contact. To avoid the rage-inducing features of a nine-to-five job, such as rush hour traffic and requests to work weekends, Banner removed himself from society. Jessica Jones got her powers as a result of an accident that killed her family (Bendis and Gaydos, 2001). This left her traumatized and after a brief stint as a hero she retired from that business, believing she could not live up to the expectations. Her career as a private investigator has not brought her riches and at one point Jessica notes that she is so poor she has ramen noodles coming out of her nose (Bendis and Gaydos, 2002).

So, what's the deal here? Why aren't heroes using their powers for the time-honored tradition of enriching themselves? At the very least they could form the best circus ever. They could be tremendously entertaining and consumers would pay loads of money to watch them. Hiring Zatanna as a consultant couldn't hurt.[6] She's been performing on stage for years and seems to be set financially.

The thing is, in the few instances where heroes try to charge for their services there is a palpable uncomfortableness. In the *Justice League* #0 (Johns and Frank, 2011), we are provided with the backstory of Shazam. Young Billy Batson is granted magical powers by a mysterious wizard. Uttering the magic word—yes, you guessed it "Shazam"—Billy is transformed into a hero with the wisdom of Solomon, the strength of Hercules, etc., etc., etc.[7] When he first gains these powers, Billy and his foster brother Freddy run around town doing all kinds of things. Shazam is big and tall, which opens doors for the young teens. However, Shazam is drawn to people who need help. In one of these instances Billy stops a purse thief. The woman whose purse was saved offers him $20, more money than Billy has ever seen. Chagrined, he takes the money and he and Freddy go on a minor spending spree. Freddy believes they have hit on a money-making scheme, but the artwork shows a look on Billy's face that makes the reader think Billy knows this is wrong.

It is in these moments where the tension level rises. It is almost like there is a hero code that has been violated by the mere suggestion that a payment is expected. Fans of heroes balk at the idea of money changing hands. Even if the hero is in dire straits, the thought of making money from their powers only crosses their minds occasionally, unless there is a business model set up, and even if there is, accepting money is frowned upon. When it is accepted, the price paid is usually far below market value.

We expect more from heroes than a hand extended for a money grab. If they say anything less than "Just doing my job mam" it is a bit off-putting. Really though, a hero has to eat too (except a couple of them who don't actually need to eat), so who are we to deny them a living? Well, as has been the case throughout this book, there is something that economics can offer to explain why a hero is better off not trying to earn a living through their powers alone. Hero work won't pay the bills unless you're willing to enter the protection racket. To understand why, let's first explore the world of the working superhero stiff. Then we'll discuss the problems they face when trying to charge the ungrateful masses.

Working for a Living

Some hero aliases are known by their occupations. Clark Kent—reporter. Peter Parker—photographer. Jessica Jones—private investigator. Hal Jordan—Air Force pilot. Barry Allen—crime scene investigator. Matt Murdock—lawyer. Diana Prince—Army nurse. Donald Blake—medical student.[8] Unless you are part of the X-Men with a salary and benefits, it can be hard to make ends meet. Costumes need to be patched, accessories need to be purchased or produced, wounds need to be mended. Being a hero means you need a source of funding to keep fighting evil and to look the part. As a result, heroes go to work.

Peter Parker is an interesting case study here. After his close encounter of the arachnid kind, Peter notices his enhanced abilities almost immediately. In Spidey's origin story, portrayed in *Amazing Fantasy* #15 (Lee and Ditko, 1962), he also conveniently comes across an advertisement offering $100 to anyone who can stay in the wrestling ring with the famous Crusher Hogan for three minutes. Seeing a chance to test his new abilities and make some money, Peter whips up a costume and takes to the ring. His amazingly easy time with Crusher and spider-like stunts attract the attention of a television producer looking for someone to put on the small screen. With the promise of big money, Peter thinks he is on easy street, and in a moment of egotism he lets a criminal escape. The money is talking and he thinks he doesn't owe it to anyone to offer help. Comic book karma rears its head and the escaped crook ends up killing his Uncle Ben. It's the money that made him do it, or, in this case, *not* do it.

Some heroes are more, shall we say, entrepreneurial. When asked which hero would accept payment for services rendered, many comic fans would put Deadpool at the top of the list. Perhaps it's his cavalier attitude about hero work, or maybe it's his history as a mercenary (or his tendency to become unhinged). Deadpool forms a team of vigilantes who dress as him to conduct business under the shingle "Heroes for Hire" (Duggan and Hawthorne, 2016). Unfortunately for the hired mercenaries, Deadpool isn't prompt on payments and he often negotiates with clients on prices. In a great scene where a number of the mercs are busy evicting deadbeats from a tenement, the owner reveals that Deadpool had agreed to accept what amounts to a positive rating on social media in exchange for services rendered. Understandably the mercs are annoyed. When they confront Deadpool he says that business will be turning up soon, only to be contradicted by his accountant who tells him he needs to get some paying customers or his business will go under. Add to this a cease and desist order from Luke Cage for the use of Luke's and Danny Rand's company name, and Deadpool changes the shingle to the blunter "Mercs for Money." Deadpool notes that "Saving the world ain't cheap, and what you're not making in money, you might make in fame" (p. 5).

Other heroes obviously use their skills to earn a living. The real "Heroes for Hire" is staffed by Power Man and Iron Fist. Jessica Jones runs a detective agency but tries to keep her use of powers to a minimum. In these situations, there are people who willingly enter into contracts with super-powered individuals who are running businesses. It is a voluntary transaction on both parts. While some heroes could follow this track, they may be less willing to meet the conditions of running a business.

For one thing, if heroes were to be paid there might be a concern about compromising their secret identities. Luke and Jessica aren't particularly discreet with their aliases so this isn't an issue for them. Other heroes are more protective, as we discussed in Chapter 2. Spider-Man runs into the problem of simply cashing a check—made out to Spider-Man—after being paid as an entertainer prior to his uncle's death (Lee and Ditko, 1963). If payment is obtained, presumably taxes would be due, and that also opens up the potential for revealing an identity (just think about the field day a group of computer hackers could have if they infiltrated the Internal Revenue Service's database and determined the identities of heroes). The main impetus of the Superhero Registration Act, the proposal to force heroes to basically become employees of the federal government, was to control hero activity. Heroes would be put on the government payroll where they would be paid and taxed. To do this, however, the heroes would have to reveal their identities. This raises the question of whether heroes would be subject to negligence if they failed to save someone when they weren't officially on the job.

Or perhaps more interestingly, what if they are on the clock and someone is injured when the hero steps in to save the day? If the police today are facing a backlash based on the way they conduct themselves, would heroes be any different?

Maybe the government shouldn't pay heroes, but what would prevent private citizens or firms from doing this? A job as a security guard at STAR Labs might be just what the doctor ordered for Green Arrow after he loses his fortune.[9] But what about a job working in security for the Falconi crime family of Gotham? Accepting payment can put you into the service of unscrupulous people. If you think paying a hero is unethical, what about being paid by a crime boss? If you think government is the way to go, as Captain America noted when presented with the option of being registered, what happens when your boss wants you to do something you know is wrong?

Nevertheless, there are certainly some unscrupulous, or perhaps naïve, anti-heroes who would accept payment for their services. In the hopes of being part of a team, the Tick joins a group called the Justly Compensated League of Heroes. His friend Arthur tries to dissuade him, questioning whether a group who would charge those they saved can really be called heroes. Tick reasons that they are saving money for some superhero equipment, but Arthur is resolute in thinking that "it's not right for superheroes to charge for doing good" (Griffith and Hopkins, 1997, p. 6).

I Suppose Now You Want to Be Paid

So heroes aren't getting paid, at least not for hero work. Much of the time, sleuthing and protection are left to the civilians. When heroes are really needed is when a cataclysmic event is about to occur. Think big, such as the X-Men battling the Dark Phoenix, or Superman fending off an attack from General Zod to save planet Earth.[10] A smaller situation might be the Green Goblin riding around New York lobbing pumpkin grenades everywhere, or Black Manta setting off undersea explosions to generate tsunamis.[11] Whenever there is treachery and destruction afoot, a hero is called to save the day. Here's the economic catch: If heroes were to wait for payment prior to doing their thing, a lot of death and destruction would likely ensue. Heroes need to jump into action at a moment's notice. This is one of the concerns of Captain America when presented with the Superhero Registration Act. What if hero services are needed but the bureaucracy prevents them from getting where they need to go quickly? Cap's position is that it's better to deal with the politics after the situation has been resolved.

If heroes charge potential victims prior to saving the world they are in an unfair bargaining position. Ruminate on this: If you are allergic to wasp stings, you know the importance of getting to your EpiPen as quickly as possible after you are stung. If you don't get the injection there is a real possibility that you will die. Now, let's say that you are out on a beautiful spring day, enjoying the mild temperatures after a brutal winter. In the rush to get to the great outdoors you left your epinephrine at home and, of course, while sitting on a red and white gingham tablecloth enjoying a tasty lunch, you are stung. Fortunately for you, a few tablecloths away is a couple also out basking in the spring sunshine. It just so happens that one of them is also allergic to wasp venom and happens to have an EpiPen, just the thing you need to potentially save your life. How much would you be willing to pay for this? As you stand there, throat swelling closed, the answer is whatever the owner of the medicine wants. If you don't like the price they offer you don't have time to negotiate. In economic lingo, this is called an inelastic demand. Because your need for the item is acute, it doesn't matter what the price is. Normally if prices rise, the amount that we are willing and able to buy drops. That is called the law of demand. If price moves in one direction, the amount of the good we are willing and able to purchase goes in the other direction. When we bring elasticity into the mix we are addressing the intensity of the change in how much you are willing and able to buy.

If price goes up and you buy a lot less, we say demand is elastic. There is a large change in the amount you buy when the price goes up, even if it rises just a little bit. Usually this is because you have lots of options on which you can spend your money. If the price of petunias goes up, you are likely to buy a lot less because there are many other types of flowers you can plant in your garden. However, if a higher price leads you to buying just a little bit less, then demand is inelastic. That's what you are facing with the EpiPen. You have exactly zero options for the medicine, and even if they existed, you have very little time to find alternatives. The life-saving injection in the possession of this nice, young couple is worth more than its weight in gold.

When a cataclysmic event is on the doorstep of Earth, or Gotham, New York, or Star City, heroes are like the couple with the medicine. They have the power to stop the destruction. No one else is capable of emerging victorious from a battle with what might become your alien overlords. Our demand for them is very inelastic. If they were to charge us prior to the fight, we might be willing to give them all of our money, our possessions, our children, maybe even sell ourselves into slavery to prevent losing all these things, including our lives, to an invasion.

The other problem facing a pre-battle payment plan is that finding the right price will certainly be tricky. Who is going to negotiate on behalf of the civilian population? Will I be subject to the payment plan adopted by the mayor of New York to entice Spider-Man to stop the Green Goblin? What if I steadfastly refuse to pay? What if I am financially unable to comply? What if I agree to a payment but don't have the money on me at the time, and after the fact I renege? If the Flash is negotiating over a price while Grod the gorilla is rampaging down the streets of Keystone City, how much more destruction will be wrought until a bargain is struck? While the haggling is going on, Flash is surely engendering ill will. He could be stopping the primate's fury but instead is trying to line his own pockets. Similarly, the negotiator for the city is sure to come under scrutiny, since he tried to drive a hard bargain at the expense of shattered windows, smashed storefronts, bashed police cars, and all sorts of monkey mayhem. In short, trying to determine how much to pay a hero immediately prior to an attack is fraught with peril.

On the other hand, perhaps heroes could do their jobs first and then ask for some financial compensation. That would eliminate the need to wait for civil servants to cut through the red tape and then people can settle-up afterwards when tensions are low. This course of action is also tremendously problematic due to a predicament known as the free-rider problem. Free-riders are the type of people who want something but don't want to pay for it. They aren't necessarily bad people. It isn't as if they believe that society owes them something, and in reaction to the cruel circumstances of life they simply take what they want. No, such backstories are often reserved for the villains against whom the hero is struggling. Free-riders typically do not do anything illegal. It isn't as if they are ignoring a bill or neglecting to pay their taxes. Free-riders just sit back and let others pay for something that the free-rider would pay for if they absolutely, positively had to. Free-riding after the world is safe is easy because the villain has been banished and the hero would not consciously allow them to return in revenge for not being paid. Therefore, if everyone free-rides, the hero does not get paid and has no recourse.

You Need to Produce Something Different

Underlying the problem facing heroes in getting paid for hero work is what they are providing. It is safe to say that almost everyone is grateful for the work heroes do, even if thanks are given begrudgingly. At the outset of DC's *The New 52*, the individual members of the Justice League find themselves in the midst of protests and general discontent as civilians bemoan the incursion of those with superpowers into their daily lives (Johns and Lee, 2011). The destruction that results from the supers' activities and the threat they pose to the world order is disconcerting, even if that threat is psychological rather than actual. When a new menace appears in the form of Darkscid, the heroes team up to defeat it. Much to the heroes' surprise, they find themselves surrounded by thankful people cheering them after a particularly dangerous battle.

But what are the heroes producing? If we could relate it to something in the non-comic world, heroes are in the protection business. Not the organized crime type of protection, rather they are more like national defense. Superman, Wonder Woman, Ironman, and Green Lantern comprise the Airforce. Hal Jordan, aka the Green Lantern, was literally an Air Force pilot. Aquaman and Namor make up the Navy. The Hulk, Black Canary, and the Flash, with Green Arrow and Hawkeye as marksmen, constitute the Army. The Marines are composed of Black Panther, The Punisher, and Wolverine. Batman and Captain America are the officers who run the show.

Protection falls under a class of goods referred to as public goods. These are things that consumers want to have. With defense we're dealing with one of the most basic services governments are expected to provide. To wit, the economic godfather, Adam Smith, considers the proper role of government in *Wealth of Nations* ([1776] 1994).[12] He stipulates that if government doesn't do three things, it is a failure. Government must provide for the national defense. That's protection for citizens from foreign threats. To this end, government can legitimately build an army. It must also protect citizens from domestic threats. This is accomplished through law enforcement and judicial bodies. Finally, it should provide some public goods, chief among them are commerce-inducing activities. That means that government should put in place an infrastructure to make it easier for citizens to conduct business. It isn't that these items can't be supplied by private enterprise as there are private security firms and private roads. Rather, they are more efficiently provided and maintained by the public sector.

We'll leave the discussion of infrastructure spending for a minute to focus on defense. The idea of having government provide defense, and to a lesser extent the police and courts, makes sense because of two key components that make them public goods. Since public goods have these two specific characteristics, the market is not likely to produce them, as these features make it difficult for the producer to earn a profit.

The first attribute is non-excludability. This means that if you don't pay for something, the seller cannot stop you from consuming it. Free-riders love this aspect of public goods. You get all the benefits and incur none of the costs. For example, if Canada decided it was going to try to invade the United States, the U.S. Army would mobilize on the border to repel the red coat-clad Canadian Mounties (after getting over the initial surprise that the good people from north of the border were engaging in hostilities, of course).

Even for those who don't pay taxes or who despise the military, defense would be provided because it is *national* defense, not "individuals who pay taxes" defense. Yet, imagine a circumstance where, due to the proliferation of data analytics, the U.S. government decides to change its tactics and use this unexpected incursion to handle a particular problem. Scanning taxpayer data, the executive branch has noticed that there is an enclave of tax dodgers clustered in eastern Ohio.[13] Due to their religious beliefs, this group of people have shunned modernity. They don't use electricity, they ride around in horse-drawn carts, and embrace pacifism. That must stop! So while the U.S. didn't invite the Canadian invasion, it is possible that it could be used to wipe out . . . the Amish.

To implement the plan, the executive branch orders the Army to stop defending eastern Ohio, but only eastern Ohio. The non-confrontational Amish will put up no resistance and will ostensibly become a southern province of Canada. This failure to defend U.S. territory will be explained with a shrug of the shoulders and the official government line: "That's what happens when you don't pay your taxes."

Of course, this is a preposterous scenario. If it were to be adopted, it provides the enemy a foothold from which to launch other attacks. It is also quite possible that the Canadian invasion force would damage tax payers' property along their march south. Perhaps the Amish are well treated and word gets out about how much better life is under Canadian rule, fomenting rebellion outside the Amish enclave. Maybe the Amish become a paramilitary force to be reckoned with. Who knows? The point is, allowing the enemy even a modicum of safety within your territory is at best a foolish military strategy, and at worst a maneuver to ensure your own demise.

So, public goods are non-excludable. You can't keep people from using them, even if they don't pay. That is true of national defense to be sure, but to be a pure public good you need a second characteristic. The good must also be non-rival in consumption. This means that the good can be enjoyed by many people at the same time without anyone losing the benefit. This is certainly the case with national defense. I am currently enjoying it. As I look out the window there are no marauding bands of Canadians (or Amish) streaming from the woods. At the same time, my cousin in Seattle is also benefitting from national defense and he lives closer to the Canadian border than I do. Similarly, my friend in Montana, who also lives close to the northern U.S. border, is protected, despite his antipathy towards the military industrial complex. The fact that we all benefit from national defense at the same time doesn't make that defense any less potent.

To reinforce this idea, let's contrast a public good with a private good. A private good might be something like a pair of pants. Pants are certainly something people want, if for no other reason than it gets cold in the winter. As customers we are willing to pay for them and firms are willing to produce them because they can profit from the sales. Unlike defense, it is possible to keep people from taking possession of a pair of pants if they don't pay for them. Try this next time you are at the mall. Pick up a pair of pants and just walk out of the store and see what happens.[14] In economic terms, pants are excludable. They are also rival in consumption. As a fun experiment, try to see how many people you can fit into a pair of pants. Unless they are some sort of magical clown pants, you will likely find that you are the only one you can fit into your jeans, dress trousers, or knickers. Putting more than one person in a pair of pants is obviously a fool's errand because your use of them makes it impossible for others to do the same. They are rival in consumption.

Now you know the problem for hero work. Hero work is a public good. When the Justice League defends the planet from an invasion by Anti-Monitor, it is providing a public good.[15] If Squirrel Girl stops Thanos from annihilating Earth, she is providing a public good.[16] When Aquaman prevents the pollution of the oceans, he is providing a public good. When Daredevil takes a gang of criminals off the street, he is providing a public good. You get the picture. All of these acts are things that the majority of people want. We prefer not having to deal with all-powerful alien invasions. We like clean oceans and safe streets. Finding someone to provide these things can be a problem, and even more of an issue is finding any entity on Earth with the capabilities of stopping those aliens. Heroes fit that bill. However, this protection, like national defense, is both non-excludable and non-rival in consumption. If heroes performed their heroics for money and some homeless guy (or an Amish family lost in the big city) says he can't pay, will Wonder Woman simply allow Anti-Monitor to annihilate the vagabond? Of course not. Does the fact that the homeless man receives the benefits of the heroes' actions in any way make the saving of the Earth less valuable to the

Amish family, or Etta Candy, or Perry White?[17] No it does not. Everyone on Earth is made better off when the superheroes fend off a galactic villain who is threatening to kill everyone on the planet.

So, if no one needs to pay for their services, or in other words, if because they are providing public goods the entire population free rides off their goodwill, then making money off their hero abilities becomes next to impossible. Heroes continue to do what they do because they are heroes. To walk away from it all, even though that occasionally happens (as noted in Chapter 2 with Spider-Man), would make them less likable to be sure. Yet, in the real world public goods are provided. Adam Smith advocated for them, which is like a voice from the heavens. Was Smith naïve enough to not recognize that in the real world these services still have to be paid for? Let's not be silly. Of course Smith knew that this could pose a problem. His solution was very straightforward and brings us to the final section of this chapter: How do you fix those nasty little blighters we have been calling free-riders?

Fixing the Free-rider Problem

Addressing the free-rider problem depends on how determined you are to stamp it out. In the most traditional sense, when you have public goods such as defense, lighthouses, or national public radio, you use some combination of taxation and fees to cover the costs. Since everyone benefits from defense, there is some sort of national level tax, part of which is used to pay for the army, navy, and air force. There will always be tax cheats but because the cost of defense is spread across all the citizenry, those tax dodgers don't significantly impact the ability of government to defend the country. Similarly, with lighthouses you might collect a tax, but upon whom do you levy it? A better option might be to place a fee on the ships that dock in the port protected by the lighthouse.[18] The point is, you try to spread the cost to those who benefit from the public good.

Public radio has some problems in this regard. Even if they are subsidized by government handouts, the government charity does not fully cover operating expenses. To make up the financing gap there are regularly scheduled fundraising drives. While the announcer does his or her level best to guilt listeners into paying, it is quite easy, and rather enjoyable, to free-ride off the other listeners whose hearts are more tender towards the voice in the box. In this case, the free-rider problem is met with great sighs and anguished pleading. "Do not let your public radio station go off the air," the voices implore, and enough people must be conscious-stricken as at the end of the campaign the station remains. Here the free-riders have a much easier time continuing to get what they like at no charge.

We've mentioned the idea of heroes becoming government employees and earning a government salary. That could possibly help heroes earn a living while providing a public good, although there would certainly be strings attached. However, there is an alternative. Let's not sugarcoat things too much. Superheroes are in the protection business, some might say the protection racket. When they fight aliens from outer space, there aren't any cameras to capture the evidence. Sometimes they prevent crimes before they happen. In many cases, their mere presence is deterrent enough. Petty thieves would have to be really desperate to commit a crime when Batman might descend upon them in a dark alley. The reduction in normal crime, and by normal crime I mean gang-related, garden-variety muggings, or petty holdups, is certainly a public good. If streets are safer because criminals know Luke Cage is walking around and will punch their lights out, then businesses are more likely to thrive, not having to worry about being robbed, and residents are more frequently out on the streets because they do not face the threat of being mugged; however, this opens the door for the mafia-type answer to free-riders: Shake downs. Surely businesses would pay for the protection offered by heroes? They would probably pay gladly, as opposed to the squeeze that is put on them by the local crime boss, knowing that they are getting their money's worth. Heroes aren't likely to beat them up if they don't pay, rather they just move to a part of town where they are more wanted. Maybe if they took the money they could spend more time punching the bad guys and less time punching a clock. Then again, would we consider them heroes if they chose that route?

And the Answer Is...

One of the more peculiar aspects of superhero life is that even the most skilled hero needs an income stream. Fighting crime might be a lonely business, but for heroes it is also an unprofitable one. As a result, we see heroes taking day jobs. The superhero creed prevents certain behaviors—heroes don't kill people and they don't bill those they save for their services. At first blush, not charging seems reasonable—they are heroes after all. Demanding payment for their services would be downright tawdry. From an economic perspective, however, the rationale is more obvious. You don't charge because there is no good collection mechanism. If you try to get someone to pay Kate Kane (Batwoman) for saving the day, and they don't, will Batwoman stand around and let the villain win? Additionally, if the hero does the work, everyone benefits from the actions equally. So, if I don't pay, my benefit isn't any less. Heroes find themselves in the unprofitable situation of providing public goods. Like a firefighter, the hero usually needs to address a problem quickly; there is no time for deliberation over prices. Once the threat has passed, there is no reason for the beneficiaries to pay for it.

Understanding the nature of public goods helps us appreciate why heroes need a day job. Their avocation can't pay the electric bill. Unfortunately though, the jobs most heroes can take are lower-paying. Heroes must skip work, disappear from the work place, and take extended vacations for the sake of their hero duties. The boss in most high-paying jobs would not put up with that. So the heroes who must work for a living are most definitely not living it up. Perhaps what they need to do is consider their nemesis. Maybe a life of crime would result in a more comfortable lifestyle.

Endnotes

1. The Jean Grey School for Higher Learning replaced Xavier's School for the Gifted and helps teach students with mutant powers to use them responsibly (2011).
2. The 1927 Yankees had a record of 110 wins and 44 losses and are considered by many the best baseball team of all time. Having Babe Ruth and Lou Gehrig, along with a lineup called Murderer's Row, just adds to their legend.
3. Two of the professor's students, Warren Worthington (aka Angel) and Emma Frost, are billionaires and presumably add to the revenue stream occasionally.
4. This estimate comes from Money Magazine (Davidson, 2015).
5. These are the heroes Iron Man, Mr Fantastic, White Queen, and Ozymandias successively.
6. Zatanna is the daughter of the great Giovanni Zatara. They are both powerful wizards from the mystical Homo Magi race. She is an adept business woman who earns an extremely good living performing what her patrons believe are illusions but are actually real magic. Zatanna teams up with the Justice League when supernatural powers are needed.
7. Shazam is an acronym that represents Billy Batson's powers. He has the wisdom of Solomon, the strength of Hercules, the stamina of Atlas, the power of Zeus, the courage of Achilles, and the speed of Mercury. By mixing the Greek and Roman mythologies you get SHAZAM! Mary Batson, Billy's twin sister, can change into a female version of Shazam (she is also referred to as Mary Marvel). She similarly uses the magic word Shazam to change, but originally this was based on a different group of mythological figures: the

grace of Selena, the strength of Hippolyta, the skill of Ariadne, the fleetness of Zephyrus, the beauty of Aurora, and the wisdom of Minerva.

8. This was the original Thor story, before it was revealed that he was a discredited son of Asgard.

9. The Science and Technology Advanced Research Laboratories, or STAR Labs, are a chain of private research facilities used in DC Comics for a variety of purposes. In the Flash television show, an explosion at STAR labs in Central City was responsible for Barry Allen becoming the Flash, along with the creation of many of the villains he faces.

10. General Zod was the leader of the Kryptonian Army who tried, unsuccessfully, to take over the planet. Superman's father (Jor-El) banished him and his minions to the Phantom Zone, which meant he wasn't on the Krypton when it exploded. When he returns from the Phantom Zone he understandably has it out for Jor-El's son.

11. Black Manta is the arch enemy of Aquaman. In their first encounter, Aquaman's father suffered a heart attack and eventually died. While seeking revenge, Aquaman accidentally killed Black Manta's father, linking the two forever as mortal enemies.

12. Smith's view of the role of government is covered in Book 5 of *The Wealth of Nations*.

13. The Amish do have to pay state and federal income taxes and any local sales taxes; however, they are exempt from paying Social Security and Medicare taxes. The Amish are opposed to the idea of insurance on a religious basis and these programs are essentially forced insurances. In the original Medicare bill, passed in 1965, an exemption for religious groups opposed to paying for insurance granted the Amish the privilege of not paying taxes for these purposes. They do, however, have to pay Social Security taxes for their non-Amish employees per a Supreme Court ruling (*United States v. Lee*, 1982).

14. The legal disclaimer here is that this suggestion is only a thought exercise. If you think that walking out of a store with a pair of pants you haven't paid for is a good idea, well, you can deal with the consequences.

15. Anti-Monitor is a power-hungry force from the anti-matter universe—a parallel universe to ours. His discovery of the existence of the positive matter universe led to the DC event *Crisis on Infinite Earths*. Anti-Monitor is one of the most powerful villains in DC, having destroyed or absorbed thousands of universes. He has also caused the deaths of heroes like Supergirl and the Flash.

16. Thanos was born a Titan, a god-like race on one of the moons of Saturn. Unfortunately for him, and eventually the rest of the universe, Thanos carried a physical mutation that left him with purple skin. Eventually he partnered with Mistress Death (not a good thing), and when he was banished from Titan he began his pursuit of the Infinity Stones, a set of crystals with mystical powers he hopes to use to control the universe (also a bad thing). Thanos is connected to the Marvel universe through his battles with the Avengers and the Guardians of the Galaxy.

17. Etta Candy is Wonder Woman's best friend and Perry White is the editor of the *Daily Planet*, the newspaper that employs Clark Kent, neither of whom has superpowers.

18. A lighthouse is one of economists' favorite examples of a public good. You can't keep people from using the light, even if they don't pay—imagine how difficult that would be, not to mention how you would be placing the paying customers at risk—so it is non-excludable. Also, since the light benefits everyone no matter how many ships' captains are using it, the lighthouse is non-rival in consumption. Ronald Coase (1974) notes that private firms built many lighthouses in England. Faced with the free-rider problem however, the lighthouse was maintained by a toll on all ships docking in the harbor served by the lighthouse.

References

Bendis, B. and Gaydos, M. (2001). *Alias*, #22. Marvel Comics.

Bendis, B. and Gaydos, M. (2002). *Alias*, #7. Marvel Comics.

Coase, R. (1974). The Lighthouse in Economics. *Journal of Law and Economics*, 17(2), pp. 357–76.

Davidson, J. (2015). These are the five richest superheroes. [Online] *Money*. Available at: http://time.com/money/3950362/richest-superheroes-comic-con/ [Accessed April 4, 2018].

Duggan, G. and Hawthorne, M. (2016). *Deadpool*, #2. Marvel Comics.

Griffith, C. and Hopkins, A. (1997). *The Tick: Karma Tornado*, #5. New England Comic Press.

Johns, G. and Frank, F. (2011). *Justice League*, #0. DC Comics.

Johns, G. and Lee, J. (2011). *Justice League*, #6. DC Comics.

Lee, S. and Ditko, S. (1962). *Amazing Fantasy*, Issue #15. Marvel Comics.

Lee, S. and Ditko, S. (1963). *The Amazing Spider-Man*, Issue #1. Marvel Comics.

Smith, A. (1994). *An Inquiry into the Nature and Causes of the Wealth of Nations*. New York: Random House (Originally published in 1776).

United States v. Lee. [1982]. 455 U.S. 252 (Supreme Court of the United States); 1.

6

Give Up Already! When Superheroes Are Fighting Crime, Who Wants to Be a Criminal?

In a world of superheroes a reasonable question might be: Why do criminals bother to break the law in the face of almost certain capture? Other than pure hubris, why would anyone take to a life of crime with Superman patrolling the sky? The players, heroes, and villains regularly face off against each other and the heroes almost always win. In *Injustice: Gods Among Us* (Taylor et al., 2016), Joker is annoyed about always losing. Yet Joker's admission demands a response from the reader of comics. Yes, Joker, you may lose nearly every time, but so what? Within a couple of months, weeks, days, or maybe even hours, you're back on the street finding new ways to terrorize Gotham. In fact, it seems like there are no prisons built, especially the ones designed to hold super-villains, that can actually hold a supervillain. Even Lex Luthor realizes this. He notes that no prison is capable of containing meta-humans for any length of time. Specifically, he has calculated that "eighty-seven percent of all violent meta-humans escape within three months of incarceration. One month if we're talking about Arkham" (Johns and Fabok, 2015, p. 85).

The revolving doors that are the famous prisons in the comic book world do a woeful job of preventing prisoners from escaping. Arkham Asylum, Belle Reve, Iron Heights, The Raft, and Ryker's Island are just some of the prisons in the superhero universe. Arkham is for the certifiably crazy DC Comics psychopaths. Belle Reve and Iron Heights, also reserved for the DC criminal element, are for the slightly more sane, but still extraordinarily dangerous, villains. The Raft, probably the most secure of these big houses, is a maximum-security facility in the middle of the ocean, created by the brightest minds in the Marvel Universe.

Think of Alcatraz with some really, really nasty inmates. Ryker's is an actual prison in New York City's East River. This is where many lower-level convicts in Marvel stories are housed.

Criminal activity is often thought of as irrational, and based on the behavior of many of the villains who appear in the comics, that presumption would be entirely correct. Economic models have a difficult time providing adequate predictions of irrational actions. In that we are not alone. It is difficult for any analysis, psychological, sociological, medical, or mathematical, to forecast the random acts that often characterize the criminally deranged. To avoid that uncertainty, economists ground their models on the assumption of rationality. The predictions of models are more likely to be accurate if people aren't unhinged. While there are some villains who enjoy wreaking havoc for havoc's sake, much criminal behavior is not as random, or as irrational, as it first appears. Criminals are often quite calculating and economists have found their behavior to be a fascinating Petri dish in which to observe how incentives work.

Beyond that though, we should be asking whether heroes themselves are part of the problem? This is a theme that arises regularly in comic stories. At some point in time, most heroes have had to face a resentful civilian who accuses them of attracting the criminal element to a city. Desperate cries of "if it wasn't for you..." are normal occurrences and typically lead the hero down a hole of critical self-examination. That makes for a good storyline, but from an economic perspective we need to dig a little deeper. Is there some justification to this claim, and if so, what is it based on? Does the preconceived notion that a hero will let the justice system run its course, meaning a villain ends up in a jail cell, however temporarily, rather than in an electric chair, alter the incentive structure of villains? Heroes are often extreme on this point. In one story, Batman goes so far as to provide evidence of Joker's innocence in a series of crimes, despite Joker's history of getting away with so many other crimes (Dixon and Nolan, 1996). Does a hero's adherence to the rule of law therefore embolden the criminal element? Interestingly, there is a parallel between this question and a thread of economic theory that focuses on safety.

Another facet driving the criminal element is related to games (but not game theory). In some contests there are payoffs for all the participants, in others only the winner gets a payday. For example, in politics, business, and professional golf there is no real prize for second place.[1] An election victor, the person who becomes CEO, and the champion of a golf match win huge monetary or fame prizes. The second-place contestant receives what amounts to a parting gift for their troubles.

This is germane to our analysis of comics because people, including lawbreakers, are expected to behave differently when they know there is a huge payday for winning and very little for coming in second.

So, let's take a path less traveled and explore what motivates villains. We all have a favorite, from the looney 1960s Batman television show rogues, to the mallet-wielding Harley Quinn, to the god of mischief Loki, to the multi-layered Magneto. The question on the minds of many readers is: Why do the villains try so hard when they almost always lose? What keeps them coming back for one beating after another is more than just entertainment; it is partially about economics.

Villain Origins: Tell Me About Your Mother

In the comics, the early villains were often relatively normal people—except for the extraterrestrial warlords—possessing interesting gadgets and gimmicks but without any real superpowers. The Penguin, Toyman, and Catwoman are all familiar Batman villains who began as petty thieves or simple burglars.

Other evildoers are intellectuals with visions of grandeur. Lex Luthor is a scientific genius who lost his hair trying to discover a cure for Kryptonite poisoning (more on this later in the chapter).[2] The Riddler wanted everyone to know how smart he was so he left clues to befuddle the Caped Crusader. The Green Goblin is another magnificent but troubled scientist, Norman Osborne, who lost his sanity but gained super strength after injecting himself with an experimental serum.[3] Dr Ock, Otto Octavious, is a gifted researcher who unfortunately went a step too far and ended up melding metallic legs to himself. Mr Sinister was yet another mastermind who mutated himself through genetic engineering, which has potentially granted him immortality (the word is still out on this). Ozymandias is believed to be the most brilliant man on the planet and had the great fortune of not transforming himself into a bizarre creature. Other supervillains are alien in origin—Brainiac, Darkseid, Doomsday, Galactus, Sinestro, Thanos, and Venom all fit the bill here—while some are mutants, such as Apocalypse, Magneto, and Mystique.

Regardless of their derivation, most villains have backstories as well. They typically come from homes with abusive parents, or they have lost a parent due to a tragic event. Essentially, their home lives were disasters. The death of a spouse or significant other is also a common character device. Many criminals are pulled into the underworld because of a lack of positive role models. Some, like Magneto, are driven to the dark side after viewing a horrific event. Eric Lehnsherr's family was killed in a concentration camp. He escaped by hiding under the dead bodies of other prisoners. As Magneto, he seeks to defend mutants by any and all means from the actions of normal people wishing to do them harm. Criminals such as Catwoman are just doing what comes naturally after spending their lives on the streets. Catwoman's burglaries are relatively minor compared to those of more vicious members of the crime community.

Some villains are in it for revenge. Others are megalomaniacs. Still others are just deranged. When it comes to committing crimes or doing bad things, it seems there is no shortage of motivations and no shortage of players on the big stage. Regardless of what inspires these scoundrels, they keep breaking out of jail and trying again, and again, and again to pull one over on the good guys. Rarely, however, does crime pay.

Crime Is Terribly Revealing

The real question for those contemplating committing a crime, as laid out by Nobel Prize winner Gary Becker (1968), is what motivates such action? Becker's famous paper about the economics of crime suggests that those who engage in malfeasance may not be as irrational as we believe. Criminals weigh the costs and benefits of their actions by balancing the payoffs from wrongdoing against the probability of being caught, and the punishment for their actions if they are apprehended. The implication of Becker's research is that economic analysis applies to the choices made by all types of people, be they criminal or hero.

When it comes to incarcerating the bad guys, choices must be made. Imposing punishments is costly, not just for the lawbreaker but for society as well. Conducting public trials and transferring prisoners like Magneto, the Green Goblin, or Gorilla Grod would be a nightmare. Dr Doom, from the country of Latveria, might not agree to extradition, and forget trying one of the alien villains like Sinestro or General Zod in a court of law. Some bad guys can't really be killed, either. Nitro can blow himself up and reform, Vandal Savage has lived for millennia and there are gods who go on like a Celine Dion song. Trying to find the least costly way of imposing those penalties is necessary for the efficient use of society's resources. If sentences are not properly deterring behavior, in other words if punishments are too light or the probability of being apprehended is too low, then we should expect more people to engage in criminal activity, or we should at least expect criminals to be more brazen.

Incentives, then, should have some impact on an individual who is riding the fence about committing an act of lawlessness, that is if they are behaving rationally. For instance, Machin and Meghir (2004) find that low-wage workers, not necessarily those unemployed, are more prone to committing crimes primarily because they have less to lose if caught. The rate of return to criminal activity is higher for those in low-wage circumstances. So, in a city where there are a lot of minimum-wage jobs we should see more crime. As we've noted before, incentives drive behavior. However, there are different kinds of incentives.

Ignoring the criminally insane for now, in the case of many non-comic-related bad guys, felonious behavior can be thought of as a natural response to two types of incentives which were discussed in Chapter 1: positive and negative. If you recall, positive incentives are the rewards you receive for engaging in certain kinds of activities. These are the pats on the back for doing a good job, the paycheck you earn from going to work, the high you get from smoking dope. However, there are desultory effects from certain kinds of behaviors as well. Negative incentives are the slaps on the wrist for doing something naughty: Tickets for speeding, a failing grade for not submitting the research paper on *The Grapes of Wrath*, jail time for possession of that dope. Positive incentives are there to get you to behave in certain ways, while negative incentives are in place to try to get you not to do something. In the case of criminal behavior, the punishments for being found guilty of a crime are intended to deter misconduct. However, if those incentives are not credible then they will fail to accomplish their goal. Thus, if prison time isn't a burden because supervillains can easily escape, malefactors will continue to commit crimes.

As if revolving door prisons weren't enough to encourage criminal behavior, the punishments themselves are so relatively soft that they fail to deter anyone. It is almost a running joke. The extent of the punishment is often a significant deterrent to would-be criminals. Ehrlich (1996) reviews the economics literature (which is a good thing because reading through economics research papers can be like doing time in Iron Heights) and finds that, at the very least, punishments, and particularly capital punishments, have the effect of discouraging murder. The presumption is that you will think twice about committing murder if there is an extremely stiff penalty attached; however, the consequences of engaging in misconduct in hero comics must not have much cachet, given the number of recurring felonious personalities. A stay at Ryker's Island is a room and three-square meals for some criminals. When the cell gets a little cramped, it's time to hit the road.

With the rap sheets of some of the regulars going back to the 1940s, and given the heinousness of some of their crimes, it is a bit strange that stronger medicine has not been administered. The only instance of a villain having been condemned to death by the justice system occurred in *Captain Marvel* #46 (Binder and Beck, 1945), where Mr Mind, a deranged worm (he was literally a worm) accused of killing over 100,000 people, is executed by electrocution.

In cities like Gotham where crime is running amok, the pervasiveness of criminal activity might inhibit the judicial system from levying the proper penalties. Research by Bar-Gill and Harel (2001) suggests that the rate of crime itself can affect the ability to properly deter the bad guys. In situations where lawlessness is out of control, prosecutions are not carried out effectively, punishments are dispensed without enough thought to deterring others, and the probability of being caught falls because law enforcement resources are stretched too thin. This is likely the case in Gotham, assuming the GCPD doesn't increase its resources (not to mention half the police force is being paid off by crime bosses). This would also explain the efforts of criminal masterminds to break others out of jail.[4] More chaos increases the chances that you'll get away with the crime.

That being said, the presence of heroes could reasonably be expected to ameliorate the mayhem. If heroes are more capable than the police department then they should be able to increase the incidence of capture and reduce the rate of return to criminal activity.[5] Curiously though, despite Batman's best efforts, crime in Gotham only seems to fall in alternate realities where he exists as a vigilante nightmare, becoming judge, jury, and executioner. For instance, in *Kingdom Come*, Batman utilizes a paramilitary police force to rid the streets of crime (Waid and Ross, 2008). It's chillingly dystopian but effective.

One final issue should be considered. Perhaps crime is a function of the existence of heroes themselves. In the case of the vigilante hero, the cops are often more interested in pursuing the vigilante than they are the villain. Batman, Daredevil, Green Arrow, and others combat criminals outside the bounds of the law. They break the rules to keep others safe. This activity crosses a line that good police officers find abhorrent, even when the aims of the vigilante are in line with the city's finest. Crime-fighters distract the police, interfere with traditional methods of stopping the bad guys, and encourage copycats, crime fighters who are far less capable than the hero. The result is that the cops are trying to hunt down the hero and the villains are roaming free.

In the comic world, it seems as if the justice system has broken down. No matter how good the lawyers are, no matter how tightly the case is presented, no matter how incontrovertible the evidence, no matter how secure the facility, criminals escape. Interestingly, even prisons built by Superman fail to keep the nasties contained. Plastic Man initiates a breakout of the legions of imprisoned people Superman has rounded up in *Injustice: Gods Among Us* (Taylor et al., 2016). Similarly, the great supervillain prison to which Supes banishes all wrongdoers in *Kingdom Come* (Waid and Ross, 2008) isn't enough to hold the concentrated villainy. Combine this with the faulty incentive structure that doesn't work to deter crime, namely inadequate sentences and a non-credible commitment to incarcerations, and you have a recipe for continued illicit mischief. So, in part we can blame the continued activity of the criminal element on the system. In this case, we can fix part of the problem by focusing on the incentive structure that has been established.

Moral Hazard, Not *Dukes of Hazzard*

Consider, if you will, a world where every action is made as safe as possible. You can drive your car as fast as you want, Thelma and Louise style, towards the edge of the Grand Canyon.[6] As you leave terra firma, the momentary weightlessness gives you a sense of flying. However, that blissful freedom is quickly replaced by an abject panic as gravity takes over and you begin to plunge into the abyss. But just before you meet your maker, your momentum is arrested. You hang, suspended in mid-air, your sense of relief mixing with a curiosity strong enough to kill a dozen cats. Ever so gently your car is lifted out of the canyon and returned to solid ground. You see a man in a cape give you a friendly wave, and without a word he rockets off into the sky, likely looking for other unfortunate souls to save. You sit there in stunned silence for a minute before a wicked grin forms on your lips. You back the car away from the cliff, turn it around, then gun the engine. Like a child being thrown in the air by their father, a voice in the back of your head screams "Again! Again!"

Moral hazard is kind of like that. If superheroes were around to protect us from doing stupid things, we might just engage in those stupid things more often. In fact, moral hazard is the result of excessive intervention in the graphic novel *Superman: Red Son* (Millar and Johnson, 2014). This alternate reality imagines how the world would have looked if Superman had landed in communist Russia instead of Kansas. Superman, unencumbered by privacy concerns, scans the country to prevent fatalities. This may sound good, and many people say that superheroes should be more involved in day-to-day activities to prevent random calamities, but Superman isn't initially keen on the idea. In a discussion with Wonder Woman he notes that "nobody wears a seatbelt anymore. Ships have even stopped carrying life jackets. I don't like the unhealthy new way that people are behaving" (p. 64). The reason people become more risk-loving in Superman's Russia isn't because they're drinking too much vodka. It's more as if they've won the insurance lottery. If super-heroes are always going to prevent untimely accidents, why not take more risks? It is like having free insurance. Jumping out of a plane without a parachute is a huge rush, or so I've been told, but no matter how it makes you feel while you're falling, the splat at the end is probably not worth it. But if Superman is going to stop me from becom-ing a human pancake, then why not give it a go? When risk is taken out of the equation, people behave differently.

This has been duly noted by economist Sam Peltzman (1975). Peltz-man's work is so important that he has an effect named after him—the Peltzman effect (you didn't think economists were going to be more creative with the naming, did you?). The Peltzman effect basically applies moral hazard to driving behaviors. When you reduce the risk of driving a car, people get a little more reckless. Of course, the driving force here is entirely unintentional. In the name of protecting people from themselves, government mandates safety features in automobiles. Seat belts, air bags, anti-crumple zones, you name it. Those things are supposed to help the driver live through an accident and they seem to have worked. As long as drivers and passengers actually use these devices, people survive car crashes in astonishingly high proportions. However, what wasn't expected was that the number of fatalities of bikers, walkers, and other pedestrians increased, and the people who were killed in car accidents tended to die in more grisly ways (that's what the driver's education videos in high school taught us, to be sure).

Peltzman reasons that if you mandate safety, people will find a way to screw it up. Maybe that doesn't sound economic enough but that is what happens. Put another way, if you try to legislate safety, people will unpredictably respond to the incentives in front of them. When you feel safer inside the car, you engage in riskier behavior. This means you drive a little faster because "if I hit something, the air bag will save me!" You pay a little less attention on the road because, once again, "if I hit something, the air bag will save me!" The problem, of course, is that mothers pushing baby strollers don't have built in air bags, and even an air bag isn't effective if you drive fast enough.

More generally, the Peltzman effect says that regulations alter people's behaviors. When you make them feel safe, they stop taking what lawyers call reasonable care. We see this in sports, too. An extraordinarily cool paper by O'Roark and Wood (2004) demonstrates that the Peltzman effect applies to NASCAR races. When you try to make auto racing safer, drivers who are already risk-loving—and you would have to be to drive at 180 miles per hour despite traveling in circles—will take even more risks, which has led to more accidents.

Safety regulations in football lead to extremely large human beings slamming into each other with the force of a rhinoceros. All those pads and helmets give men who are young enough not to fear much a reason to fear even less. The contact between two average-sized football players can generate 1,600 pounds of force (Higgins, 2009). As players get bigger, faster, and stronger, the force exerted during a tackle can be massive, leading to severe injuries, "but don't worry ma, I've got my helmet on."

Criminals in the comic world are similarly encouraged by the Peltzman effect. We'd like to deter criminal behavior but the way crime is regulated isn't effective. In fact, the weak system of enforcement creates incentives that lead to more misconduct, or at least to more supervillains. Fame and fortune are accolades in the criminal world. Add to this the reality that heroes won't kill you and that villains are rarely successfully prosecuted for a capital offense and you've got the making of the Peltzman effect for criminals. Why do villains in the comics keep coming back for more? Other than the occasional fight-induced bruise or cut and a week-long stay in the slammer, what reason can you find not to be a criminal? If you are risk-loving, a little crazy, and are looking for the potential to earn a spectacular income at little to no cost, then this might be the job for you.

Tournament of Champions

Speaking of dream jobs, who among us has never once imagined being up on stage in front of thousands of people while millions more watch on television? Maybe your daydream isn't performing, rather you fantasize about a last lap pass to win the Monaco Grand Prix, blasting a backhand down the line to best your opponent at Wimbledon, or draining a putt on number eighteen to win the Masters. Surely you have considered that if you ran for political office, you would do a much more competent job than the clowns currently in power? Perhaps you've had the thought of taking over the top boss's position and really setting things right where you work. In these instances, the reality of being in the spotlight that accompanies a job like a superstar entertainer or athlete, a political veteran, or CEO is far-fetched for most of us. Serenading millions of fans is laughable if you can't carry a tune in a bucket and winning an automobile race isn't realistic if driving over 100 miles per hour scares the dickens out of you. Running for office is almost a literal slog through a pig's trough, and becoming the CEO requires a level of schmoozing that you don't possess. The point is, while you might be able to visualize yourself in these positions, attaining them is ludicrously difficult. If you try and don't succeed, you'll be cast aside like the legions who have tried and failed before you. Becoming a star, be it as an entertainer, athlete, politician, or business executive can be extraordinarily profitable, but to quote Blake from the movie *Glengarry Glen Ross* "first prize is Cadillac Eldorado. Anybody wanna see second prize? Second prize's a set of steak knives. Third prize is you're fired" (1992). If you don't win the top spot, there is a huge drop-off to second and third place, so much so that if you're in third you might as well be on the street.

To an economist this incentive structure is fascinating. It's basically a winner-take-all proposition. Sure, there are nice parting gifts for second but the notoriety granted to the world's great second place finishers usually comes from parents and immediate family. Young children (and adults, too, for that matter) have a hard time naming former presidents of the United States. Ask them who the losers of previous elections were and if you're lucky you'll get a blank stare. The winner-take-all contests that make up certain kinds of professions are studied under the moniker of tournament theory in economics.[7] Consider jousting in the Middle Ages. As depicted in the movies, a jousting tournament consists of combatants charging at each other on horseback with long poles, attempting to knock each other off their mounts. If you fall off, you lose. The last knight standing typically wins the hand of the king's daughter in marriage, or some other highly sought-after prize. It seems barbaric, but the winner is usually the one the princess wanted to marry anyway, so all's well that ends well, right? At least in the movies. The relation to tournament theory is that, as in jousting, a tournament can have only one victor, and that is what makes tournament theory so interesting.

People behave differently when they know there is a huge payday for winning. Just consider the depths to which candidates for office will sink to sully the image of their opponents. For CEOs and athletes, the cost of their position typically takes the form of insane hours at the office or on the practice field. They sacrifice relationships with children, spouses, and friends, driven by the golden ring of success. If everyone in tournaments were simply given a participation trophy and a bag of orange slices, the behaviors that go along with the tournaments would likely dissipate. But if that were the case, the intensity would go out of a lot of the entertainment that we enjoy so much. Sure, there is still the underlying drive to beat an opponent in a contest, but if you end up sharing the spoils of the battle it's like sharing the king's daughter, and that gets rather uncomfortable.

This helps to explain part of the manic behavior of villains in their pursuit of their nemeses. For most of us, after a few defeats at the hands of a superpowered adversary, we'd just give up, break out of prison one last time, and try to get a job in some quiet, little town that doesn't have superheroes patrolling the streets. Supervillains don't give up that easily. Eventually the real prize sought by the true arch-nemesis of a hero, the real reason to break out of prison, the driving force in their lives, is to become the one who whacks the hero. These villains are vengeance seekers. They are obsessed with destroying or discrediting a hero for some real or perceived affront. Possibly the most obvious example of this is Lex Luthor. Luthor's backstory involves a bit of a man crush on the young Superman. They both live in Smallville and, upon hearing that Superman's only weakness was kryptonite, Luthor, already a budding genius, begins working on a way for Superman to resist the green mineral. Unfortunately, his skills in the lab are slightly deficient and a fire breaks out. Superman comes to the rescue and extinguishes the flames, but in the process Luthor loses his hair and his research and is ever after trying to convince the world that Superman is a threat to civilization (Siegel and Plastino, 1960).

One part of Luthor's hatred of Superman is jealousy. Luthor envisions himself as humanity's greatest hope for a brighter future, but the rabble are blinded by the flying man from outer space. Another part of Luthor's obsession is xenophobic. Superman is an alien, after all, and if you aren't from here you can't be trusted. This hysteria is most palpable in *Superman: Red Son*, where at the end of his long life, Luthor concedes that his greatest achievement was not being president of the United States, curing cancer, or ending war, but defeating Superman (Millar and Johnson, 2014).

Luthor is consumed with killing Superman, and no one had better get in his way. This is nowhere more obvious than in the famous story of Superman's death. In the DC animated version, Luthor's reaction when Doomsday kills Superman is basically to go crazy. He is apoplectic that his prize has been taken by an intergalactic interloper (*Superman: Doomsday*, 2007). Luthor reacts similarly after Silver Banshee kills the Man of Steel (Byrne and Williams, 1987).[8] Luthor has also prevented the death of the Big Blue Cheese by others because he insists that it be him who ends the Kryptonian.[9] When Superman battles Metallo, a kryptonite-powered villain, the end seems near for our hero. In the nick of time, Luthor's forces show up and haul Metallo away. In *Superman Villains Secret Files*, #1, Lex tells his infant daughter the story of how he couldn't allow "a fool like Corben [Metallo's secret identity] to enjoy the killing blow" (Immonen, 1998, p. 10).[10]

Don't You Touch Him

This is the issue faced by vengeful villains. They have a bone to pick with a hero, for whatever reason, and their mania drives them. The ultimate goal isn't so much taking down the hero as it is being the one to take them down. This is the "take what you want from the rest but leave (fill in the blank with a hero name) to me" reaction. As there is only one prize and only one person can claim victory, the bad guys are in a tournament. Second place is the first loser. As a result, they engage in activity that they might forego in other circumstances, even if that means turning on other villains.

In *The Amazing Spider-Man* #12 (Mackie and Byrne, 1999), Sandman gets the Sinister Six back together,[11] reluctantly allowing Venom to join the gang.[12] Sandman's goal is to finish off Doc Ock (long story). In the next episode, continued in *Peter Parker: Spider-Man* #12 (Mackie et al., 1999), Venom agrees to help the Six track down Ock but warns them to stay away from Spider-Man. If anyone is to kill the Web Slinger, it is to be Venom. When Sandman tells Spider-Man he can go free, Venom freaks out and attacks Sandman.

In a similar DC storyline, (beginning with *Justice League* #23 [Johns and Reis, 2013]) evil doppelgangers of the Justice League from another dimension called the Crime Syndicate believe they have killed the members of Earth's vaunted hero society. Aquaman's arch-nemesis, Black Manta, is stricken. He has been hunting Aquaman to avenge his father's death for years. In *Aquaman* #23.1 (Bedard, Johns, and St. Aubin, 2013), Manta is seen kneeling near his father's grave, apologizing for failing to kill Aquaman. In retaliation, he swears to wipe out the Crime Syndicate for depriving him of his revenge. By the end of the story arc the heroes are back, and to set things right Manta returns Aquaman's trident with the attached message: "I'm glad you're not dead" (Johns and Finch, 2014b). The thinly veiled intent of the communication is that Manta would be fine with Aquaman's death if it had been Manta's doing.

We think of Joker as wanting Batman dead and this is true, but only if it is at the hands of Joker. In the interesting crossover *Spider-Man and Batman*, the Joker keeps the villain Carnage from killing Batman because that is the Joker's job. After all, Gotham is "my [Joker's] town—and [he is] my Batman!" (DeMatteis and Bagley, 1995, p. 43). Even Robin isn't immune from the Joker's revenge fantasies. In the series *Robin II: Joker's Wild*, Tim Drake has taken over for the recently deceased Jason Todd. Robin catches Joker while Batman is away on holiday (sort of). Once he's back at Arkham, Joker menaces the inmates, warning "none of you touch him [Robin]. He's the Joker's property from now on" (Dixon and Lyle, 1991, p. 24). If you recall, Joker already killed one Robin. Now Tim Drake is on Joker's hit list.

These examples all point to an unhealthy obsession with killing a hero. In part, this has to do with a deep-seated psychosis. These are bad folks who are looking to do bad things. But it isn't all psychology, there are some economics involved too. For an arch-nemesis, winning the hero-killing tournament is like being elected president, becoming a movie star, and drinking from the Stanley Cup all at once.

And the Answer Is...

Villains may be cowardly but they're not stupid. The arch-enemies of heroes are some of the most intelligent characters in the comic world. Sure, they might go a little mad, but they know how to solve problems that have stymied lesser intellects, be it inter-dimensional travel, living forever, or curing cancer. Nevertheless, the main reason bad guys do bad things is that they are, at their core, bad people. There's no getting around this. Whatever your backstory, it is difficult to say that blowing up a school full of children, distributing mind-altering drugs, kidnapping and selling kids into slavery, or eating planets are excusable behaviors. To compound the problem for villains, it seems as if their actions are doomed to failure. Every time they try to get away with something they are confronted and, except for very rare circumstances, defeated by superpowered do gooders.

But villains don't go quietly. If at first they don't succeed, they try, try again, because they know that the heroes won't kill them and the prisons won't hold them. There is a moral hazard in place. The negative incentives that might normally cow a run-of-the-mill criminal aren't nearly strong enough to alter the actions of super-criminals. When the punishment is taken away, the villains come out to play, and they never go home. Additionally, because of the self-imposed regulation that most heroes have adopted not to kill the bad guys, that cowardly lot gets more brazen. As we have seen in this chapter, the Peltzman effect comes into full force as that part of the hero code makes villains feel safer, with catastrophic results.

Some of the more jilted villains find themselves attempting to win the title of taking down a hero. This tournament of destruction results in the repeated interactions with an arch-nemesis, but more than that it sometimes leads to villain on villain crime. If Lex Luthor isn't going to take down Superman, no one will! Lex wants to win the tournament of killing the Man of Steel. Not only does he see this as his duty as the smartest man in the world, but it will bring with it an everlasting fame. There is no prize for second place. Lex is playing to win, no matter how many tries it takes and regardless of who gets hurt.

Endnotes

1. In golf, for example, the money might be good for coming in second at the Open Championship, but there is no Claret Jug for second place.
2. Lex Luthor first appeared in *Action Comics* #23 (Siegel and Shuster, 1940).
3. The Green Goblin first appeared in *The Amazing Spiderman* #14 (Lee and Ditko, 1964a).
4. Using an intricate plan that involved breaking the criminally insane out of Arkham, Bane surprises Batman at Wayne Manor after the caped crusader is worn out from collecting those who were AWOL from the asylum. Bane beats Batman badly and breaks his back, leaving him a paraplegic, but only temporarily (Moench and Aparo, 1993).
5. In comics, the corruption in law enforcement is a regular theme in cities where criminal activity is rampant, as is the excessive bluster on the part of the judicial system advocating against the "vigilantism" of a hero. Part of this is certainly in the public interest. Amateur, masked crime-stoppers often end up dead in the comics. However, part of this is a reaction to the success of the hero and the threat to the corrupt members of the police department.
6. If you've never seen the movie *Thelma and Louise*, then I fear I may have spoiled the ending. Oh, and there are no superheroes in that movie, so you can imagine what driving a car off a cliff might look like at the bottom of said cliff.
7. Tournament theory was introduced to the economics field in the seminal work of Lazear and Rosen (1981).
8. Supes wasn't dead of course, but Luthor didn't know this.
9. Captain Thunder called Superman the "Big Blue Cheese" in *Superman* #276 where DC is poking fun at Captain Marvel. Captain Marvel has been called the "Big Red Cheese" (Maggin and Swan, 1974).
10. There is a silver age comic story where Luthor kills Superman by exposing him to massive amounts of kryptonite radiation. He rejoices but is sent to the

phantom zone as punishment. Fortunately (or frustratingly), this is just an "imaginary story" (Siegel and Swan, 1961).

11. The Sinister Six was a group originally organized by Doctor Octopus (Doc Ock) to fight Spider-Man (Lee and Ditko, 1964b). All of the members held a grudge against the wall-crawler. In typical criminal teaming up fashion, ulterior motives abounded and the team failed to achieve its objective. The members all turned against Doc Ock and, after he was killed, one more effort was made at reconstituting the group with Sandman as the leader. This version met with no more success than prior incarnations.

12. Venom is a combination of Eddie Brock and an alien symbiote, a lifeform that acts as a parasite living off the emotions of the host. Brock's hatred of Spider-Man drove the symbiote mad, and the symbiote provided Brock with a super suit and powers to battle his nemesis.

References

Bar-Gill, O. and Harel, A. (2001). Crime Rates and Expected Sanctions: The Economics of Deterrence. *Journal of Legal Studies*, 30(2), pp. 485–501.

Becker, G. (1968). Crime and Punishment: An Economic Approach. *Journal of Political Economy*, 76(2), pp. 169–217.

Bedard, T., Johns, G., and St. Aubin, C. (2013). *Aquaman*, #23.1. DC Comics.

Binder, O. and Beck, C. (1945). *Captain Marvel*, Issue #46. Fawcett Magazine.

Binder, O. and Papp, G. (1958). *Superboy*, #68. DC Comics.

Binder, O. and Pastino, A. (1959). *Action Comics*, #254. DC Comics.

Byrne, J. and Williams, K. (1987). *Action Comics*, #595. DC Comics.

DeMatteis, J. and Bagley, M. (1995). *Spider-Man and Batman: Disordered Minds*. DC Comics.

Dixon, C. and Lyle, T. (1991). *Robin II: The Joker's Wild*, #4. DC Comics.

Dixon, C. and Nolan, G. (1996). *The Joker: Devil's Advocate*. DC Comics.

Ehrlich, I. (1996). Crime, Punishment and the Market for Offenses. *Journal of Economic Perspectives*, 10(1), pp. 43–67.

Glengarry Glen Ross. (1992). [Film] New York: James Foley.

Higgins, M. (2009). Football Physics: The Anatomy of a Hit. *Popular Mechanics*. [Online] Popular Mechanics. Available at: http://www.popularmechanics.com/adventure/sports/a2954/4212171/ [Accessed April 4, 2018].

Immonen, S. (1998). *Superman Villains Secret Files and Origins*. DC Comics.

Johns, G. and Fabok, J. (2015). *Justice League*, #37. DC Comics.

Johns, G. and Finch, D. (2014a). *Forever Evil*, #2. DC Comics.

Johns, G. and Finch, D. (2014b). *Forever Evil*, #7. DC Comics.

Johns, G. and Reis, I. (2013). *Justice League*, #23. DC Comics.

Lazear, E. and Rosen, S. (1981). Rank Order Tournaments as Optimum Labor Contracts. *Journal of Political Economy*, 89(5), pp. 841–64.

Lee, S. and Ditko, S. (1964a). *The Amazing Spider-Man*, #14. Marvel Comics.

Lee, S. and Ditko, S. (1964b). *The Amazing Spider-Man*, Annual 1. Marvel Comics.

Machin, S. and Meghir, C. (2004). Crime and Economic Incentives. *Journal of Human Resources*, 39(4), pp. 958–79.

Mackie, H. and Byrne, J. (1999). *The Amazing Spider-Man*, #12. Marvel Comics.

Mackie, H., Brevoort, T., Isherwood, G., and Romita, J. (1999). *Peter Parker: Spider-Man*, #12. Marvel Comics.

Maggin, E. and Swan, C. (1974). *Superman*, #276. DC Comics.

Millar, M. and Johnson, D. (2014). *Superman: Red Son*. Burbank, CA: DC Comics.

Moench, D. and Aparo, J. (1993). *Batman*, #497. DC Comics.

O'Roark, B. and Wood, W. (2004). Safety at the Racetrack: Results of Restrictor Plates in Superspeedway Competition. *Southern Economic Journal*, 71(1), pp. 118–29.

Peltzman, S. (1975). The Effects of Automobile Safety Regulation. *Journal of Political Economy*, 83(4), pp. 677–726.

Siegel, J. and Plastino, A. (1960). *Adventure* Comics, #271. DC Comics.

Siegel, J. and Shuster, J. (1940). *Action Comics*, #23. DC Comics.

Siegel, J. and Swan, C. (1961). *Superman*, #149. DC Comics.

Superman: Doomsday. (2007). [Film] Hollywood: Timm, B., Montgomery, L., and Vietti, B.

Taylor, T., Redondo, B., Sandoval, S., and Tarragona, J. (2016). *Injustice: Gods Among Us: Year 4*. Burbank, CA: DC Comics.

Waid, M. and Ross, A. (2008). *Kingdom Come*. Burbank, CA: DC Comics.

7

Who's Going to Clean Up This Mess?

Civilian characters in comic books have a love-hate relationship with the heroes who defend their cities. There are the fan boys and girls like Flash Thompson,[1] Snapper Carr,[2] and Doreen Green who stand by their favorites through thick and thin.[3] Even erstwhile protesters who fear meta-humans recant and shower heroes with adulation when they realize the supers have saved the planet from alien forces.[4] Many heroes are capable liaisons to the civilian world. After meeting her, little girls want to be Wonder Woman, and Captain America embodies all that's right with the land of the free and the home of the brave. Heroes aren't always role models, but even if their motives may be questionable at times (think Batman, the Punisher, and Rorschach), in the end they seem to do so much more good than harm. Usually.

Heroes almost always get their man when it comes to crime-fighting. One of the attractions of comics is that no matter how bleak the outcome, no matter how improbable the odds, the good guys come away at the end of the day with a victory snatched from the jaws of defeat. They evacuate the burning buildings, get the civilians away from the lines of battle, and fight the fights that are unwinnable through established means. Nuclear weapons aren't going to work against the planet-eating Galactus.[5] He eats planets, what's a nuclear warhead going to do to stop him? When magical forces from the great beyond that are not subject to the laws that govern this world appear, who you gonna call?[6] If an intellect far beyond the normal human capacity develops technologies that dwarf those of the conventional military, how will you prevent the genius madman from taking over the world? To accomplish any of these things, you need more than a hero. You need a *super* hero.

It's a perfect solution to an unwinnable dilemma. The heroes want to hero. That's what they do. Nevertheless, just about every hero runs into an unbreakable stone (or kryptonite, or adamantium) wall of community-wide resentment at some point in time. For some reason, the general public look askance at their champions and ask whether the presence of these masked marvels is at least as dangerous as the forces against which they are fighting.

One of the more famous frictions between a person of influence and a hero is the antagonistic approach that editor J. Jonah Jameson takes towards Spider-Man. There are various explanations for his hostility but the original cause revolves around Jameson's jealousy. His son, John Jameson, is a test pilot who has taken his share of risks. Test piloting is a harrowing business, but despite his efforts he toils in obscurity. The public is only interested in the exploits of the web-slinging, masked man. As a result, Jameson generates public antipathy towards Spider-Man by focusing on how only a miscreant would wear a mask, but the source of his deep-seated hatred really stems from Spider-Man stealing the spotlight from his son.[7]

Mutants are particularly despised. It might be because they look different from everyone else; it might be because their powers were gained by a genetic mutation rather than coming from a science experiment gone wrong, or some cosmic force; or maybe it is due to the threat that continued gene mutations mean for the human species. Regardless, the X-Men and most mutants are "feared and hated by the world they have sworn to protect" (Claremont and Cockrum, 1975, p. 1). People understandably distrust the vigilantes as they seem to work outside the rules to which the rest of us must adhere. There are lots of reasons to worry about the existence of superheroes. In fact, if one lives in your town, you can bet that a protest mob is on its way.

This might ruffle a hero's feathers from time to time, but usually they don't let the demonstrators get them down. The right to protest superheroes ranks right up there with freedom of the press and the right to a jury trial, but the general *Sturm und Drang* of anti-hero sentiment misses a significant economic point. J. Jonah Jameson, the anti-mutant crowds, and general hero-bashers would have a larger following if they spent a little less time in front of the cameras and a little more time in front of an economics book. The most effective argument against superheroes isn't that their powers pose too great a danger to humanity, it isn't that they represent a bastardization of the gene pool, it isn't even that they dress strangely. There are two economic reasons that the haters should emphasize. First, heroes don't have insurance. Second, heroes generate lemons.

Why You Should Hate Superheroes
Too—Part I: Insurance

In the course of life people sometimes find themselves the beneficiaries of the activities of others. There is some remuneration that basically falls into their laps over which they had no control. For instance, due to the hard work and expense of a neighbor, your evening constitutional is improved because you stroll by their home, surrounded by its beautiful garden. The colors are impeccably balanced, the beds expertly mulched, and the lawn fed and watered to perfection. It is the highlight of the evening and you didn't have to pull one weed.

There is also the benefit that can spill over to the population from a more highly educated citizenry. This is one of the reasons why governments spend so much on the education system. If the populace is literate it means they are more employable. If they are employable, they can pay income taxes. If they can pay income taxes then government can spend more money on social programs. Those social programs can help those less fortunate. Thus, those less fortunate benefit tangentially from the jobs they didn't get. In fact, much of society benefits from a governmentally-funded school system. People can understand a bit about civil responsibility, they can sign their names on contracts, and read enough to know who they are voting for on a ballot, even if they don't fully recognize what the candidates stand for. Perhaps those educated on the public dime will go on to university and solve the world's great problems.[8] A cure for Alzheimer's disease, a cost-effective way to desalinize water, a cure for the heinous traffic snarls on the roadways of major cities, or a way to let people with whom you are nominally friends see the cat video you made, are all possibilities that result from an educated workforce, and from which we all benefit. The problem with these good things is that the producer of them may not be paid properly for their altruism. Teachers aren't paid enough based on the value they generate for society and the people who get the inoculation, or tend their gardens, almost always have to pay for it, yet they are providing benefits to others.

Again, think about walking around your neighborhood. You pass this quaint bungalow with the charming garden. You stop to admire it and notice something that wasn't there the night before. Strapped to the picket fence is an enchanting, little box with some words carved on the side. You step up to it and read "For your enjoyment. Please contribute what you can." The homeowners, realizing what their garden means to those around them, are trying to monetize their work! You huff indignantly. The no-good deadbeats. Who would pay for this? It's their choice to tend this garden, how can they dare ask for a handout? You pass by the box, as do most of the evening stroller crowd. Next year, you notice the garden isn't quite as well maintained, and you think to yourself "those homeowners are slacking off, I wonder what their problem is." The box is still there but for some reason it doesn't look as cheery as it did the first time you saw it (as if boxes could look cheery). The next year the garden looks a little more unkempt and you notice some crab grass in the lawn. The box is still there and now you are sure it looks menacing. The next year, there is no garden at all, but at least the box is gone.

What happened here? Why did the homeowners let their garden slide? Keeping up a garden is hard work and can be very expensive. The attempt to crowdfund the gardeners' work backfires for a reason we discussed earlier in Chapter 5. The garden is a public good. The homeowners are the source of something that certainly brings value to the neighbors, but in this case it is clearly non-excludable. In order to try to cover the costs of their efforts, your green-thumbed neighbors place a collection box on the fence, but because the view is non-excludable, free-riders, like yourself, can walk by without paying. Over the next few years, the financial and physical toll of keeping up the garden catches up with the homeowners and they no longer provide what everyone enjoyed. This garden is the classic case of something that generates a positive externality. A positive externality is a benefit to a third party that accrues even though they have no role in creating it. All you do is walk by the house, but the industriousness of the gardeners is what produces the benefit.

Activities that beget positive externalities are viewed as good things, but sometimes, because the producer has difficulty finding users willing to compensate them financially, they aren't as widespread as society would like. We might enjoy soothing musical performances while waiting for the subway, but musicians don't oblige us because too many commuters pass by the suitcase without paying, and getting up early in the morning to make a small sum of money playing Vivaldi on the violin for the ungrateful cretins who populate the subway stations is a real drag. To address such underproduction, governments will sometimes subsidize activities. Education, the arts, and preventive medical care generate positive externalities, but the gains are difficult to capture fully. As a result, government writes a check to ensure these ventures continue. Similarly, superhero work, a public good, generates positive externalities. They presumably keep crime at bay and save us from becoming slaves to alien overlords.

That's all well and good, and to an extent we have covered this ground already. Where we haven't gone is the dark side of externalities. As you may have already guessed, not all externalities are making people's lives better. Sometimes people are the victims of a harm over which they had no control: A polluted water source, a construction project going on outside of the bedroom window, even someone's overpowering perfume. These are examples of negative externalities. Negative externalities arise when, despite being an innocent third party minding your own business, an activity causes you some kind of harm. Be it the inability to use a body of water for swimming or drinking, a bad night's sleep, or the nausea that results from the overpowering bouquet of Calvin Klein's *Obsession*, negative externalities are difficult to avoid because, other than to be carrying on our day-to-day activities in the proximity of the source, we have no role in generating them. Consequently, society would prefer less of these activities, but because those who generate the harm do not bear the full costs of the production process, these things are made in excess.

One explanation for why negative externalities exist is that the cost they are imposing upon the rest of the world is not accounted for in the production decisions of those who generate them. The reason a river is polluted is because that's the easy, affordable way to dispose of toxic waste. No one holds title to the river, so there isn't a litigious property owner taking the factory boss to court. The folks who live downstream might be prevented from using the water, but since that water isn't theirs to begin with, their claims of being harmed might fall on deaf ears. What needs to happen, assuming we want there to be less pollution, is that the folks affected must be moved to another town. That way they are not harmed and the factory can pollute to its dirty heart's content.

Wait a minute! That doesn't sound right. Why should the noble townsfolk be forced out of their homes? It isn't their fault the evil factory is discharging such noxious emissions. Ah, but are you so sure? This is one of the points of Nobel Prize winner Ronald Coase's work (1960).[9] Coase notes that when property rights are unclear, we have a problem. In the case of pollution, the question is who has the right to the air, water, quiet, whatever is being damaged? This must be determined by a court if the property right is in question, and as established by precedent, a good jurist will apply the Hand Formula to the case and deduct an answer. Named after Judge Learned Hand, the practicable formula says that the burden should be placed on whoever can avoid the harm most easily (United States, 1947).[10] If we know the pollution is coming from a factory, getting that plant to stop is almost certainly less costly than moving every town that is downstream from the pollution source. In essence, you have assigned the property right of clean water to the town, and you will force the factory to literally clean up its act.[11]

Superheroes As the Factory

Now, think of superheroes as the factory and everyone else as the town and you've got our first reason to hate superheroes. In the superhero world, there are lots of negative externalities, and failure to deal with them can cause disgruntled crowds to turn against heroes. In comics we see significant destruction when a hero battles a villain, especially when the villain possesses their own set of superpowers. For instance, in the epic *Death of Superman* (Jurgens and Breeding, 1993), the otherworldly Doomsday falls from the sky and is marching, like William Tecumseh Sherman, to Metropolis, demolishing roads, bridges, towns, and anything else that gets in his way. The damage is almost incalculable. The military is called out to no avail and it is up to the Man of Steel to stop the destruction. All the damage is in no way the result of the actions of people who will now find themselves homeless or stuck in traffic because they have to drive on alternative routes to school or work. They are subject to externalities. The Brobdingnagian battles depicted on the big screen of hero movies provide a more palpable context for the destruction imposed on the innocent bystander. When heroes and villains battle they engage in terrifying encounters that leave smoldering ruins, torn up highways, and precariously leaning structures. Rebuilding after the destruction will cost hundreds of billions, if not trillions, of dollars, and the tantalizing question of "who's going to pay for it all?" begins. If you're lucky, the casualties will be minimal, but after the glow of being saved wears off, the remaining devastation is enough to invoke the ire of survivors and cause tremendous acrimony towards the perceived source of their discontent.

One of the most poignant examples of the negative externalities imposed by superhero activity can be found in Astro City. With all of the *tête-à-tête* between good and bad actors, there have been many civilian casualties. In order to provide comfort to those who have lost loved ones, Mike Tenicek starts a support group called Miranda's Friends, named after his deceased wife. As much as he wants to help others, this group is balm for his own soul. The members of the group are trying to find solace in a life turned upside down through no fault of their own. Like support groups for victims of diseases such as Parkinson's or cancer, these people are trying to work out their grief, the source of which was beyond their control. The members of Miranda's friends didn't ask to be party to the travesties that took their sons, daughters, and spouses, but because of where they live they are put in harm's way (Busiek and Anderson, 2018).

So how do we deal with externalities? In the case of pollution, the goal of policy-makers is to get the polluter to consider what they are doing by making them pay the full cost of their actions. You want to pollute the river? That's fine, but if you're going to do it you must incur the cost of not only dumping your waste in the water, that obviously isn't costing you much, but also the costs you are imposing on the folks downstream. This is what we call internalizing the externality. When you internalize the negative externality, you consider and deal with the full costs of the action. Governments might decide to tax the polluting activity. Or, they might force the factory to install some sort of cleaning equipment to scrub the effluents of toxins prior to dumping any materials in the water. Perhaps they forbid dumping in the river altogether. Maybe they choose the nuclear option and shut the factory down, and for good measure condemn the executives to jail to set an example for anyone in the future who might dare to sully the pristine waters of the nation's rivers. Whatever the punishment, the idea is to get the factory to consider the true costs of what they are doing so that they will cut back on production.

So, how might heroes realize the costs they impose on others from battling evil? There are a couple of ways this can take place. In the Astro City situation, someone, presumably a remorseful hero, is secretly funding the activities of Miranda's Friends and paying Mike's bills. This personal response isn't common though, nor is it practical. Trying to compensate every survivor out of pocket will bleed you dry quickly. Instead, heroes need to think on a grander scale, and that means insurance. Before explaining how that might work for hero activity, let's take a slight detour and consider the draconian option of internalizing externalities: Superhero jail.

Superhero Perp Walk

As we have established, super-powered individuals might at any time be involved in a battle, resulting in considerable damage. This arouses the indignation of non-supers, especially if the good guys are unapologetic. Heroes could respond that if it wasn't for them, people would have been killed or the world would have been destroyed, and they would, of course, be correct. But what if the heroes are battling each other, Greek god-style? What if the fights causing destruction aren't life-altering conflicts of galactic proportion? What if it's just bored and boorish heroes letting off some steam? In Mark Waid's futuristic *Kingdom*

Come, that's just what is going on as the story gets under way (Waid and Ross, 2008). The protagonist, Norman McCay, explains that the children and grandchildren of the superheroes of the past lack the morals of their elders. They "no longer fight for the right. They fight simply to fight, their only foes each other" (p. 22). As he describes the scene in front of him, wanton destruction is occurring all around. There are some of the old guard, Flash, Hawkman, and Green Lantern, who continue to keep order, but they are more local patrols rather than protectors of the planet, and in the case of Batman, more a dictator than a hero. Wonder Woman finds Superman cloistered in a holographic reality where she tries to convince him to wrest control from those who are making chaos their own form of entertainment. Finally, Superman agrees, bringing with him the legends of yesterday. Their goal is to restore order to the world and their plan is a relatively simple one. Superman recruits those he believes can be redeemed and instructs them in the ways of heroes. He has those unwilling to be part of his new order incarcerated in a superhero prison constructed precisely to hold the most dangerous of criminals; however, if you've read Chapter 6, you know this won't work.

Why did Superman let the world get to the point where the young, powered whipper-snappers fought and wreaked havoc without a care? Years earlier a new hero emerged called Magog. He didn't share the values of Superman's generation. He considered letting villains essentially get away with a slap on the wrist as a poor excuse for justice. Jail time ended too quickly as the jails built to hold them proved inadequate to this task (this probably sounds familiar). Magog took it upon himself to begin executing the bad guys with prejudice. He murdered Joker on the steps of Metropolis' city hall, and during his trial Magog was unrepentant. The jury was equally frustrated with the failure of heroes to permanently end the activities of villains and found Magog innocent. In frustration, Superman left Metropolis, yielding the torch of protection to Magog, whose *modus operandi* might have been more visceral but was certainly effective. Until...a battle erupted that led to the annihilation of millions of innocent lives and the irradiation of much of the breadbasket of the United States. Magog is gripped with remorse, and when Superman finds him, he meekly submits. He begs for death but is condemned to the ultimate prison as a consequence of his actions, or to internalize the costs he imposed on others. Incarceration is one way to deal with externalities but it does so poorly in this case because Magog was already bereft and had stopped generating negative externalities. Additionally, he isn't bearing the full costs of the devastation he caused. For this we turn, finally, to insurance.

Fifteen Minutes Can Save You Fifteen Percent

Most situations concerning property damage, or even physical harm imposed on civilians by hero battles, are not as dramatic as what is seen in *Kingdom Come*. A block of damaged buildings or some smashed cars are much lower stakes than the deaths of millions of people. Additionally, they are much easier to come back from. A structure can be rebuilt and a car replaced. When those unexpected calamities occur, insurance is in place to help limit the financial expense we would face if we needed to replace these big-ticket items.

Insurance also exists to internalize externalities. If I fail to take the proper amount of care while driving, I could really hurt someone. Without insurance I could be sued by a victim, but there is no guarantee that, even if a court found me liable, the victim would receive any payments. I could refuse to pay. I might not have the means to pay. I could run away, change my name, and rely on my lawyers to drag the process out until the victim gives up. But with insurance, any damages I cause can be covered. I pay for that insurance so I am paying for the harm I cause.

Insurance of all kinds is big business, but in this case we will ignore most types of protection. We're not worried about life insurance, body part insurance, pet insurance, ransom insurance, multiple birth insurance, UFO insurance, zombie insurance, or any other number of crazy things that people are willing to pay to be protected from. Superheroes might fight aliens or zombies but that isn't what the public needs to be defended against most. They need to be safeguarded against the actions of the heroes themselves. So of course, in a market-based economy an enterprising individual is expected to step up and provide such a service. Enter the folks from the Flatiron Building: Mrs Hoag and Damage Control.

In *Marvel Comics Presents* #19 (Harras and Lim, 1989), we see Mrs Hoag, the intrepid leader of Damage Control, trying to hire John Porter, a superhero insurance broker. Porter is currently selling policies to victims of superhero activity. In New York this is an important business, but it doesn't internalize the externality heroes are imposing because such insurance is paid by the victim rather than the source of the externality. What sets Damage Control, the company, apart from other insurance brokerages is that they contract with the heroes, not the people who are harmed by hero activity. In other words, Damage Control cleans up superhero messes. They advertise "When the super heroes need help, they call Damage Control" (McDuffie and Colon, 1989a, p. 20). When things are wrecked during the course of their adventures, a hero's insurance policy kicks in and, in an impossibly short time, damage is repaired and life goes on.

In the original 1988 issue of *Damage Control*, the estimate of annual superhero demolition was $20 billion.[12] Even in a city as large as New York, where Damage Control is headquartered, this is an untenable amount. The city's budget wouldn't be able to cover such cleanups year after year. If the burden were placed on individuals, insurance rates would be astronomical. Damage Control attempts to internalize the externality by placing the burden of payment on the cause of the harm. They provide insurance for heroes who now pay a premium to fund the cleanup activities surrounding their adventures. As former Avengers chairperson, Janet van Dyne, aka the Wasp, testifies "[Damage Control] has provided absolutely fabulous service to the Avengers almost since the beginning." At an event promoting Damage Control's business, Iron Man announces that Stark Enterprises has always used the company to clean up their "super-messes" (McDuffie and Colon, 1989b, p. 81).

We're Running a Business Here

To ensure that risks are properly assessed, insurance companies rely on actuarial tables that attempt to impose higher premiums on those more likely to use the insurance. Younger drivers pay more for auto insurance, as do home owners who build on a flood plain. The objective is that those more likely to use the insurance pay more. While the rate schedules are never discussed in *Damage Control*, it is likely that the Hulk pays more than the Wasp, as due to the Hulk's strength and rampaging he is more prone to smashing things than the petite fashion designer Janet van Dyne.

You see, Damage Control isn't a bunch of superhero groupies trying to enter the orbit of celebrity heroes. It's a business, meaning they have to be conscious of their revenues and costs. Clients can be hard to come by and insurance requires a large pool of customers to cover for the catastrophes that befall other members of the pool. As a result, Damage Control is willing to take on some unusual clients, as long as they pay their bills. In *Damage Control* #2 (McDuffie and Colon, 1989c), the supervillain Dr Doom's latest weapon malfunctions, damaging one of his facilities. Doom's cronies turn to their insurance company for help. Albert Cleary, Damage Control's accountant, insists that Doom is six months behind on paying his premium and they shouldn't honor his claim until he has paid up. His adamant stance lands him in the position of collection agent. Ignorant of the danger to himself, he marches over and confronts Doom, who, fortunately for Cleary, understands the need for strict order and pays up.

On the cost side, we see that Damage Control won't just let a client slide if they don't have the proper form of insurance, either. When the supervillain prison, the Vault, is attacked, the warden makes an inadvertent call to Damage Control. Damage Control employees John, Gene, and Bart head to the Vault to reconnoiter and find themselves in the middle of a breakout. Fortunately for Damage Control, having eyes on the ground is good for business. The company won't have to pay for this because, unfortunately for the Vault, it doesn't have insurance for prison breaks.

So, insurance helps to shift the burden of superhero work onto the heroes and villains who cause the damage. By internalizing the externality, we can hate the heroes a little less. Still, there is another reason why heroes might be unlikable. It's not quite as obvious, and certainly more personal in nature, but it drives storylines in a way that few other economic issues can.

Why You Should Hate Superheroes Too—Part II: Lemons

Even heroes lose people they love. Sometimes the losses are tragic, other times the pressures of hero life strain a relationship to the breaking point. As noted in Chapter 2, this is one reason to maintain a secret identity. Just because you are dating a superhero doesn't mean you should be hunted down like a rabid dog; ask Gwen Stacy—a former love interest of Spider-Man who is thrown to her death by the Green Goblin (Conway and Kane, 1972)—Aquababy—who was killed by Black Manta (Michelinie and Aparo, 1977)—Karen Page—the former girlfriend of Daredevil who was killed when she walked in on a fight between the devil of Hell's Kitchen and the villain Bullseye (Smith and Quesada, 1999)—or Alexandra DeWitt—Green Lantern Kyle Rainer's girlfriend, whose dismembered body was found in a refrigerator (Marz et al., 1994).[13] These examples of collateral damage are directly attributable to getting involved with a hero. In that sense, you can imagine that the harm that befalls these characters is partly of their own making (except for Aquababy, he's a baby for goodness sake). The rest of those who were so unfortunately killed at least had an inkling of what they were getting into—unless they weren't told. Alexandra DeWitt had only been dating Rainer a few weeks and wasn't aware of his second self. Other love interests are kept in the dark for long periods of time before they are told about the hero's identity. Keeping that special someone guessing about why you were late for a date makes for a necessary tension in the relationship, but by keeping this information secret it prevents the paramour from making a fully-informed decision about whether or not to cut you loose. Those in the dark are subject to asymmetric information, which is commonly connected with the lemons problem.

In 1970, economist George Akerlof (another economist who pocketed a Nobel Prize) published a paper explaining why the market for used goods was subject to distrust. Given that one side of the market, usually the seller, has information about the quality of the product that they do not share with the other side of the market, usually the buyer, the prices of goods in the market tend to be lower than they should be. Using the example of the used car market, Akerlof demonstrated that because buyers are unsure if they are getting a bad car—a lemon—or a good one—a cherry—they are not willing to pay the price that equates to the actual value of the vehicle. As a result, prices in the used car market are depressed, leading to a lack of quality cars on the market. Since prices are lower than they should be, high-quality used cars appear less frequently in dealers' inventories. Sellers do not want to supply cars that will fetch a lower price if it is actually a high-quality vehicle. Thus, both the price and the quality of cars is lower in the used car market than they would be if the buyers and sellers were able to perfectly communicate information about the condition of the cars. The lack of information prevents mutually beneficial exchanges from taking place. If you could tell that a used, late model car had been salvaged from a flood, you might still be willing to buy it, but only if the price were sufficiently low. The seller has no incentive to provide this information, and in some cases they may not know the car's history and couldn't tell you even if they wanted to.[14] Due to the asymmetry of information, a beneficial trade fails to materialize because the buyer doesn't trust the used car salesman and, let's face it, the reputation of used car salesmen has been earned over time.

This is analogous to the naïve or simply clueless associate of a hero. Being connected to a celebrity has its advantages and disadvantages. Sure, your new squeeze is an icon with legions of fans, but is being seen with someone whose Q Score is off the charts worth the stress?[15] Hero news is A1, above the fold.[16] Their lives and exploits are explored by every blogger, tweeter, and reporter alive. Add to this the obsession of some in the criminal element who are doing everything they can to bring down the hero and you've got the recipe for a dangerous relationship. However, if you know what you are getting into then you can make a more fully-informed choice about whether or not to try and make it work. Mary Jane's and Peter Parker's marital problems are in full bloom in *The Amazing Spider Man* #12 (Mackie and Byrne, 1999), when Peter can't help but web-sling around New York City (he does have that great power and you know what that means), despite having told M.J. that he wasn't going to do that anymore. At least she knew what she was getting into when they got married.[17]

It is a show of trust to divulge a secret identity to someone, but when is the right time to take that step? Sharing this information too early in the dating process might scare off a viable match. It might also mean that the potential love interest falls for the hero role, not the real person. Of course, there are the common misunderstandings that occur if you're dating a superhero but don't know it. You're bound to get irritated when they are late for dinner, forget a birthday, or don't call when they are supposed to. If you are left in the dark about the identity of a date, being attacked by a maniacal villain would come as a pretty big surprise. The hero knows the costs of being a hero, but without confiding that to their companions there is a serious information asymmetry and that's unfair. If someone has hoarding issues you don't know about when you start to date, that's one thing; when a crazed arch-nemesis who wouldn't hesitate to kill you is on your tail, that is something else entirely.

There is an externality connected to being in the sphere of a super-hero, and because people are purposefully kept ignorant of the truth, it places them at risk of potential harm, but this obliviousness is not only relevant for a love interest. What about the other people with whom the disguised hero comes into contact? If Clark Kent's co-workers at the *Daily Planet* knew he was Superman, would they continue to work there? Most would, but not all. There is a significant threat that if an identity is revealed, the business might be attacked, and there's the even greater chance that Kent will be off saving the world and you will get stuck picking up his slack at work. The lack of information, even now, might be the reason why you have to work this weekend. Do you really know what your co-worker two desks over does when she leaves the office?

A more palpable example of this situation is found in *Daredevil* #118 (Brubaker, Lark, and Lucas, 2009), where we see a split between Matt Murdock and his best friend Foggy Nelson. While Foggy knows that Matt is Daredevil, Matt's recent actions are causing problems for Foggy's business as an attorney. Matt has aligned himself with the criminal Kingpin, and when he tells Foggy it isn't any of his business, Foggy explodes. "When you put on that mask and go out there and do stupid &$%# [sic] like that—it puts us all at risk, Matt!" (p. 18). Foggy is irate because "I can't even list our firm's address because frigging Stilt-Man or the freaking Toad might fire-bomb us!" (p. 18). In a similar rant in the Netflix *Daredevil* (2015) serial, Foggy lets Matt know that he and Karen [their secretary] are now, by proximity, part of what Daredevil is doing. The difference here is that in the television program, neither Foggy or Karen had a say in it. The lack of information that came from working with Matt Murdock has put them both in jeopardy.

And the Answer Is . . .

There are a lot of questions in the hero world about the damage inflicted during normal superhero activities. There are third parties, typically your innocent passersby, who become part of the action whether they want to or not. Some are taken hostage or used as human shields to promote escapes. People lose their homes, cars, phones, and other physical property due to the immensely destructive confrontations that arise when good guys battle bad guys. Sometimes there are bumps and bruises, but in more extreme circumstances human frailty is on display when those in the wrong place at the wrong time die. To limit negative externalities, heroes (and villains) need to be forced to include the costs they impose on others in their decision-making calculus. Society wants to be protected from the blackguards but they also don't want to deal with the externalities that are sure to accompany a fight. The optimal amount of hero and criminal confrontations is almost surely less than what actually occurs; however, since villains don't care about civilians (and prison sentences don't deter them), heroes will likely bear most of the burden of any negative externalities generated. This is one reason why they try to talk the villain out of their plans prior to engaging in battle.

Insurance is one way to redistribute the costs of an action away from the inflicted to the inflictor. If you hit a pedestrian while driving carelessly, your insurance kicks in to cover their medical bills. The aggrieved party had no reason to expect to be injured and they presumably were not part of your commute—they didn't build the car, they weren't involved with the construction of the road, and they weren't behaving erratically. Your actions caused them harm and they should, at the very least, have their medical bills compensated. Because they were taking sufficient care by walking on the sidewalk, they shouldn't be financially responsible for what you did.

Providing decision-makers with the proper information is another way to reduce the ill will shown toward heroes. In the non-comic world, laws and regulations are imposed to help ameliorate the lemons problem. When transactions are undertaken, certain information must be revealed to the participants. In the case of a home purchase, inspection reports noting termite damage provide important details about the structural soundness of a building, and if such relevant aspects are hidden, or if they are proven to be false or misrepresented, the sale can be voided. In a world of superheroes, for normal people to take proper care it might be helpful to know who has powers. Not disclosing that information might be good for heroes' associates but because proximity puts you in harm's way, heroes might not be entitled to all of their secrets.

When information or insurance isn't available, we see predictable problems. Relationships are strained when a secret identity is kept under wraps. People feel unsafe and distrust heroes when the physical world around them is repeatedly damaged during the routine activities undertaken by super-powered people. The unfortunate consequences of superhero activity are part of the costs of living in a world where extreme powers exist. When you have groups of people with different abilities existing in the same space, there is the potential for serious conflict.[18] "With great power comes great responsibility" is another way of saying that with great power come costs.

But let's not leave this chapter on that depressing note. Sure, there are costs that must be faced by the third parties living in the comic world, but there are benefits—dare we say positive externalities—too. Many heroes have extraordinary powers, but some rely on a set of skills that are not alien or supernatural in nature to combat criminality. For some heroes, their powers are intellectual. In addition to all of the saving and good deed-doing, those powers of the mind have the potential to spill over into the lives of everyday people in the form of something amazing.

Endnotes

1. Thompson bullies Peter Parker but is a huge fan of Spider-Man. In *The Amazing Spider-Man* #17, he even forms a Spider-Man fan club (Lee and Ditko, 1964).
2. Snapper becomes a sidekick for the Justice League of America, first appearing in *Brave and the Bold* #28 (Fox and Sekowski, 1960).
3. Despite her own powers and hero identity as Squirrel Girl, Doreen was enamored with the hero group the New Warriors, especially Speedball (Nicieza and Medina, 2006).

4. This happens often, but as an example see *Justice League* #6 when the team saves the world from Darkseid (Johns and Lee, 2012).
5. The last of a race of humanoids who existed prior to the Big Bang, Galactus survived the ending of his universe and the beginning of the new one wrought by the Big Bang. His source of sustenance is absorbing the life energies of planets by consuming them.
6. If you said Ghostbusters, kudos to you for getting the reference, but this is a book about superheroes, not comedians in goofy costumes... OK, it's not a book about comedians.
7. The complete analysis of Jameson's Spidey-based psychosis can be found in *The Amazing Spider Man* #10 (Lee and Ditko, 1963).
8. This example comes from Gruber (2007, p. 287–9).
9. Coase won a Nobel Prize for his work on transaction costs in 1991. Transaction costs are the costs involved in carrying out a transaction. These are above the dollar price paid for a good and include things like the cost of negotiation or transportation.
10. The formula itself is pretty basic algebra: $B = P \times L$, where B is the burden of taking precaution, P is the probability of an event occurring, and L is the harm that might occur. If you do not take the proper amount of care when the burden on you for doing so would prevent a greater value in damages, then you can be found negligent of imposing harm on someone. This means that if $B < P \times L$ and you didn't take care then you are guilty of negligence.
11. The question of environmental rights is a relatively new one. People en masse don't start thinking seriously about environmental costs until well into the twentieth century. In the United States, this culminates with the creation of the Environmental Protection Agency. The agency sets environmental standards and enforces the laws and regulations which ensure polluters stay in line.
12. Adjusting for inflation, that amounts to $43.67 billion in 2018 US dollars.
13. This is the source of the crude term "fridging." Comic writer Gail Simone (n.d.) noticed that the device of killing off female characters assumes the sense of the macabre far more often than for male characters. She writes about this at her website: Women in Refrigerators.
14. Used car dealers often purchase vehicles at auction and they are subject to the lemons problem like any other buyer.
15. We know Lois Lane continues to date Clark even after she finds out he is Superman, but she had a crush on the Man of Steel first. Others don't want the hero life; ask Bruce Banner's former flame, Betty Ross.
16. This antiquated allusion refers to the location of a prominent story in a newspaper. A1 is the front page of the first section. Above the fold means it is one of the two or three stories you see when you look at the front of the paper before you unfold it. If you have never seen a newspaper before, think about this as the headline story on a news website, or the notification of news stories you get on your phone, or... Oh forget it. If you don't know what a newspaper is, this reference is probably lost on you anyway.

17. Peter and M.J. were married in 1987 in *The Amazing Spider-Man* Annual #21 (Michelinie, Shooter, and Ryan, 1987). M.J. knew Peter was Spider-Man. After all, prior to the nuptials she complained about cleaning footprints off the ceiling. That, and they have taken web-slinging tours of the city together.
18. O'Roark (2010), O'Roark (2011), and O'Roark, Wood, and Demblowski (2012) discuss how bifurcated tournaments, which include drivers of very different abilities, apply to NASCAR racing. It turns out there are more accidents when you have those with mixed skill levels competing against each other. Knoeber and Thurman (1994) examine these dual tournaments in the broiler chicken industry.

References

Akerlof, G. A. (1970). The Market for "Lemons": Quality Uncertainty and the Market Mechanism. *Quarterly Journal of Economics*, 84(3), pp. 488–500.

Brubaker, E., Lark, M., and Lucas, J. (2009). *Daredevil*, #118. Marvel Comics.

Busiek, M. and Anderson, B. (2018). *Astro City*, #50. Vertigo Comics.

Claremont, C. and Cockrum, D. (1975). *X-Men*, #96. Marvel Comics.

Coase, R. (1960). The Problem of Social Cost. *Journal of Law and Economics*, 3, pp. 1–44.

Conway, G. and Kane, G. (1972). *The Amazing Spider-Man*, #121. Marvel Comics.

Daredevil. (2015). [Television series episode]. Nelson v. Murdock. Burbank, CA: Pokaski, J. and Petrie, D.

Fox, G. and Sekowski, M. (1960). *Brave and the Bold*, #28. DC Comics.

Gruber, J. (2007). *Public Finance and Public Policy*, 2nd ed. New York: Worth Publishers.

Harras, B. and Lim, R. (1989). *Marvel Comics Presents*, #19. Marvel Comics.

Johns, G. and Lee, J. (2012). *Justice League*, #6. DC Comics.

Jurgens, D. and Breeding, B. (1993). *Superman*, v. 2, #75. DC Comics.

Knoeber, C. and Thurman, W. (1994). Testing the Theory of Tournaments: An Empirical Analysis of Broiler Production. *Journal of Labor Economics*, 12(2), pp. 155–79.

Lee, S. and Ditko, S. (1963). *The Amazing Spider-Man*, #10. Marvel Comics.

Lee, S. and Ditko, S. (1964). *The Amazing Spider-Man*, #17. Marvel Comics.

Mackie, H. and Byrne, J. (1999). *The Amazing Spider-Man*, v. 2, #12. DC Comics.

Marz, R., Carr, S., Auccoin, D., and Banks, D. (1994). *Green Lantern*, v. 3, #54. DC Comics.

McDuffie, D. and Colon, E. (1989a). *Damage Control*, v.2, #1. Marvel Comics.

McDuffie, D. and Colon, E. (1989b). *Damage Control*, v.2, #3. Marvel Comics.

McDuffie, D. and Colon, E. (1989c). *Damage Control*, v.2, #2. Marvel Comics.

Michelinie, D. and Aparo, J. (1977). *Adventure Comics*, #452. DC Comics.

Michelinie, D., Shooter, J., and Ryan, P. (1987). *The Amazing Spider-Man*, Annual #21. Marvel Comics.

Nicieza, F. and Medina, P. (2006). *I Heart Marvel*, #2. Marvel Comics.

O'Roark, B. (2010). Chasing the Buschwackers: Unintended Consequences in NASCAR. *Pennsylvania Economic Review*, 17(1–2), pp. 52–64.

O'Roark, B. (2011). Buschwhacking in NASCAR: Mixing Skill on the Road in NASCAR's Junior Circuit. *Virginia Economic Journal*, 16, pp. 1–11.

O'Roark, B., Wood, W., and Demblowski, B. (2012). Tournament Chasing NASCAR Style: Driver Incentives in Stock Car Racing's Playoff Season. *Eastern Economic Journal*, 38(1), pp. 1–17.

Simone, G. (n.d.). *Women in Refrigerators*. [Online] WiR. Available at: http://lby3.com/wir/ [Accessed April 4, 2018].

Smith, K. and Quesada, J. (1999). *Daredevil*, v. 2, #5. Marvel Comics.

United States v. Carroll Towing Co. [1947]. 159 F.2d 169 (2nd Cir.); 1.

Waid, M. and Ross, A. (2008). *Kingdom Come*. Burbank, CA: DC Comics.

8

Where Do They Get Those Wonderful Toys?

How does someone like Bruce Wayne, Oliver Queen, Clint Barton, or Kate Bishop end up in the company of Wonder Woman, Spider-Man, Flash, or the Hulk? That first group of comic book aliases comprise a few of the non-powered, albeit extremely skilled, heroes in the superhero world. Batman, Green Arrow, and the two versions of Hawkeye—a bow-based sharpshooter with a bit of kung-fu fighting thrown in—along with a number of others, comprise a curiosity in a culture where flight, superhuman strength, and invulnerability to projectiles are common traits. Other instances where innate powers are noticeably lacking involve Tony Stark, aka Iron Man, who has a great suit but no obvious powers that make him extraordinary, and Nightwing, the grown-up first Robin, Dick Grayson, whose abilities stem from being a child circus performer. Another member of the Bat Family, Barbara Gordon, aka Batgirl, is really smart and ranks among the world's most adept computer hackers, taking on the mantle of Oracle after she is paralyzed by the Joker, but her power factor equals zero. The same can be said for Batwoman, minus the hacking skills. She's in the Bat Family but she just kicks bad guy butt, as does the Huntress, who may not technically be in the Bat Family but she hangs around the periphery. She and Batgirl form two thirds of the traditional all-female, crime-fighting force, the Birds of Prey, but they are skilled combatants, not super-powered like their teammate Black Canary. Put simply, there are some supremely skilled, albeit non-powered people, who are accepted into the superhero fraternity. Their abilities have been developed over time, rather than having powers since birth, or having those powers result from a bizarre, catastrophic occurrence.

This should give those of us who aren't from outer space or who don't hang around the science labs some hope. Perhaps we can earn our superhero stripes through good old-fashioned hard work and ingenuity. What might give us pause, however, is that those heroes' skills are often augmented by radical technologies that make the hero that much more accomplished. If you want to fight the bad guys it helps to have better tools than they do. Batman's kit impresses the Joker who, in the 1989 movie *Batman*, asks "where does he get those wonderful toys?"

In the real world, the police are obliged to work within palpable resource constraints. Budgets are limited and sometimes political negotiations prevent the money from flowing to where it is most needed, but superheroes are not so constrained. Because they work as private citizens, they can funnel their monies in the direction they deem most important, without the red tape and bureaucracy facing the men in blue. This leads to the innovations that help the under-powered heroes stay one step ahead of their sometimes very powered adversaries.

This chapter will examine the role technology plays in the world of superheroes. For those with deep pockets, they can advance and support a technological agenda that will give them an advantage when battling criminals, but this is no different than a company that invests in research and development to remain one step ahead of its rivals in the business world. In fact, the ability of heroes to allocate resources efficiently is akin to the way firms determine how best to use their own resources. From an economic perspective, these advanced developments can be used to manipulate production functions and production possibilities curves, and that can make a super-powered wannabe into a contributing member of the superhero community.

It's Good to Be Rich

You know things are real when they show up in *Money* magazine. *Money* ran the numbers and arrived at a list of the top five richest superheroes (Davidson, 2015). The world's only trillionaire is the leader of Wakanda, currently T'Challa, the mythical Black Panther. T'Challa has an estimated net worth of $90.7 trillion as a result of being the sole owner, the monopolist if you will, of a resource called Vibranium, a metal deposited on Earth eons ago by large meteorites.[1] In *Doomwar* #1 (Maberry and Eaton, 2010), we are told that T-Challa has a vault that contains 10,000 tons of Vibranium. That may sound somewhat impressive but it gets better. Vibranium, a super strong alloy that is used to make Captain America's shield, goes for roughly $10,000 a gram. There are 453.59 grams in a pound and 2,000 pounds in a ton, so, if you do the math, you end up with one insanely rich king of a mysterious country somewhere in Africa.

The slightly more down-to-earth measures of wealth find Tony Stark, the fabulous industrialist, in the $12.5 billion range, enough to design and manufacture a series of those awesome Iron Man suits, with a little left over to fund the Avengers' missions. Bruce Wayne has an estimated $9.2 billion which helps keep the Batcave running and pays for the off books research and development at Wayne enterprises. Running a school for mutants isn't cheap, so Charles Xavier must have a little cash stashed under a mattress somewhere. Approximations of his wealth are in the $3.5 billion range. That might not be quite enough though, so the aid of fellow mutant Emma Frost and her $1–$3 billion fortune comes in handy. Frost used to be an evildoer but has reformed her ways and uses her income as the CEO of an electronics conglomerate to funnel money to Xavier's School for Gifted Children.

Money has some notable omissions from its list. Green Arrow might be nearer the top as heir to the multi-billion-dollar Queen enterprises, although his alias Oliver Queen is on and off of the board of directors. Perhaps the most peculiar oversight is Ozymandias. The *Watchmen* depicts Adrian Veidt as the world's smartest and richest man. His other-worldly retreat in Antarctica aside, Veidt inherits money from his parents, then parlays it into a multi-national enterprise by putting his astonishing intellect to work finding patterns in the market that help increase the value of his fortune in an era before data analytics.

Regardless of who you think is the top money dog, being rich endows you with significant advantages in life, especially if you want to play at heroics. For instance, Batman and Green Arrow, being the lineage of successful industrialists, have an almost limitless supply of resources. If you are a trust fund baby on one hand, and an aspiring superhero, notably without powers, on the other, it helps to have a comparative advantage in funding over your colleagues who might have powers but who also have to work a day job. Additionally, if you plan on spending your nights fighting bad guys you need to consider two things. First, are you able to do this job more effectively than the police? If not, why get involved? Second, are you able to be in any way successful? If you have no powers then you need one of two things, or even better, you need both. Your skill set must be second to none, including the ability to physically overwhelm the criminal element. Absent that, if you can't beat them up, you're going to need better tools than your adversaries.

It is no mystery then that you aren't going to find a financially desperate person fighting crime unless they have superpowers. Lists of the poorest heroes include Clark Kent, Peter Parker, Luke Cage, and

Jessica Jones, who are all working for a living in jobs that pay fairly low wages, and college students such as Firestar and Squirrel Girl who have no consistent income stream and are thus struggling to make ends meet. The only consistent element between them is that they all have powers.

So, to fight crime the non-powered folks need a leg up, something that is going to level the playing field. For most of them, that special something is not their fighting skills. Sure, they have physical talents and they certainly come in handy. All the hours spent training with monks and shadowy figures who teach them life lessons, along with killer ninja-type moves, provide great backstory fodder, but the bad guys they fight aren't usually ninety-pound [forty-one kilogram] weaklings. Even if they are, they will hire their own death squads or resort to weapons with deadly force to accomplish whatever diabolical aims they have in mind. This means heroes must rely on their ingenuity. It is the creative element of the hero that can often win the day. Bat shark repellent may on a rare occasion keep our heroes from a watery grave, but those Bat-a-rangs work wonders on a regular basis. It might seem cheesy but an arrow with a boxing glove at the end of it can be the difference between life and death.[2] An Iron Man suit not only ups your celebrity status, it also gives you a fighting chance against alien invaders. The thing is, the remarkable innovations that come from heroes and the development of ideas have an analogy in economics.

You May Not Want to Know How the Sausage Is Made

One of the most important decisions a business must make is how to produce the goods or services it is selling to its customers. Rarely do firms think about what to produce. That is determined by the market. If you aren't making things consumers want, you'll know about it pretty quickly. Sales will fall, revenues will fall, then the axe will fall as jobs get cut. In market-based economies, there is something referred to as consumer sovereignty. This means that consumers dictate what a company will produce because they vote for goods with their dollars. If a firm isn't satisfying the customer, it will be out of business because consumers will flee the market like rats from a sinking ship. Henry Ford famously said that consumers can have any color Model T they want "so long as it is black" (Ford and Crowther, 1922, p. 72). Today, that approach would get even the great Henry Ford fired. Consumers dictate their wants to sellers. They rule the market and sellers ignore this at their peril.

As a result, the firm must find a way to produce what the consumer wants. To be profitable, they must do this in a way that most efficiently employs the resources at their disposal. Generally speaking, a firm has four inputs they utilize in the production process. These inputs are traditionally listed as labor, capital, land, and entrepreneurship. There are only four inputs because economists try to keep the tally as short as possible. Don't think too badly of economists for doing this. It does make things much simpler, even if it means you need to be more imaginative about how inputs are classified. That being said, we're talking about economics and comics in this book, so imagination is something that comes with the territory.

Any part of the production process that has to do with people, save one which we'll get to in a minute, falls under the heading of labor. Most people think of the physical aspect of building something as labor, and that way of thinking is correct but it does leave out a substantial, and an increasingly important, part of the human contribution to production called human capital. These non-physical facets, such as the thoughts you have about how to make your job more efficient, are also part of the labor input. Furthermore, human capital is also manifested in any experience you bring to the job, or the skills you contribute, or the wisdom you add, or the knowledge you possess. All of these things are vital parts of labor's contribution to production. Employers want to hire folks who aren't just book smart. Anyone can memorize a book, but value lies in what additional attributes a person brings to the table. If you can add human capital then you are more likely to be hired.

Of course, human capital can be built up over time. That is what your resume reflects. Your past work experience tells of your opportunities to increase your human capital. It's like looking at the early years of a superhero. They are far more effective after learning how to harness their powers. Such development is often accomplished with the aid of a mentor. Whether it is Stick to Daredevil, the Ancient One to Doctor Strange, or Jonathan Kent to Superman, heroes are made better with the guidance of their Yoda. Put another way, gurus focus the abilities of heroes, which improves their human capital.

Entrepreneurship is also an aspect of human capital but it is separate because of its uniqueness. This input is difficult to teach but is of such vital importance that no matter how much of the other three inputs you have, if you don't have entrepreneurship you probably have nothing. There is no commonly accepted definition of entrepreneurship or entrepreneurial ability. It can be considered jointly as risk-taking ability and competence at coordinating the other inputs. When you start a business there are risks involved, and the one upon whom those risks fall is the entrepreneur. If you hire employees, it means that you are likely going to have to make a payroll. If your workers don't get paid, you don't get paid. Failure is an option and that means your reputation is on the line. You are probably putting up your own money, perhaps even money you have saved for a while. It might be your retirement savings or you kids' college fund. You take risks and your personal wealth is on the hook if you fail.

While that might sound terrifying, part of the reason for starting a business is because you think you can do something better than the way it is currently being done. Your ideas are worth taking a risk on because you have insight and skill and a willingness to chance it all that other people do not possess. One of the great problems facing former communist countries as they transition to market systems is that they don't have entrepreneurs. For years, communist nations told their citizens what to produce and how to produce it. The government didn't know the answers to these questions any better than anyone else, so not only were entrepreneurs shackled and their abilities squashed, but budding business owners had no good examples to follow. In the years succeeding the fall of the Iron Curtain and the Chinese tepid adoption of market reforms, advances were minimal. After decades of being strictly conditioned to follow the lead of the government, entrepreneurial aptitudes were nearly stamped out. Recently, especially in China, it seems that these necessary skills are being fostered and encouraged. But don't be misled. Not everyone can be an entrepreneur. For many of us, being the boss isn't something we can handle. The ulcers that come with the job are just too much.

The next input is land. This essentially consists of the natural elements that are used in the manufacture of goods. Another way of describing this would be to say that land includes anything that is not man-made. Anything you dig from the ground, anything you harvest, anything that exists without the plans of man is land. This includes any wind, water, air, or fire, and anything else born of mother nature.

Where Are Your Toys, Mr Terrific?

Land, labor, and entrepreneurship are all necessary for business, but what about squaring off against your nemeses? Heroes obviously possess significant quantities of human capital. Tony Stark, Ray Palmer (the Atom), and Michael Holt (Mr Terrific) are almost inhuman in their ability to apply complex theories of mathematics, engineering, and physics, in their heads no less, to create solutions to problems that stump your run-of-the-mill hero. Bruce Wayne has mastered chemistry and forensics, Barbara Gordon knows computers inside and out, and almost all of these characters have found time to develop their bodies with some form of martial art. Still, it is their application of the final type of input that really makes them interesting.

A science nerd might make a great hero, but if they were only solving equations for closing gateways to other dimensions or discovering the properties of an alien metal, they would likely get shunted to the status of role player on a team, called upon occasionally to provide some scientific insight. This is why, for as terrific as Mr Terrific is, you may have never heard of him. Contrary to Stark and Palmer, he doesn't have a suit. Unlike Bruce Wayne or Barbara Gordon, Mr Terrific's utility belt is empty. There is no Terrific-mobile, Terrific-cycle, or Terrific-cave that accompanies his character. He sits in the background being really, really smart, helping the Justice Society of America (a second-level superhero team) to solve problems. In effect, he's relegated to the B-team. With Batman around, the Justice League (the premiere league superhero team) doesn't really need him. What is Mr Terrific missing that might make him more valuable? Capital.[3]

One point about capital that needs to be firmly established before we move on is that capital is not necessarily money. Sure, firms need money to acquire inputs. Workers on the automobile assembly line, for instance, want to be paid in currency, not car parts. But capital isn't money because money isn't actually used to produce anything. It is a means by which you acquire the input needed. You can tear apart your car, leaving its individual components scattered on the garage floor, and other than the loose change you find—and that isn't needed for the car to function, it fell out of your pocket—no where will you find a piece of currency or a coin executing a material function to ensure the car performs as expected. Currency isn't strong enough to be built into the frame, nor is it fluid enough to be poured into the engine. You need steel and oil, and money can buy those for you, but it isn't what makes up the physical car itself. Instead, capital is the man-made materials that are used in the production of a good or service. Typically, we think of capital as the tools and machinery employed in production. The robots used on the assembly line do not grow on trees and they are not human. That makes them capital.

In a comic book sense, the accoutrements used by heroes, powered or not, are capital. Every gadget or gizmo in your utility belt, the suits you invented and don to fight off the forces of evil, the cars, planes, boats, motorcycles, bows and arrows, computer systems, you name it, that aren't part of your human capabilities and do not appear in nature, are all forms of capital. If you don't have superpowers, using capital is what you rely on to fight the bad guys. In other cases, such as in Wakanda and

Astrocity, it is that capital that sets your world apart from everyone else. While capital can be used to make individuals super, it can also be integrated with other inputs to increase overall efficiency.

Production Function—Just a Little Bit of Math

The transformation of inputs into outputs is a very microeconomic idea. Microeconomists study the smaller units of decision-making. By smaller we certainly don't mean insignificant. It is the individual choices that make up the aggregated whole. You may decide to sleep in today, which means you are late for work, which means a report isn't completed on time, which means information that is vital to the decision-makers at the Central Bank isn't received, which means the policy-makers have poor data, which means their decision to raise interest rates is the wrong one, which means collective investment gets more expensive, and the economy slows. The lack of information stemming from your lassitude has macro consequences, but it was the micro decision to hit the snooze bar that started the chain of events. Micro decisions are thus very important. They are considered micro because of who is making the decision. It isn't a group of people or the leader of a country who, when they make pronouncements, have the ability to shake markets world-wide, rather micro decisions come from a smaller economic unit such as an individual or a firm. Call it ripples in the pond, the butterfly effect, chaos theory, a sheep sneezing in the desert, whatever you like, the micro choices we make can have significant macro implications.

Take, for instance, the determinations firms make every day about how to produce things. One of the more important aspects of these decisions is how to combine resources to generate output. In a mathematical sense, this choice is illustrated in what economists call a production function. This is an equation that says outputs, the stuff that gets sold, results from putting your inputs, the things used to make the outputs, together in a particular way.

One of the most basic forms of this relationship is referred to as the classical production function. It involves only two inputs for simplicity's sake and reflects a view from the industrial revolution that if you have labor and capital you can produce just about anything. The function looks like this:

$$Y = f(L, K)$$

The equation says that output, which is represented by the letter Y, is a function of the combination of labor, L, and capital, K. How much output you get depends on two things. First, how much of the inputs you actually have, and second, how you combine them. From a crime-fighting perspective, this means that the number of crimes you stop (the output) depends on how much labor (and remember that this means actual number of workers and the human capital they possess) and capital each hero has. Batman isn't more renowned than Mr Terrific because he has been around longer (although he is technically three years older).[4] It could be that Batman has had better writers over the years, but more importantly those writers provided the Caped Crusader with access to capital. Assuming that Batman and Mr Terrific are equally gifted intellectually (which is probably giving Batman too much credit as Mr Terrific has 14 Ph.D.s), and assuming they are equally skilled fighters (which probably gives Mr Terrific too much credit as, even though he is a world class decathlete, he never trained with Ra's al Ghul and the League of Assassins), Mr Terrific is woefully lacking on the capital side of things. Take a stroll through the Batcave one day, or visit Batman's tech gurus, variously himself, Lucius Fox, and Harold Allnut, who provide such a veritable cornucopia of gadgets, gizmos, vehicles, and weapons that he can practically fall out of bed and be more productive than Mr.Terrific. Put in terms of the production function above, if L is the same for both heroes, but K is far greater for one than the other, the hero with the largest K will be the most productive.

Using Your Toys to Get the Bad Guys

Now, let's take this knowledge and expand upon it. Firms are in business to make profits, and economists have fallen back on the position that firms are interested in maximizing those profits, though there is certainly debate about how assiduously they pursue this objective. Many firms give dump trucks full of money away, which might engender good will with the community, but it does hurt the bottom line. In other firms, executives fritter money away on parties and junkets that makes one wonder if the objective of running a business isn't just to impress your friends. Still others use corporate resources to buy private jets and limo services, which may make their lives better and make them slightly more productive (after all you can't easily discuss business if you're sitting in the middle seat in coach), however, those amenities reserved for the executives are awfully expensive. Nevertheless, and especially for publicly traded firms, profits still seem to drive the bus. If you aren't profitable, the executive might find herself in the unemployment line. A warning to investors that a company is going to miss profit projections is a real kick in the teeth for shareholders. Profits are, if nothing else, the safe bet for the objective of the firm. To ensure those profits persist, a business needs to produce things consumers want in a way that is cost effective. Production functions help firms identify the most efficient way of combining their inputs to achieve the objective of profit maximization. However, because firms often have the ability to produce different goods in various amounts, it would behoove us to return to a tool we have discussed previously to make sure our heroes are allocating their scarce resources appropriately.

We introduced the production possibilities curve (referred to as the PPC from here on) in Chapter 3. As a reminder, the PPC shows a series of options a person, company, or country has in terms of production. In that discussion, we laid out the constraints of the PPC. For our purposes here, recall that only two goods can be produced. As an example, many older college text books used guns and butter to indicate military and civilian goods. Students might consider how their resource of time can be split between studying and partying, or those out of school might think about the trade-off between work and leisure. The point of this assumption is to simplify the analysis in order to place it in a two-dimensional space, as shown in Figure 8.1. With one option on each of the axes, you can plot points that represent potential production amounts of both goods.

Let's say we are examining the activities of Barbara "Babs" Gordon. In her dual roles of Batgirl and Oracle she can fight crime in two ways. Batgirl is on the street pounding the pavement. Oracle is in front of

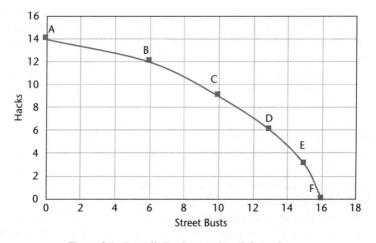

Figure 8.1. Batgirl's Production Possibilities Curve.

multiple computer screens tracking and hacking her way through mounds of data, camera footage, and firewalls. Limiting her to busting crime on the street and taking down criminals in cyber space means she is using her talents in only two ways. We can label the x-axis of the graph as hacks and the y-axis as street busting.[5] Figure 8.1 shows what Babs' production possibility curve might look like.

That brings us to the second assumption. Babs would like to be as productive as possible but she is faced with the harsh reality that she can only do so much in the course of a day. The limits that are placed on her—limited time and human capital—prevent her from being as productive as she would like to be. Additionally, she starts out her crime-fighting career with a specific quantity and quality of physical capital and technology and, for now, she is stuck with what she's got. You might not remember the days of the Apple IIe, or the Commodore 64 computers, but the superior computing power of today's desktops, not to mention laptops and tablets, so vastly outpaces the early days it is as if the Guardians of the Universe looked down with pity upon Earth and said "we can't have a so-called advanced race of sentient beings using such primitive equipment" and thus bestowed upon us a micro-gram of their advanced technology.[6] Using the Apple IIe would be like arming your police force with clubs and asking them to battle Kingpin. They wouldn't last ten seconds. For now, though, Babs is going to have to deal with whatever is at hand. The quantity and quality of her tech and capital are fixed, as is the quantity and quality of her human capital.

Again, this might sound like a rehash of Chapter 3, but there is one significant difference. The curve itself is not a straight line. This is contrary to the PPCs we saw in Chapter 3, which were, admittedly, rather simplified. Because of the limitations she faces, she must give up some of one activity to get more of the other. However, this situation is more realistic than Chapter 3's portrayal because we now presume that the crime-fighting techniques are not perfectly interchangeable. If they were, Batgirl would face a constant trade-off of hacking for busting. It might be that she can hack one criminal syndicate for every two street criminals taken down. If that were always the case, the slope of the line would be constant, not curved, and the line itself would be straight, not bowed. To say this more precisely, the trade-offs Babs makes as she moves from one type of crime-fighting to another get progressively more expensive in terms of what she has to give up. Let's take a look at Table 8.1 below, from which Figure 8.1 was built.

If Babs is acting as Oracle and is just hacking then she can break into fourteen bad guys' computer systems. At that time, however, she is not busting anyone on the street. If she wants to move to the streets to fight

Table 8.1. Batgirl's Production Possibilities Data

Option	Hacks	Street Busts
A	14	0
B	12	6
C	9	10
D	6	13
E	3	15
F	0	16

criminals the old-fashioned way she can reduce her hacking activity by two in order to bust six crimes (option B). The trade-off in terms of what she gives up relative to what she gets is two hacks to six busts, or 0.33 hacks to one bust.[7] If that doesn't sate her taste for being where the action is then she can move to the next option (option C), which would be nine hacks and ten street busts. Notice how the trade-off she faces changes. She is now giving up three hacks, moving from twelve to nine, but she only gets four busts in return. That means she must give up 0.75 hacks to get one bust. Busting street crimes is now more expensive as it costs more hacks for each bust she gets in return (0.75 > 0.33). If she continues to decrease her hacking, going from nine to six (option D), she conducts three more busts, moving from ten to thirteen, meaning her trade-off costs her one hack per bust. Street fighting is now three times as expensive as it was when she began. Looking forward, if she gives up being Oracle altogether and engages in no hacking activity she only gains one bust (the difference between fifteen and sixteen at option F) but gives up her remaining three hacks, making the cost three hacks for only one bust in return. While each option in the table means Batgirl must give up the opportunity to hack, the return for doing so gets smaller and smaller so the comparison of costs to benefits gets higher and higher.

Making Batgirl Great Again

So, what can Batgirl do? She wants to be proficient at fighting crime—that's what drives her—but she faces these restrictions on her abilities. Well, let's change that. If we allow Barbara to get some training on how to be a better hacker, or provide her with access to Wayne technology's "Batman division", we might just see that the curve that had been so limiting is no longer keeping Batgirl down. This is where those wonderful gadgets come in, and why heroes have them and invest so much in creating new and better versions. Like any skilled worker, they want to

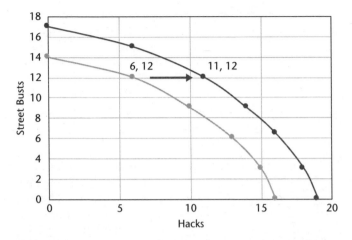

Figure 8.2. Production Possibilities Curve with New Technology.

be better at their jobs. For the non-powered hero, they can do this by augmenting their skill set, researching their area of expertise to keep up with the latest in the field, practicing their techniques, and investing in new gadgets—also known as capital. In the context of the PPC we are relaxing the assumptions that you are stuck with your initial resource allocation. When you start using new tools, this shifts the production possibilities curve outward, allowing those previously unattainable points to become attainable, as shown in Figure 8.2. If her tech gets better, this moves the curve out from the starting points. She can hack more and bust more than she could originally, making a point like eleven hacks and twelve busts, that was initially beyond the PPC, a realistic and efficient possibility. Whereas before to get twelve busts she could only complete six hacks, she now has the option to hack nearly twice as much without giving up patrolling. In fact, with the new tech there are all sorts of options that are now achievable that weren't before. Those wonderful toys the heroes have to play with are major components of successful crime-fighting, turning extraordinary people into extra-extraordinary people who can fight evil on multiple fronts in ways that make the criminal element tremble.

And the Answer Is . . .

There are two points that bear noting as we wrap up this chapter. The first is that, of course, some of the bad guys are pretty smart too.

The villains don't sit around with resignation and wait for the heroes to increase their productivity. They can play that game, too. Lex Luthor's clone of Superman shows that he has the tech skills to go toe to toe with the smartest heroes.[8] Other mad scientists develop poisons, weapons, and other means of destruction that strike fear into the hearts of people everywhere. Dr Doom has a legion of robots, a form of capital, that he uses to try and take over the world. Joker's Venom literally causes you to die laughing. Brainiac's tech can shrink cities and put them in bottles.[9] Shocker's gauntlets throw vibrational punches at buildings and people to blast them apart.[10] Basically, he can bring down structures with a punch, utilizing some tech he developed in the garage.

The second point is more economic in nature. Enhancing technology and human capital are some of the ways in which economic growth takes place. By pushing the production possibilities curve outward, more can be produced, and that is the definition of economic growth. Generally, more growth in a nation results in higher standards of living. There are some incredibly valuable technologies that heroes, and villains for that matter, implement in comic stories. If the technological innovations found in superhero comics could be applied to the world of today, the standard of living would be higher for everyone. Luthor has said he could cure cancer. Unfortunately, he's too busy trying to mess with Superman. The Wakandian communications tech puts Apple watches, and all other forms of communication, to shame. In Astrocity, transportation is taken care of by teleport doorways, reducing transportation costs and pollution by magnitudes. Such innovations are a bit of science fiction but they are used as ways to make people more productive, and in so doing they shift the PPC. For the non-powered hero, the adoption of capital makes them more capable crime-fighters, thereby allowing them to contribute to the battle against evil on a level with those who are gifted with powers. Without these tools they would be shunted to the background of stories or, like so many others, relegated to the dustbin of comic history.

Endnotes

1. There are actually two geographic locations where vibranium is found: Wakanda and Antarctica. Wakandan vibranium behaves differently than Antarctic vibranium. While the former absorbs vibrating energy that is nearby, the latter breaks the atomic and molecular bonds of metals that are in proximity (Marvel, n.d.).
2. This is one of Green Arrow's most used trick arrows. As far as I can tell, it first appeared in *Action Comics* #436 (Maggin and Dillin, 1974).

3. Mr Terrific can become invisible to electronic detection with a technology he developed, making himself a sort of one-man stealth fighter. He also utilizes T spheres, which are floating mechanized balls that project holograms, block surveillance cameras, and connect to data networks. All really fine techy stuff but nothing Batman doesn't have or can't have made for him.

4. The first appearance of Mr Terrific was Terry Sloane who appeared in *Sensation Comics* #1 (Reizenstein and Hibbard, 1942), whereas Batman first graced a page in *Detective Comics* #27 (Finger and Kane, 1939).

5. Technically it does not matter where we place each activity. The shape of the production possibilities curve is what is important. Conveniently, it will take the same shape regardless of which activity is on which axis.

6. The Guardians of the Universe from the planet of Oa are the remnant of an ancient race of scientists and thinkers who try to keep the universe orderly and free of evil. They are responsible for the creation of the Green Lantern Corp and other events in the DC Universe.

7. This is determined by taking the two hacks she gives up and dividing by the six busts she is now able to accomplish. $2 \div 6 = 0.33$. The ratio of hacks to busts is therefore 0.33 hacks for 1 bust.

8. Luthor has created a few clones of Superman, including Bizarro (Byrne, 1986 and Fisch and Johnson, 2013 as a few examples), and Conner Kent—who is a clone of Superman and Lex Luthor (Kessel and Grummett, 1994).

9. Brainiac is a supremely intelligent villain who often confronts Superman. In addition to having an intellect that far surpasses most beings, Brainiac can work through human or robotic surrogates. One of his favorite moves is to shrink a city down and put it in a bottle. This gives him the perfect vantage point for studying the goings on in that city and storing any knowledge the people of that city possess.

10. Shocker's alias, Herman Schultz, was another in a long line of brilliant, but misunderstood, characters who use their abilities for evil. Shocker is often found battling Spider-Man.

References

Batman. (1989). [Film]. Buckinghamshire, England: Tim Burton.

Byrne, J. (1986). *Man of Steel*, #5. DC Comics.

Davidson, J. (2015). These are the five richest superheroes. [Online] *Money*. Available at: http://time.com/money/3950362/richest-superheroes-comic-con/ [Accessed April 4, 2018].

Finger, B. and Kane, B. (1939). *Detective Comics*, #27. DC Comics.

Fisch, S. and Johnson, J. (2013). *Superman*, #23.1. DC Comics.

Ford, H. and Crowther, S. (1922). *My Life and Work*. New York: Garden City Publishing Company.

Kessel, K. and Grummett, T. (1994). *Superboy*, #0. DC Comics.

Maberry, J. and Eaton, S. (2010). *Doomwar*, #1. Marvel Comics.

Maggin, E. and Dillin, D. (1974). *Action Comics*, #436. DC Comics.

Marvel Database. (n.d.). Vibranium. [Online]. Available at: http://marvel.wikia. com/wiki/Vibranium. [Accessed August 20, 2018].

Reizenstein, C. and Hibbard, E. (1942). Who is Mr Terrific? In: M. Gaines (Ed.), *Sensation Comics*, #1. DC Comics.

9

Why Don't Superheroes Take
Over the World?

The Watchmen are a band of superheroes, none of whom have powers except the nuclear reactor on legs, Dr Manhattan. The rest of the group are vigilantes, attempting to make the world a safer place. Their tactics are usually above board but a few of them, in their zeal to protect the innocent, utilize some questionable methods. As they try to help the government contain rising social problems, graffiti artists start spray-painting walls with the question "Who Watches the Watchmen?" (Moore and Gibbons, [1986–7] 2014, p. 60). In the case of the Watchmen, this is a real concern because the members of the group are morally suspect. The Comedian is off his rocker, in part due to a traumatic stint in Vietnam. Ozymandias is a narcissist and Nite Owl is essentially a coward. Rorschach is probably a paranoid schizophrenic, but at the end of the day he holds most true to the call of eradicating the source of society's ills. This graphic novel by Alan Moore and Dave Gibbons (2014) strikes at the heart of civilian's discontent with superheroes. There is a lingering threat that those with powers may wield them and subjugate the population. Lord Acton said that "power tends to corrupt, and absolute power corrupts absolutely" (Acton, 1887, p. 9). If this applies to humanity, would it not more so to super-humanity?

To limit the corrupting nature of power, society adopts rules. These rules set limits on what is and what is not acceptable behavior, and how to adjudicate any violations of norms. Rules may be burdensome at times, and we probably won't agree with all of them (consider how many people try to cheat on their taxes), but they are important for any number of reasons. Economically, countries don't really start to develop until acceptable practices are adopted that promote prosperity for all. Perpetually poor countries are typically war-torn or governed by dictators who keep the military well-paid and fed, but no one else. In a world of superheroes, economic prosperity still requires a clear set of rules that apply to all, even the super-powered. Following the rules is essential because if supers try to supplant the limits placed on everyone else, it will be difficult to stop, let alone contain them, and that leaves society no better than those under a non-powered tyrant.

But which rules are we talking about? Research into economic growth demonstrates that there are certain conventions that tend to lay the foundation for persistent increases in standards of living. Many of those underpinnings are political in nature. Other rules are social, forming the framework for how we interact with each other. Still other rules are economic and provide guidance for how people acceptably satisfy our unlimited wants with limited resources.

Rules are frequently referred to as institutions. Without institutions, there would be chaos, and while many villains thrive in a world where anarchy reigns, heroes generally prefer order. By turning our attention to institutions, we can better understand the behavior of heroes that has come up in earlier chapters. For example, heroes who are beholden to following an institution that preserves the rule of law—innocent until proven guilty, guaranteeing a jury trial and the right to face your accuser—won't indiscriminately kill villains they find objectionable.

Heroes could step over the line in the name of justice. In fact, they could eviscerate the line and they might at first be congratulated for doing so because the mob wants blood. This ersatz justice might result in fewer casualties and property damage than allowing villains to commit crimes, go to and break-out of prison, and repeat ad infinitum. It also would be more economical. Costs of running a trial, incarceration, and recapturing villains would be minimized, not to mention that externalities imposed and the potential harm to civilians in the future could be avoided. But heroes are supposed to be immune to mob mentality. How long would it be until some other calamity arose requiring a vicious response to maintain order? And what degree of force would that response demand to forestall similar future behavior? Where does the hero stop acting as an executioner and become a despot? Even if such behavior would end multiple threats from Jokers, Dr Dooms, Purple Men,[1] Kingpins, and Mantas, does it really make the world safer? Would we be better off if superheroes kicked the squabbling political powers that be to the curb and took over the world? To answer that question, we turn to the most super of superheroes—Kal-El, son of Krypton.

Superman's original story establishes him as the doer of good deeds, but these actions have an ulterior motive. No, Superman's creators did not consider this while writing the story. It is impossible to imagine that two kids, Jerry Siegel and Joe Shuster, were subliminally attempting to equate their creation with economic institutions. There is no economic symbolism hidden in the cartoon they drew. Nevertheless, this character who has worldwide recognition upholds the institutions that make successful economies thrive. That's part of who this character is. Even as comics have evolved over time, and writers have come and gone, Superman's roots run deep. He could stop defending truth and justice, but that would fundamentally alter his character. He's a man who works within the system, regardless of what system that is. Before we get to that, let's consider what it means to work within the system.

Superman and the Economic Way

Even if you've never seen the original television broadcast, the lines introducing the Man of Steel during the 1950s television series are familiar:

> "Faster than a speeding bullet! More powerful than a locomotive! Able to leap tall buildings in a single bound!
> Voices: Look, up in the sky! It's a bird! It's a plane! It's Superman!
> Announcer: Yes, it's Superman, strange visitor from another planet, who came to Earth with powers and abilities far beyond those of mortal men. Superman, who can change the course of mighty rivers, bend steel in his bare hands, and who, disguised as Clark Kent, mild-mannered reporter for a great metropolitan newspaper, fights a never-ending battle for truth, justice and the American way."

Interestingly, the "American way" part was not originally included in Superman's radio show introduction when it premiered in 1940. Until then, Superman was battling for plain old truth and justice. As a way to rally people to the cause, Superman became a patriotic icon in 1942 by not only fighting for truth and justice, but also the American Way (Cronin, 2010). This not-so-subtle reminder of what the boys overseas were fighting for during World War II solidified the image of Superman as the great Boy Scout of the comic world. He's a company man. A man invested in the system under which he has flourished. Superman stands for the American Way, and paired with truth and justice, it is safe to say that the American Way is part of the institutions that make America work.

In the early comics, right and wrong are clearly defined. You know who the bad guys are and who the good guys are. Unlike many recent storylines where the heroes become evil (Spider-Man becoming Venom, Jean Grey becoming the Dark Phoenix, Hal Jordan killing everyone in Coastal City and assuming the role of Parallax, to name a few), the lines of good and bad are blurred only by mind control, and even then any complications are usually cleared up by the end of the issue. Superman's job is to bring the bad guys and girls to justice.

In the first Superman comic, *Action Comics* #1 (Siegel and Shuster, 1938a), a short origin story introduces the main man to the readers. Very quickly thereon, Superman is seen speeding to the house of the governor (presumably of New York) to present evidence that will save the life of a woman condemned to be electrocuted. He then moves on to save a woman being abused by her husband. During his last stop, Superman brings to light the actions of a corrupt politician who is getting a kickback for working on a bill that will embroil the United States in Europe. Creators Jerry Siegel and Joe Shuster depict Superman as a defender of the disenfranchised, a protector of the weak, and the guardian of democracy. Unknowingly though, Siegel and Shuster enshrine in their creation a symbiotic link between Superman and the institutions that define America.

Economist Douglas North (who won a Nobel Prize in economics in 1993) said that "Institutions are the rules of the game in a society, [...] the humanly devised constraints that shape human interaction. [...] They structure incentives in human exchange, whether political, social or economic" (1990, p. 4). Institutions are more than economic, legal or political in nature. They include all the things that order life, including religious strictures, societal norms, and cultural approbation. Institutions are the things that help a society maintain order and, importantly, are often more powerful than governmental dictates. Banning religious groups in China and Russia, for instance, did not diminish their influence. Similarly, variously banning Catholicism or Protestantism in Europe did not make people any less prone to following the teachings of the Pope or Martin Luther.

The thing about institutions is that they are oftentimes the glue that holds society together. Whether they are codified or not, when perpetrators step outside the accepted bounds of social institutions they are sometimes punished, sometimes shunned, and sometimes banned from reintegrating into society. They must recant to be offered readmittance. Going beyond the confines of what society deems permissible is often grounds for excommunication. As long as everyone knows this, and as long as the rules apply to everyone on an equal footing, society works pretty well.

We know heroes have institutions of their own. They are usually referred to as a code. When new members join a hero team, especially if Nicky New Guy has a checkered past, the old timers' refrain is consistently "that's not how we do things!" For example, when Lex Luthor joins the Justice League (Johns and Mahnke, 2014) he is constantly reminded that killing or maiming a villain isn't good form. Similarly, in *Action Comics* #775 (Kelly, Mahnke, and Bermejo, 2001), titled "What's So Funny About Truth, Justice, and the American Way?", a new group of super-powered humans, called The Elite, show up and begin executing wrong-doers with reckless abandon. Superman is appalled that they callously disregard the system. "You're murdering people and calling yourself 'heroes!' This is not the way the job gets done!" (p. 15). The Elite's leader, Manchester Black, retaliates "Good pounding the snot out of evil in bright tights. No questions. No 'grey areas'.... Reality is a mite bloodier than sitcoms or comics. The greys stretch out further" (p. 15).

The Elite arise in part because of that peculiarity that we examined in Chapter 6. Depositing villains in jails that almost certainly won't hold them means that the rules sustaining order are failing. When that happens the populace can easily become disenchanted with the political and economic institutions governing them. If people don't believe law and order will be upheld, if the negative incentives put in place to discourage bad behavior don't accomplish what they are supposed to, civil society has a tendency to deteriorate.

OK, so back to Superman, the defender of two of the most important institutions as far as economics are concerned. In economic research on institutions, there are certain rules which, when adopted, provide a good predictor of economic success. If you guessed "truth and justice", move to the head of the class. Perhaps, then, Superman isn't just fighting for the American Way. Maybe he isn't fighting for that at all, but rather a much grander idea: the Economic Way. By defending institutions that make it more likely that the economic welfare of society will improve, Superman might just be the greatest defender of economics since Adam Smith.[2]

Not convinced? Vollum and Adkinson (2003) explain the differences between Batman and Superman in the crime-fighting world, noting that while both are effective, Supes "works within the boundaries of the law and in cooperation with official law enforcement" (p. 101). Gavaler (2012) illustrates Superman's devotion to the rule of law in his work on the Ku Klux Klan and superheroes. He notes that the first punch Superman ever throws is against a Klan-styled leader attempting to lynch a man who has not had his day in court. The scene was added to the opening sequence in *Action Comics* #1, when Siegel and Shuster moved on to write *Superman* #1 in 1939.

Superman is the purest of jurists. He believes everyone should have a fair shake and will step in front of an angry mob to ensure that happens.

That is part of what it means to support the Economic Way. So, does that mean we shouldn't be afraid of the rogue hero who might install themselves as emperor supreme? That depends entirely upon the hero.

Be Afraid, Be Very Afraid

Some heroes are so obviously unsuited for taking over the world that we don't have to consider them seriously. For example, Deadpool is as likely to adopt an Alexander the Great complex as Big Bird. He's usually in it for the money, and when he's not he can't keep his thoughts straight enough to formulate a plan for world domination. The biggest problem he faces, and this applies to most heroes, is that his powers aren't significant enough to take over the world. Similarly, the Tick isn't nearly smart enough to get the job done. To accomplish this, you need to be clever as well as powerful. You must also possess a sense of narcissism that leads you to believe you are the savior of the world. Someone like Squirrel Girl fits the first two categories, but certainly not the last one. Luke Cage has no ambition beyond cleaning up Harlem. Aquaman just wants the seas to be Spic-and-Span. Imagining the Flash, at least Barry Allen's Flash, contemplating world domination draws a smile. He's a nice guy who wants everyone to be safe. His job is crime-fighting, not nation-building.

There are others, though, who should be looked at with a little more suspicion. At the top of the list is Dr Manhattan from the Watchmen. His moral compass is, at best, tilted. He knows things about the past and the future and isn't afraid of changing either. Similarly, Ozymandias, another one of the Watchmen, is a concern. He actually puts in place a plan that Dr Manhattan finds defensible, even though it ends with the deaths of millions. This is a seriously crazy dude, both intellectually dominant and psychologically unstable.

The Authority, a Warren Ellis creation, involves a group of heroes who start out with all the best intentions, but they adopt more and more aggressive tactics in their pursuit of enforcing justice. The Authority initially defends the Earth against alien and interdimensional attacks, but they move from a policing role to engage in more proactive, inter-national meddling. The president of the United States attempts to corral them, but the Authority dismisses the effort out of hand. They exercise very little restraint and thus fear of them spreads. Human groups start to speak out against them, questioning the *moral* authority of the Authority and equating their actions to those of rogue nations. Nevertheless, the Authority continues to work to protect the Earth from extraterrestrial threats, but they ultimately have enough of the meddling and hypocrisy from democratically elected people and take over the United States (Morrison and Portacio, 2004).

While other heroes or groups let the power go to their heads, this is an unlikely scenario for Superman. The Man of Steel may occasionally question his role on Earth, but it is never an issue of whether he should continue to fight on the side of good. Instead he questions whether he should continue fighting at all. In *Superman* #713 (Straczynski and Roberson, 2011), Clark Kent does some quiet introspection and decides he can do as much good without a cape as he can being Superman. A Superman fanboy reads some of Clark's musings and chafes at the reporter's lack of understanding of the role model Superman is for so many people. The Superman devotee drags Clark around town as he interviews one person after another about their thoughts on the Man of Steel. One person is asked about whether Superman kills people. He answers "Superman is a 'law and order' guy ... Everybody has a right to a fair trial and innocent before proven guilty, all that jazz ... [p. 20] ... I guess if I was the one accused of a crime, I'd want a court to decide if I was guilty or innocent, and not some guy, super or not. Wouldn't you?" (p. 22).

At the end of it all, Clark's faith in people is restored and he drops the idea of abandoning his life as Superman. The world needs someone to maintain order, not take over, and that's what Superman does, and because of it he promotes the Economic Way. He defends institutions.

You Say You Want an Institution

Institutions are important in economic development because they establish certainty. When you know the rules of the game, you are able to plan accordingly. Nevertheless, not all institutions are created equal. Dictatorships have certainty. If you talk bad about the czar, you're going to disappear in the middle of the night. The vanishing of malcontents might keep the government in power, but it also makes for a distrustful society, and trust is a valuable commodity in an economy. In his book *Trust: The Social Virtues and the Creation of Prosperity*, Francis Fukuyama (1995) explains why economic and social life go hand in hand. In societies where trust is absent, economic activity will flounder. At the microeconomic level, trust is needed to form contracts and to build connections that will help a company grow. Without trust, businesses stay small and inefficient because they can't find the networks they need to provide inputs into the production process. Thus, each business has to do everything for themselves. As Adam Smith ([1776]

1994) pointed out, the inability to specialize in production ensures inefficiency.[3]

So what institutions are needed to promote a healthy economy? By protecting truth and justice, Superman is practically following the playbook an economist would write to promote economic vitality. The question is, how do these manifest themselves in a society? We all want to know the truth. When justice is denied, it makes us a little less certain about the world in which we live. No one is against these things but they don't just appear. There need to be sanctioned mechanisms that promote and encapsulate these ideas. Truth and justice aren't institutions, they are notions. Institutions are the bodies and structures that protect the ideals a society values. Superman is aided in his defense of truth and justice by three of the most important institutions the world has ever seen, and while there are a myriad of other conventions a state could adopt, as far as economic development is concerned, these are possibly the most important: Impartial courts, protection of property, and eliminating corruption.

Here Comes the Judge, Here Comes the Judge, Here Comes the Judge

Courts are in place to arbitrate disputes. Parties who come before the court will presumably abide by the decision and the court system will preferably dole out justice equitably. Without this properly functioning institution, the laws of the land hold little sway over people. The courts might only be the adjudication mechanism, not the enforcement mechanism for society, but they do give credence to those who would coerce compliance. If the court system doesn't perform its duties impartially, if it favors the elite, connected, or wealthy at the expense of everyone else, fewer cases will come before it and more justice will be carried out Old West-style; however, the lack of faith in the court system imposes negative economic consequences beyond the potential loss of employees to duals.

In order for economic transactions to be carried out in a complex economy, it is vital that there be clearly defined and enforceable contracts. As noted earlier, this is based on trust, not just trust in the folks on the other side of the table, but also trust that if there is a dispute the courts will dispassionately enforce the terms of the agreement. If you have a court system that enforces contracts, you may be able to get past any trust issues. Additionally, it expands the scope of potential trading partners. You no longer have to actually know the people you do business with, because after negotiating the terms of the pact, you are satisfied that they will be carried out, and if the other side reneges you have the court to back you up. This increases the number of trades that people engage in and allows for greater degrees of specialization in production, both of which are very good for economic activity and standards of living.

Dude, That's My Car!

The court system doesn't matter, though, unless there is a firm commitment to the protection of property rights. When property is owned, the possessor can benefit financially from its use or sale. One of the classic papers in economics, written by Ronald Coase (1960), established that when property rights are not clearly defined, economic outcomes are suboptimal. Defined property rights ensure that transactions that do occur move goods to those who value them most. As such, the agents who need resources to be productive will get them. This outcome also encourages investment in businesses (Besley, 1995). If it is well established that courts will protect the investments that individuals make in their businesses, then business will begin to expand. This leads to more production, more hiring, and eventually greater incomes.

Protection of property rights also expands the scale of market transactions. Consider the process of buying a house. Most of us will buy a house that has had previous owners. When you sit down to close the sale, you might be overwhelmed by the number of forms that require signatures. Among the stacks of papers is an acknowledgement that the seller is the owner of the house and they are transferring ownership to you. This is possibly the most overlooked aspect of the purchase. Imagine if in the process of buying a house this part of the transaction was missing. Yes, there is a for sale sign in the front yard and a real estate agent walks you through the structure, answering all of your questions. Inspections are conducted and papers are signed, but on the first night in your new home someone appears on the doorstep claiming that the house is theirs. You call up the police to help settle the, admittedly odd, dispute and come to realize that you do not have the deed to the property. Neither, it turns out, does the interloper, nor do the people who sold the house to you. Possession might be nine tenths of the law, but a legal document wouldn't hurt. In developed countries, the papers get filed and property ownership is firmly established, especially in the case of large purchases like a home, but in some parts of the world this paper trail simply doesn't exist. Establishing who owns something is a much more difficult process. Buying property in a place such as Haiti might just be done with a handshake. Identifying the proper owner can take years of trying to track down former transactions. If it becomes enough of a problem, one of three things is likely to happen. First, the transaction might not take place. If that is the case, the buyer is deprived of an asset they wished to possess and the seller is deprived of the income from that asset (although it wasn't theirs to sell). Fewer transactions are a bad thing. People trade because they believe the transaction will make them better off. If trading is limited because no one is sure who owns the goods being traded, then people are prevented from improving their lot in life in a way they see fit.

The second potential outcome is that the property might be seized by force. In this case, whoever is the strongest, or has the bigger guns, gets the property. Third, the courts might step in to solve the dispute and, without a tradition of protecting property rights and no paper trail to establish the rights, they favor their friends and the connected people in society, so the poor end up being prejudiced.

In short, if courts can't or won't deliver justice to the correct party, the number of transactions is likely to fall. If property rights aren't protected, innovation will slow. Why spend time developing new products if someone can come along and steal your ideas? Without an impartial judiciary you might be arrested for a crime you didn't commit because you ended up on the wrong side of a local politician. Any of these situations will lead to less economic and political freedom, and consequently a poorer populace.

Authority Plus Monopoly Minus Transparency Equals Corruption

The final of our three institutions in focus involves limiting corruption. Corruption is a way for the connected to get what they want at the expense of everyone else. The corruption tends to enrich a small group of people (like the judge you paid off) at the expense of a larger group. Simply, corruption reduces economic growth. This is the main finding of papers by Mauro (1995) and Jain (2002). If the only people who are able to do business are the ones connected to the government, there is no incentive to experiment, innovate, or create. No matter what you do, there is some impediment keeping you from getting ahead. Corruption can also cause resources to flow from where they are needed to pet projects of bureaucrats. Think about taking food aid from the poor due to tight budgets. That tight budget might be the result of a sports stadium that was built for a politician's favorite team. Perhaps it is the case that in order to open a shop you need to pay off the local sheriff. This will ensure that no competitors enter the market; that is unless they pay more than you do. While it might be the way business gets done in parts of the world, corruption is not efficient, nor does it encourage business activity. In many cases, it drives activity away.

While these three institutions might seem obvious, there are still plenty of countries where they do not apply. Annual measures published by Transparency International (2017) regularly note that corruption is rampant in the overwhelming majority of the countries it surveys. The Economic Freedom of the World Index (McMahon et al., 2017) compiled by the Frasier Institute shows that the protection of private property rights and a fair court are key components in free nations. Yet, establishing these institutions are most definitely not priorities in many places. Then again, Superman is defending the American Way, not the Eritrean Way. Which reminds me, all of this discussion of institutions is supposed to be illustrating the importance of Superman. So where does he fit into this?

Superman Began As a Law and Order Man

Remember the endeavors of Superman in *Action Comics* #1? Supes is shown preventing the death of a woman for a crime she did not commit. In *Superman* #1 he stops a lynching because not only is it bad to lynch someone, there is no evidence that the man is guilty. In both situations Superman is not just protecting the innocent, he is also trying to uphold the integrity of the court system. People need to trust that justice will be served. This is the very first act of super-heroics the Man of Steel carries out.

The woman who is being beaten by her husband is, in essence, having her property rights violated. The most personal thing you can own is yourself. When a life is being threatened, that property should be protected post-haste. It may not be possible for the police or the courts to act in a timely fashion, but Superman can. He won't carry out a punishment against the abuser, but he'll put a stop to it.

The corrupt politician is violating the trust of the electorate. Sure, it happens all the time but we don't have to like it, and in this case there are repercussions far beyond Washington. The lobbyist, in no uncertain terms, tells the lawmaker he will be well taken care of. In *Action Comics* #2 (Siegel and Shuster, 1938b) we find out that the bribe originates from a weapons manufacturer who figures to get rich if America enters a war

157

in Europe. Very shady dealings are afoot, and Superman not only wants to prevent getting involved in a war, but he also wants to keep politics as clean as possible.

Working Within the System . . . The Economic System

In economics, we divide macroeconomies into systems.[4] These systems coordinate how societies allocate resources, goods, and services by answering three questions: What will we produce, how will we produce it, and for whom will things be produced? To put systems in the most succinct fashion, they can be considered along a continuum; at one end is the pure capitalist system, the other the pure command system.

Capitalism is typically accompanied by economic and political freedom, higher standards of living, and more innovation. This system answers the three questions of what, how and for whom through the market. The interaction of buyers and sellers, driven by self-interest, will determine what to produce. If buyers want something and are willing to pay for it, sellers have an incentive to provide it. How will those things be produced? In the most efficient way if you want to earn the largest profit possible. If you don't do it well and sell goods at a price buyers are willing to pay, then either you'll immediately be out of business, or someone else will step in and do the job and you will eventually be out of business. Whatever is produced will be available to whoever can pay for it, which brings us to the largest drawback for the capitalist system: Inequality. There is the potential for great wealth to be generated in a capitalist system, but that income need not find its way to the poorest. The rich are free to give away what they make to help the less fortunate, but there is no compulsion to do so. To put it bluntly, capitalism is not fair.

Command systems are characterized by strict governmental control. All production decisions, resource allocation, and goods distribution are determined by a government bureaucracy and thus, the what, how, and for whom questions are answered by government. The attempt is to create equality across the society. If one group has more than they need, a benevolent dictator will reallocate material goods so that no one has more than anyone else. Fairness is a focal point. Unfortunately, the determination of what is fair is usually made without consulting the people. There is little to no freedom of choice economically or politically. Profit motives that drive innovation are absent, resulting in slow economic growth and very slow changes to the overall living conditions of people.

In reality, neither of these systems actually exist. A society chooses how to organize itself and inevitably mixes components of the two types of systems depending on the evolution of the culture. A capitalist system is likely to have some restraints on what firms can acceptably do to earn a profit. Employing children might be profitable but it is outlawed. Environmental activists can't be shot on sight if they are blocking a pipeline that would speed natural gas to markets, and toxic chemicals must be disposed of properly, even if polluting the ground water would keep costs down. Potentially life-saving medicines must be tested in the lab first, even though people might die while waiting for treatment. Additionally, capitalism isn't anarchy. Government still exists and must be paid for, so tax collection plans are imposed even though this hurts the bottom line.

Similarly, command systems have some aspects of capitalism. Innovations happen and markets exist, even if the innovations occur more sporadically and the markets survive outside the view of government officials. There are rich people living in command economies, they just tend to be the ones making the rules. The rich have found a way to profit from the economic system in which they live, even if it is at the expense of those who are otherwise prohibited from doing the same.

Regardless of which economic system a society chooses, institutions govern the system. Systems and institutions go together like Superman and Lois Lane. It just so happens that capitalist systems have the growth-promoting institutions, such as a fair court system, protection of property rights, and less corruption, that coincide with Superman's mission statement. It isn't that capitalist systems never have problems with their institutions; rather, the choice of a capitalist economic system and the institutions that tend to accompany capitalism are more likely to lead to economic growth. By defending this system over another, Superman is promoting economic well-being. That being said, you still have to do the work.

I Will Defend Truth, Justice, and the Economic Way . . .

Superman can improve the lot of humanity, but he doesn't. At least not on a wide scale. The Man of Steel can change the course of rivers but he hasn't ended drug smuggling. He battles physically powerful aliens and defeats them but regular street crimes are still committed. He has resources and technology at his fingertips that are light years ahead of Earth-based kit, yet he hasn't destroyed nuclear weapons. Despite his powers, Superman doesn't save us from ourselves. In fact, there are times when he just bails out altogether. He has run away from Earth and left the public eye at times, feeling pressured, unwanted, or just needing a break.[5] While he wants the best for humanity, and could accomplish that by being more involved and interfering with the day-to-day lives of humans, he hasn't. This behavior is both vexing (see Lex Luthor below) and liberating. While he could be a benevolent dictator, he chooses not to be.

Supes follows the rules even when it hurts. An early 1970s story arc finds the Man of Steel trying to stop a volcano from erupting and killing the inhabitants of an island (O'Neil and Swan, 1971a). Unfortunately, the location of the volcano is the private property of a wicked plantation owner called Boysie Harker. Harker tells Superman to vacate the premises or else face the law. Superman knows he can't legally get to the volcano, so he comes up with an alternative plan. He is bound and determined to obey the law even as the volcano threatens hundreds of native residents of the island. Nevertheless, Superman notes that "if worst comes to worst, I'll have to defy Harker—and take the consequences! Because there's a moral law that's above some man-made laws!" (p. 9).

Here he is, thirty-three years after his creation, still toeing the line. Private property protections apply not just to individuals, but to the hero as well, and Superman never sees himself as above the law. He will only intervene if there is no other alternative. *Superman* #247 (Maggin and Swan, 1972) expands on this point. Here we find the Man of Tomorrow working with the Guardians, an alien species who oversee the universe. While healing him after a successful mission, the Guardians plant an idea in his mind that he is creating a cultural lag on Earth. This leaves Superman confused about how much he should be interfering with events on his adopted home planet. When he returns to Earth, he comes across a migrant boy being beaten by a field boss. After saving the boy, the oppressed workers cheer and begin asking Superman to do all manner of things for them, from throwing the boss in jail to rebuilding their houses. Superman begins to think that perhaps people are not evolving culturally because they are too dependent on him to fix their problems.

This point is further illustrated in the graphic novel *Kingdom Come*. Heroes are not supposed to interfere. When they do and people no longer have to fend for themselves, they stop being productive. Pastor Norman McCay remembers his friend Wesley, who lamented that the aging heroes had given way to a new generation of superhumans. Norman recalls Wesley saying that "human initiative began to erode the day people asked a new breed to face the future for them" (Waid and Ross, 2008, p. 17). The dilemma Superman faces is that there are things a superhero should do, but creating dependency isn't part of the plan. Heroes should work within the system, not replace the system, even if the system is flawed.

. . . But What If I Didn't?

For the majority of Superman story arcs, he is the unassailable fighter for truth, justice, and the American Way. Superman has continually defended the system, battling all manner of organized crime, insanely smart evildoers, and alien invaders. While he may not always agree with the people in charge, it is the system to which Superman adheres. In *The Dark Knight* (Miller, 2016), Superman is asked by the President of the United States to reign in Batman's use of excessive force. In the guise of Clark Kent he is engaged in a discussion with Bruce Wayne about where he thinks this is going, which concludes with Clark's assessment that "it's like this, Bruce—sooner or later, somebody's going to order me to bring you in. Somebody with authority" (p. 110).

Later, as he reflects on their conversation, Superman admits that Batman has an agenda, and he will not waver no matter the cost. While the rest of the superheroes have come to terms with some degree of government oversight, Batman does not acquiesce. Superman contemplates that "Nothing matters to you [Batman]—except your holy war. They were considering their options and you were probably still laughing when we came to terms. I gave them [the government] my obedience and my invisibility. They gave me a license and let us live. No, I don't like it. But I get to save lives—and the media stays quiet. But now the storm is growing again—they'll hunt us down again—because of you" (p. 130).

The question of what would happen if Superman followed his own agenda, as Batman does, has led to some intriguing storylines regarding Superman. One of the better known of these alternative realities is *Superman: Red Son* (Millar and Johnson, 2014). In this Elseworlds story-line,[6] Kal-El lands on a Ukrainian collective farm rather than in Kansas. Instead of fighting for "truth, justice and the American way" he becomes one "who as the champion of the common worker, fights a never-ending battle for Stalin, socialism and the international expansion of the Warsaw Pact" (p. 5). Underneath the Soviet trappings, Superman is, at least initially, the hero readers expect. He saves America's Metropolis from certain destruction when a satellite falls out of orbit and is heading for what will be a cataclysmic impact. Mid-flight he concedes that he isn't a soldier. He didn't hate the enemy or fight only for his people. He "fought for what was right" (p. 11). Notice the past tense.

Repeatedly, Superman turns down political advancement in the Communist party, claiming he doesn't want to be the leader. He even notes that his "privileges" should disqualify him from influence in the socialist republic. He's still toeing the company line, but now it's in a command system. If equality is the rule then that's how he'll play the game. That all changes when he sees an old friend and her children in a bread line. Seeing hungry people prompts Superman to act. His friend Lana tells him that "it's not your fault. It's just the way the system works...you can't take care of everyone's problems" (p. 46), but in a command economic system he can, and Superman is nothing if not a man who works within the system. By the end of *Red Son* he has become a dictator, whose subjects are entirely subservient to the Man of Tomorrow. People have given up taking responsibility for themselves and have given over control of their lives to Superman so much so that they stop wearing seatbelts or life jackets. Superman can save them from any catastrophe and they are willing to give up responsibility for their lives. The difference between being in a capitalist system and a command system is that in the capitalist system Superman would be convicted of stepping beyond his bounds, of moving outside the system. In the command structure, while Superman feels a little guilty at first about taking too much control, he gradually consolidates power, eventually demanding obedience from all. In his global Soviet Union, only the United States resisted, and it was beset by civil war. Everywhere else "every adult had a job, every child had a hobby, and the entire human population enjoyed the full eight hours sleep which their bodies required. Crime didn't exist. Accidents never happened. It didn't even rain unless...everyone had an umbrella. Almost six billion citizens and hardly anyone complained. Even in private" (p. 98). Dependency on government is part of the command system. And no matter what, Superman defends the system.

The most gloriously terrifying example of Superman becoming unhinged is in the series *Injustice: Gods Among Us* (Taylor, Raapack, and Redondo, 2016). In a sadistic twist, the Joker leaves Gotham for Metropolis and tricks Superman into killing Lois Lane and their unborn child. To top it off, when she dies it sets off a nuclear bomb that levels Metropolis. During the interrogation, Batman wants to know why the Joker hit a different target. The Joker's response was that fighting Batman is hard and he wanted something easy. As their conversation continues, the Joker muses about what will happen to Superman now that he's lost everything. Batman became "an all-punching, all-kicking little ball of angst" (p. 40) as a result of losing his parents. Batman replies that even Joker can't corrupt Superman. Almost before the words are out of his mouth, Superman breaks through the wall of the prison and rips Joker's heart out of his body. From that moment, Superman engages in a worldwide effort to rid the planet of villains. He becomes the dictator people feared, and then some. More people die at his hands, both civilians and heroes. The world is safe from criminals but not from the Man of Steel. When Superman decides to become a tyrant, he does it very well.

And the Answer Is . . .

Superheroes in general, and Superman in particular, have powers that amaze. In some ways, it's miraculous that they are so restrained in the use of those powers. As noted in Chapter 2, villains such as Lex Luthor can't believe that a powerful being such as Superman wouldn't try to take over the world. Nevertheless, heroes tend to play within the boundaries constraining everyone else, despite the constant fear that they might one day decide to put themselves in charge.

If you aren't going to take over the world then you must subjugate yourself to the existing regimes. Hopefully the system you find yourself in is a respectable one. Superman's attachment to the American Way is good for everyone, as long as you aren't a criminal. The American Way is the Economic Way, but defending the Economic Way is a balancing act. When you have superpowers it would be much easier, and much less messy, to just take over, subject everyone to your will, and eliminate the opposition. But if Superman did this he would be the personification of the evil being fought in Europe when his credo was established. This is what Hitler and Mussolini would do, and taking such actions wouldn't fit the character of Superman.

From his first appearance to the present, Superman has been a hero who sets the standard for heroes. He fights for truth and justice for all. Superman also fights to uphold the process by which truth and justice themselves are protected. He defends the institutions that govern society so that he doesn't have to be the judge. He lets the system play out and subjects himself to the rules that he works so diligently to uphold, even though he doesn't have to. When we see what the alternative could be, we shudder and realize it's a good thing Superman landed in Kansas.

Endnotes

1. Purple Man is a heinous villain who uses deception and mind control to get Jessica Jones to act as his slave. He so cripples her emotionally that she gives up being a superhero.
2. Of course, Superman isn't the only hero who holds up the virtues of truth and justice. He's just the most obvious. Tony Stark is worried about keeping heroes

accountable to the elected officials of a country. This is the premise for *Civil War* (Miller and McNiven, 2007). Stark's concern is that if heroes are able to do whatever they want, whenever they want, innocent lives will be put at risk and that isn't just.

3. Smith discusses the importance of the division of labor in the opening chapter of *Wealth of Nations*.
4. Macroeconomics is defined in the introduction to the book.
5. For examples see Bates and Swan, 1967; O'Neil and Swan, 1971b; and Straczynski and Roberson, 2011.
6. Elseworlds is a DC series of alternative reality storylines.

References

Acton, B. (April 5, 1887). *Letter from Lord Acton to Archbishop Creighton, April 5, 1887*. [Letter.] Available at: http://lf-oll.s3.amazonaws.com/titles/2254/Acton_PowerCorrupts1524_EBk_v6.0.pdf [Accessed August 22, 2018].

Bates, C. and Swan, C. (1967). *Superman*, #201. DC Comics.

Besley, T. (1995). Property Rights and Investment Incentives: Theory and Evidence from Ghana. *Journal of Political Economy*, 103(5), pp. 903–37.

Coase, R. (1960). The Problem of Social Cost. *Journal of Law and Economics*, 3, pp. 1–44.

Cronin, B. (2010). Comic Book Legends Revealed, #276. [Online] CRB.com. Available at: http://www.cbr.com/comic-book-legends-revealed-276/ [Accessed April 4, 2018].

Fukuyama, F. (1995). *Trust: The Social Virtues and the Creation of Prosperity*. New York: Simon and Schuster, Inc.

Gavaler, C. (2012). The Ku Klux Clan and the Birth of the Superhero. *Journal of Graphic Novels and Comics*, 4(2), pp. 191–208.

Jain, A. (2002). Corruption: A Review. *Journal of Economic Surveys*, 15(1), pp. 71–121.

Johns, G. and Mahnke, D. (2014). *Justice League*, #33. DC Comics.

Kelly, J., Mahnke, D., and Bermejo, L. (2001). *Action Comics*, #775. DC Comics.

McMahon, F., Gwartney, J., Lawson, R., and Hall, J. (2017). *Economic Freedom of the World: 2017 Annual Report*. [Online] Frasier Institute. Available at: https://www.fraserinstitute.org/studies/economic-freedom-of-the-world-2017-annual-report [Accessed April 4, 2018].

Maggin, E. and Swan, C. (1972). *Superman*, #247. DC Comics.

Mauro, P. (1995). Corruption and Growth. *Quarterly Journal of Economics*, 110(3), pp. 681–712.

Millar, M. and Johnson, D. (2014). *Superman: Red Son*. Burbank, CA: DC Comics.

Miller, F. (2016). *Batman: The Dark Knight Returns, 30th Anniversary Edition*. Burbank, CA: DC Comics.

Miller, M. and McNiven, S. (2007). *Civil War*. New York: Marvel Comics.

Moore, A. and Gibbons, D. (2014). *Watchmen*. Burbank, CA: DC Comics (Originally published in 1986–7).

Morrison, R. and Portacio, W. (2004). *Coup d'Etat*, #1. WildStorm Productions.

North, D. (1990). *Institutions, Institutional Change, and Economic Performance*. Cambridge: Cambridge University Press.

O'Neil, D. and Swan, C. (1971a). *Superman*, #234. DC Comics.

O'Neil, D. and Swan, C. (1971b). *Superman*, #240. DC Comics.

Siegel, J. and Shuster, J. (1938a). *Action Comics*, #1. DC Comics.

Siegel, J. and Shuster, J. (1938b). *Action Comics*, #2. DC Comics.

Siegel, J. and Shuster, J. (1939). *Superman*, #1. DC Comics.

Smith, A. (1994). *An Inquiry into the Nature and Causes of the Wealth of Nations*. New York: Random House (Originally published in 1776).

Straczynski, M. and Roberson, C. (2011). *Superman*, #713. DC Comics.

Taylor, T., Raapack, J., and Redondo, B. (2016). *Injustice: Gods Among Us: Year One*. DC Comics.

Transparency International. (2017). *Corruption Perceptions Index 2016*. [Online] Transparency International. Available at: https://www.transparency.org/news/feature/corruption_perceptions_index_2016 [Accessed April 4, 2018].

Vollum, S. and Adkinson, C. (2003). The Portrayal of Crime and Justice in the Comic Book Superhero Mythos. *Journal of Criminal Justice and Popular Culture*, 10(20), pp. 96–108.

Waid, M. and Ross, A. (2008). *Kingdom Come*. Burbank, CA: DC Comics.

10

Who Is the Greatest of Them All?

Now it is time to discard the more rigorous academic inquiry and have some real fun by focusing on a bar room debate, the fool's errand if you will, of deciding who is the best superhero. Like Don Quixote tilting at windmills, we may be deluding ourselves if we think we'll actually settle this age-old question. Instead, we might be adding fuel to the fire of a war that is perpetually in an unsteady truce. Or it could be that hardcore comic fans look at what is to follow and, with a mighty groan, begin to assault economists as the latest impostors wading into streams in which they do not belong. All of these outcomes are equally possible, of course. Throwing stones at the hardened combatants from the sidelines is easy. When they inevitably get tired of being pecked at and turn their guns toward you, then you can see what you are made of. But that again is what makes the subsequent shindig fun, and why the debate goes on. There isn't an answer that satisfies everyone. We all have opinions and perspectives that can be as zany and far-out as we want them to be. This concluding chapter isn't trying to explain unusual behaviors or provide insight into the psyche of a made-up character. Instead, these final musings takes a crack at the argument comic readers have been having since the second superhero came onto the scene: Who is the greatest of them all?

I'll See Your Superman and Raise You a Batman

As most people who have read comics know, the powered-up people first appeared in 1938 with the appearance of Superman in *Action Comics* #1. There were comic heroes prior to this, of course, they just didn't have otherworldly powers. One of the most popular precursors to Superman, the Shadow, was a masked vigilante, similar to Batman but without the utility belt. For the science fiction fan, Flash Gordon displayed extreme courage fighting battles in outer space. The Phantom was orphaned after his father's ship was attacked by pirates off the coast of Africa. Despite an absence of powers, he relied upon his physical adeptness to fight bad guys, especially (and perhaps predictably) pirates, but he's not opposed to using firearms either. If you want your super-heroes with powers, you could dust off your Greek language skills and take a crack at the mythology of the ancients. Of course, we still see the gods making guest appearances in comics today. The problem with them is that you never really know where they stand morally.

Truly, the first super-powered, non-deity, good-versus-evil protagonist is Superman. In 1938, he is the undisputed king of the hero mountain because he's the only one. He is the monopolist, the only seller in a market that is about to get crowded. Monopolies are criticized for a number of good reasons, for example, prices are usually higher when a monopolist is running the show, but economists are hung up on one in particular. Markets that are ruled by a single seller are prone to inefficiencies. Benefits that are generated through the exchange process disappear. It's like a villain aims a ray gun at the markets and POOF! Valuable trades are gone. In a market where a monopolist lurks, some of the value that buyers would have received from a transaction is transferred to the seller. After all, when you pay more the seller takes more of your money. However, unless the demand for a good is perfectly inelastic (remember the EpiPen in Chapter 5?), when prices rise the amounts that people buy go down. So, compared to a competitive market, fewer consumers buy things than they would have if the market were competitive. The result is that less value is created through the market system. Even if the monopolist is made better off, the total market shrinks, and the overall economy is harmed because the gains to the monopolist are more than offset by the losses to consumers. This annihilation of value is known as a deadweight loss.

While economists focus on deadweight loss, the rest of society looks at other problems arising from monopolies. Those higher prices relative to competitive markets is one bone of contention, but another one is that in some cases quality suffers. For instance, comic story arcs go through ebbs and flows. Sometimes you are on pins and needles waiting for the next issue, while other times you wonder if you should shift your attention to another book or genre entirely. If there was only one hero option, the writers might have a tendency to get a little lazy and story-lines might be less innovative.[1]

Governments, too, realize the negative impact monopolies pose for an economy and have created rules to discourage their formation.

Antitrust laws, so called due to the insistence of lawyers that we cling to the old-fashioned way of referring to monopolies as trusts, lay out the ground rules for what it means to act in an un-competitive manner. It isn't that being a monopoly is illegal; in fact in some industries governments sanction monopoly and actively keep potential competitors away. These so-called natural monopolies are protected because a larger firm is more cost-effective than many smaller ones. In the case of power production, for example, a single large power plant faces lower average costs of generating electricity than multiple small producers, in part because, on average, distribution costs go down as you provide power to more homes. Therefore it is better for everyone if there is a single producer. (Not to mention if there were a dozen power companies there would likely be a dozen sets of power lines crisscrossing the town where you live, and if you ever wondered what it would be like if Spider-Man was swinging through your neighborhood and his webs never went away, well, you would now have some idea.) Governments grant a single firm a monopoly and prevent entry by others. But, just as there is no such thing as a free lunch, there is also no such thing as a free monopoly. In return for keeping competitors away, the firm gives up the right to set their own prices. Government then attempts to regulate prices as carefully as governments can regulate anything.

The point of this little discourse on market structure is to say that competition is usually a good thing. It provides us with variety and, for consumers, almost always keeps the price for what we buy lower than alternatives. In terms of superhero debates you need some competition, otherwise you get to the drinking that accompanies such controversies far too quickly and the convoluted reasoning that is facilitated by alcohol makes even less sense because you and your fellow disputants are arguing about the same person. Thankfully for comic fans, there is another.

Batman enters the cosmic, comic consciousness in 1939. While he doesn't have super-human abilities, he does have a costume and gadgets, and more importantly, staying power. In the late 1930s and early 1940s, after Superman premiered, a series of super-powered flops rose like zombies in a B-rated horror film, only to be crushed out of existence due to the consolidation of small comic publishers and a paucity of good writers. But this time period also brought with it a huge increase in the number of heroes and some of the most famous names in comics. Some, such as Captain Marvel (now known as Shazam), even began to outsell Superman. In 1940 alone, the Daredevil, Dr Fate, Flash, Hawkman, Green Lantern, and Robin made their first appearances, followed in 1941 by Aquaman, Captain America, Hawkgirl, Plastic Man, and Wonder

Woman. What a wonderful time to be alive, except for that nasty World War II. Kids at home, wondering what might become of their fathers on the front could, at least for a little while, escape in the pages of the comics, and with a treasure trove of characters to choose from, the debates over who was the greatest could begin in earnest.

In This Corner...

To possibly reach a consensus of greatness, we need to lay out some ground rules. First, we need to establish up front what is meant by "the best". Remember, the issue at hand isn't who your favorite hero is, but who is the best. Initially this sounds like a pretty subjective question. There are many choices and many opinions depending on story arcs, the era of the hero in question, and the villain being fought. Fear not good citizen! Economists have a tool to help in making this determination. The best hero is the one who accomplishes his or her objectives. For nearly all those who dare call themselves heroes, this means helping people, and because you need to help people, this immediately disqualifies some from the greatest list. Characters like Black Adam, Impossible Man, Lex Luthor, Magneto, and Swamp Thing began as villains and have now switched sides or are ambiguous in their allegiance, yet their past is too tainted for consideration here. Furthermore, while Jean Grey is undoubtedly a force to be reckoned with, her time as the Dark Phoenix (a really, really bad thing) is a persuasive mark against her. Ditto that for the Sentry. His power is undeniably awesome but his interactions with the enigma that is the Void make him a question mark.

Second, I will include heroes from any reasonable comic publisher, but there are a few characters who aren't really consequential enough to be in the conversation. Matter Eater Lad, who can eat his way through anything, and the pair Yank and Doodle, who have super strength but only when they are together, won't be on the list.

Third, the hero must be formidable. Therefore I will start the debate with a list of superheroes who are over the top powerful. You may not have heard of them all because these ridiculously over-powered characters are so awe-inspiring that their escapades are, frankly, a little boring. There is no tension about whether they will emerge victorious from a fight. Any moral dilemma they might face centers on how they will win, not if. It's more a question of containing and controlling their powers, rather than having the ability to accomplish a task. Of the people on this list there is no doubt that they are great, but being great doesn't mean you are good, nor does it mean you are the best. So, in alphabetical order, the first contingent of contestants for the best superhero are: Black Bolt, Dr Fate, Nate Grey, Hulk, Dr Manhattan, Martian Manhunter, Franklin Richards, Shazam, Silver Surfer, The Spectre, Superman, Thor, and Wonder Woman. Again, these are characters who have awesome, world-altering, potentially world-ending powers. If they go nuts and try to take over the world, you're better off letting them do it. Combining the requirement that they must be mighty with the expectation that they have to help people will allow us to begin to winnow the list.

Dr Manhattan lacks the empathy necessary to care about people. He is obscenely powerful, able to manipulate atoms, transport himself wherever in the universe he wants to go, has near omniscience as he can see the past, present, and future together, and he can repair himself whenever necessary. He just doesn't care to make the world a better place. In *Watchmen*, you get the feeling he is resigned to the way history will turn out, even if it seems like the future will be terrible. So, sorry Dr Manhattan, you are not the best. Others who lose the title right off the bat due to their lack of empathy include Dr Fate, Silver Surfer, and the Spectre.

Similarly, because the Hulk's primary characteristic, his colossal strength, only comes with uncontrollable rage, we have to kick him, ever so gently as to not make him mad, to the curb as well. There is no doubt that Hulk is powerful but you know the line about having great power, and Hulk is not responsible with that power.

A couple of the folks on the list are still kids and don't have enough control over their powers to wield them responsibly, including Nate Grey and Franklin Richards. Shazam isn't a kid when he's powered up, but his alter ego is Billy Batson, a teenager who, despite being pretty selfless some of the time considering the trouble he's seen, is still a kid. That child-like personality comes through too often to trust Shazam. Black Bolt's problem is that he can't really motivate anyone. His voice is one of his weapons, and with it he can literally flatten mountains. If he tried to give a speech to rally the troops, he might just destroy the planet. So, pretty quickly we are down to Martian Manhunter, Superman, Thor, and Wonder Woman.

Of this list though, we have to drop Martian Manhunter. One of the criteria of being the greatest has to be that you like what you do. Manhunter can't be happy. He's seen his race wiped from existence by his twin brother and is constantly on the verge of succumbing to madness. Being a hero should be a happy coincidence. Sure, as we discussed in Chapter 2, a hero's life isn't perfect. It can be hard to get by as a hero and life can get a little lonely, but there is joy in saving people. Protecting the weak and doing good deeds, that's a value proposition.

That leaves us with three contenders for the crown still on their feet. It is now time to pull out a slightly more objective tool to help advance our analysis. In other words, we're going to seek the guidance of some real economics to help us answer the question about greatness. It is time to return to utility.

...And in This Corner

As previously noted, economists sometimes make it difficult for everyone else to understand what they are talking about. Nowhere is this more obvious than with the term utility. In Chapter 1 we reviewed the history of this concept and concluded that, no matter how bizarre, it is the way economists measure happiness. As even heroes want to be happy, we can apply utility analysis to our remaining contestants. Let's begin with the Man of Steel.

Superman not only possesses awesome power but he willingly stands up for those who can't defend themselves. Superman is also a good example of a number of economic ideas that aren't covered in this chapter but were covered in prior chapters: He has a comparative advantage in nearly everything—that is why he never adopts a permanent sidekick—his opportunity costs are very low for all of his activities because he can act so quickly, and his powers enable him to be incredibly productive. He also gets a lot of satisfaction out of being a good guy. Layman (2008) offers an interesting application of Spider-Man's credo to Superman. He suggests that for Superman, the doctrine could be "With great power comes great personal satisfaction" (p. 195). Powers certainly could be used to help yourself, your friends, and your family, and harm those who get in your way. But heroes don't do that. Why not?

A series of essays, of which Layman's is a part, deals with superheroes and philosophy, where the question of superhero morality is debated. Using economics, utility can explain the idea that a hero derives a sense of well-being from doing what is right. Helping people makes the hero happy and that means the job yields higher utility. Rational people engage in activities that provide them more happiness, so heroes are just following the natural, economic order of things. If stopping an alien invasion makes you happy then bully for you. This also explains why heroes don't just take what they want. Sure, having more stuff makes you happy, but the moral compass of a hero points them away from stealing. Philosophers don't focus on utility, at least not in those terms. Instead, they discuss things like peace of mind, and in fact Layman goes on to suggest that one reason for a hero to be good is that it soothes their souls. Helping others is its own reward.

Of course, there are the costs and benefits to remaining within the rules. As we considered in Chapter 9, Superman doesn't try to take over the planet, even though this move could increase his utility. He might be happier if he didn't have to fight all the time. He could help others by being proactive to eliminate crime, rather than reactive. Some say that other heroes wouldn't let him take such drastic actions, but economics presents us with a more nuanced view. Superman has chosen to be bound by the rules of the game, partly because he finds utility or satisfaction in doing so. Forcing compliance makes him a dictator, and Superman doesn't want to be a dictator.

Superman's behavior is vexing to friend and foe alike. Lois Lane considers, with some dubiousness, that this man from the sky who can do anything with this power repertoire decides to "be a hero" in a world where "nobody sticks their neck out for anybody . . . here's this . . . this . . . man sticking his neck out for everyone. Way, way out" (Loeb and Sale, 1999, pp. 66–7). The preconceived notion of what it means to be powerful keeps both Lois and Luthor (remember Lex's incredulity in Chapter 2?) from identifying the obvious: Clark Kent is Superman. Consider it a form of rational ignorance. Becoming fully informed shatters their world view.

While it sounds impossible to Lois, Superman likes helping people. He derives value from making others safer. Even when he doesn't don the cape there are instances of Clark Kent protecting people from harm. In *Green Arrow* #28 (Percy and Ferreyra, 2017), Green Arrow teams up with Superman to take on a criminal financier. In one panel, we see Clark Kent walking down the street and, in the span of about ten seconds, he thwarts a robbery, prevents a kid from being clocked by a falling paint can, and opens a taxi cab door for a little old lady (p. 5). Even if the task seems impossibly difficult, as is his effort at feeding the world in a day in the graphic novel *Peace on Earth* (Dini and Ross, 1998), Superman is going to give it the old college try. Economists say that being a Boy Scout is utility-enhancing for Superman. Everyone else says such acts make him happy.

The Mighty Thor also enjoys power. Using that hammer to battle aliens and protect Askaard is what he was born to do. Like Superman, Thor is also an alien to Earth, but rather than being from a different planet, he's from a different realm. That's like being from a different universe or plane of existence. Nevertheless, Thor's origin is significantly more convoluted. Supposedly he was banished to Earth as punishment for breaking a truce with some storm giants (Lee and Kirby, 1968). He took the appearance of a lame (as in he couldn't walk, not that he was uncool, although he was totally uncool) doctor who finds a cane in a cave in Norway that he uses to transform into Thor. The cane eventually becomes a hammer and the banishment is finally lifted. Of course, Thor has a bit of a wild streak in him so he sometimes does things that make him unworthy of lifting the hammer, which makes his selection as the greatest a bit problematic. Another concern, at least for people of Earth, is that Thor doesn't permanently live here. Thus, when there is trouble it is possible that Thor is occupied elsewhere. Still, when he's on his game, Thor is strong, resistant to injury, and is able to tap into cosmic forces to further enhance his powers. He's fearless too, willing to fight any and all comers.

To conclude our list of challengers, Wonder Woman stands apart from other heroes not just because she's a woman, but because her inspiration is to fight war and evil, guided by wisdom and love (Moulton and Peter, 1942). Wonder Woman brings a civilizing touch to the world of mostly male superheroes. But don't be fooled, Wonder Woman is a force to be reckoned with. She has incredible strength, and in the mid-1980s she ditched her invisible jet and was given the ability to fly. Her lasso works as a truth detector that demands whoever is bound by it to reveal their deepest, darkest secrets.[2] Wonder Woman's biggest limitation for being the greatest is the fickle nature of her writers. The Amazon pincess's history is filled with retcons that are utterly bizarre. The most distressing of these was the silver age decision to have Diana Prince give up her powers to remain in the world of men, where she opened a boutique and attempted to become a fashionista. A wizened mentor appears to train her in martial arts, and she enters the world of espionage as a non-powered, super-secret, super spy. Still, Wonder Woman has a lot going for her, especially these days as she is depicted as the direct descendent of Zeus. Her philosophy that love conquers all makes her mission of peace believable, until she punches your lights out.

Right Makes Might

Staying on the philosophical road for a little while longer, the great heroes are guided by an unquestionable pursuit of right. Brenzel (2008) notes that "to be a plausible character at all, the super-powered individual must *choose* to be good, and must go on being good in some broadly recognizable way" (p. 149). This is manifested in an exchange between Spider-Man and the Green Goblin. Goblin asks Spider-Man why he bothers trying to protect people who hate him. The reply is that it is the right thing to do (*Spider-Man 2*, 2002).[3] While a reluctant hero might make for an interesting storyline, constantly dragging someone out of their self-imposed exile can get exhausting. Similarly, the anti-hero has a niche in the comics, but because their integrity, or lack thereof, borders on the profane, they can't be part of the pantheon of greatness. To bring our analysis into focus, we need to examine the motivations of heroes a little more carefully. What drives them to do good in the first place?

Layman (2008) suggests that one reason to be good is to avoid unintended consequences. Henry Hazlitt (1979) emphasizes the unintended consequences of actions, particularly when policy goes amok, in his classic work *Economics in One Lesson*. Policies are designed to change people's behavior. Consider a policy that almost everyone agrees on: People who work hard deserve a fair wage. To some, that translates as a higher minimum wage. The problem is that if the minimum wage is raised to a high enough level, it provides an incentive to business owners to consider alternatives to labor. A very low minimum wage can be increased without having much of an impact on how many workers get hired. This is because a negligible mandated wage is likely to be below the wage set by the market. However, if the payment to workers is forced up by fiat, then options that were not previously cost-effective to employers become so. Self-serve kiosks at restaurants allow patrons to order off of a digital menu and then use their credit card for payment. This eliminates the need for an employee to run the register. That's one fewer worker the store needs to pay. Other workers may lose hours because the kiosk doesn't need a break (or benefits). Now, because the wage is artificially set higher than what the market can bear, fewer workers are employed. Thus, the unintended consequence might be that while wages go up, there are not as many people working. Even more nefarious though, the unintended consequence may be that young workers have fewer entry-level job opportunities and find it more difficult to gain the valuable work experience that will allow them to be hired for better paying jobs in the future. This isn't the intention of legislators who pass higher minimum wages, but it is something that should be considered when a wage hike is being debated.

In the comics, unintended consequences happen frequently. Sometimes they occur because heroes are standing up for what they believe in. In Marvel's *Civil War* (Millar and McNiven, 2009), the fighting hero teams end up killing Goliath. The fighting wasn't supposed to kill anyone, but in his zeal to win Tony Stark didn't have full control of some of his technology. Other times, unintended consequences reveal themselves when you don't do what you can to stop crime. In a fit of selfishness, the criminal goes free and someone you love dies. Just ask Peter Parker about this. In these two circumstances, being good would have avoided the undesired results, and in both cases Parker ends up in the middle. Gripped by remorse, Parker assumes the mantle of Spider-Man to help people. Gripped by determination not to lose to Captain America, Tony Stark enlists criminals to help his cause and nearly kills Peter Parker.

Waid (2008) provides what might be the best insight for understanding hero motivation. While his focus is on Superman, this could apply to any hero. By being heroic, Superman is *"acting in his own self-interest"* (p. 10). Regardless of why they do it, superheroes receive an internal benefit from saving the day beyond any gratification the public might bestow. They do it because it is part of their being and to not act heroically would yield less happiness. This idea of self-interest underpins all motivations for economic activity. Adam Smith notes in *Wealth of Nations* that "It is not from the benevolence of the butcher, the brewer, or the baker, that we expect our dinner, but from their regard to their own interest" (Smith, 1994, p. 15). That doesn't mean that the butcher is a bad guy, although he might be. What it means is that the reason the butcher is in business is because it allows him to provide for himself and his family. It is in his self-interest to provide a quality product at a fair price. If he doesn't then the consumer will go elsewhere and the butcher will be out of business, which is not in his self-interest. Being good is its own incentive. If they are good, the hero derives more satisfaction from their actions.

Utility Assemble!

Satisfaction or happiness can be difficult to attain, but it is even more difficult to measure. While utility means happiness, because we live in a world beset by scarcity we can't have unlimited happiness. We haven't yet talked about how happiness is restricted, and make no mistake, it is restricted. Limits on happiness are typically examined through the prism of a constraint. For example, having a beachfront house might make you happy (increasing your utility), but unless you are able to pay for it you aren't going to be able to buy the house. Income is a constraint. It limits the level of utility you can reach. While heroes have abilities that allow them to accomplish great feats, even heroes are limited. As noted in Chapter 5, heroes need an income so they find a job.

Additionally, there are some things a hero just cannot do. Sometimes this manifests itself in a power a hero doesn't have. Deadpool can't fly, and perhaps that is a good thing, but if he could fly, some of the crazy things he does, such as throwing himself off a bridge to follow a criminal, wouldn't have the same impact (no pun intended). The lack of flight inhibits his superhero work. Similarly, those non-powered superheroes—Batman, Green Arrow, Hawkeye, Iron Man, et al.—are prevented from achieving levels of proficiency because they don't have powers. It is these constraints that keep some heroes from being as great as others. And of course, no hero has unlimited time.

Because superheroes are incentivized by being good, we can develop a set of utility curves for them and perhaps answer the question motivating this chapter. Utility curves are graphical representations of happiness. Faced with a budget constraint, meaning you can't have all of everything that you would like, we must make choices—that's why most of us live where we do, rather than on a beach. A utility curve represents all the potential combinations of two goods you could acquire that would make you equally well-off.

Right away you have probably identified a problem. Are we talking about the two goods again? Why only two? This is to make the analysis simple. Remember the multiple dimension problem of illustrating a production possibilities curve from Chapter 8? It applies here, too. You can make the category of goods as broad as you like though, so this isn't that restricting of an assumption.

Another thing to note about utility curves is that there are lots of them and they never cross. Any level of utility will have its own curve but they must remain parallel. For the mathematically inclined, this involves the notion of transitivity. If A equals B, and B equals C, then A must equal C. A combination of goods identified by point A can only yield the same utility as that at point C if the lines cross at point B, and that is a big no-no for utility curves.[4] The problem here is that A should never equal C because A can be a combination where you have more of both goods, and C a package where you have less of both goods. Those two things cannot be equivalent.

Finally, the most preferred utility curve is the highest one you can reach. As you will see in Figures 10.1 and 10.2 below, the higher the curve, the happier you are. This means that you are getting more of what you want. Regrettably, getting to that highest curve may not be possible because of the constraints the actors face. For you that might be income, for heroes that constraint is going to be their powers.[5]

To build a utility curve we first need to determine what the two goods will be. For heroes, I am going to broadly define these as hero work and a personal life. The hero would love to have a better personal life, that is to be further to the right on the horizontal axis; however, given a predilection to heroic deeds, a hero won't trade crime-fighting for peaceful evenings on the couch. We see this inherent behavior in the comics all the time. Peter Parker and Mary Jane's marriage is falling apart because Peter just can't quit being Spider-Man (Mackie and Byrne, 1999). Storm's involvement in the X-Men places a significant strain on her marriage to Black Panther, which ends in separation (Aaron and Kubert, 2012). Tony Stark's assistant, Pepper Potts, marries Stark's bodyguard (whose name is Happy but that's just ridiculous so I won't mention it). Happy (whoops I mentioned it anyway) is punch-drunk on being the stand-in for Iron Man, so he isn't the supportive husband Pepper had hoped for. They divorce and try to reconcile but Happy eventually dies from injuries sustained while fighting the Spymaster (Knauf, Knauf, and Zircher, 2007).

Because of the obsession with saving the day, the utility curves for a typical superhero are flat, as shown in Figure 10.1 below. This means that at any given level of good deeds, no personal life is as satisfying as a great personal life. The curves are mapped upwards, so that the preferred line is higher regardless of how much of a personal life is possible. U2 is preferred to U1, and U3 is preferred to U2. Notice, the curves never cross. This outcome indicates that the hero will give up a spectacular personal life if it results in more hero work. Point A on utility curve U1 is less preferable than point B on utility curve U2, even though B includes no

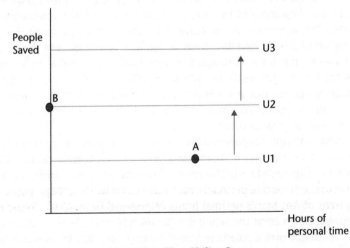

Figure 10.1. Hero Utility Curves.

personal life, because heroes derive more utility from hero work than anything else.

The only real issue now is upon which utility curve the hero finds themself. They want to be on the highest one, in the graph that would be U3, but that is dependent upon the constraint. Once we have that constraint in place, we will be able to determine the utility curve and the optimal amount of a personal life they should have. And most importantly, we will be able to identify the best hero.

Normally, the constraint facing an economic actor is their budget; however, in the case of heroes, the constraint will be physical. Heroes want to do as much as they can, yet their ability to do so is subject to some physical limitations. Most heroes must recover at some point. They need to eat, sleep, and heal. Even characters with rapid healing powers, such as Wolverine and Deadpool, need a little time to recover now and then. After all, stab wounds and bullet holes don't repair themselves instantaneously. To determine the optimum point at which the hero reaches the highest utility curve, we locate where the constraint just touches—or is tangent to—one of the utility curves. Now we have an answer to the question of "who is the greatest superhero." The answer is "whoever can reach the highest utility curve taking into account their physical constraints."

Figure 10.2 compares two heroes: Superman and Ant-Man. Even though he has some great tech to work with, Ant-Man has far more physical limitations than the Man of Steel. His main ability is to shrink, and while that's pretty cool, it does hinder the extent of his work. As a result, his optimum point occurs on utility curve U2, as shown by the white dot. Superman faces fewer physical strictures, and as a result he reaches U3, as shown by the black dot. Superman's constraint shown in Figure 10.2 is labeled SM, while Ant-Man's is labeled AM. Based on this we can reach the conclusion that Superman is a better hero than Ant-Man. Sure, heroes have abilities that allow them to accomplish prodigious deeds, but at some point even heroes are limited. There are just some things a hero cannot do. Those constraints keep some heroes from being as great as others.

Superman's optimal personal life involves more downtime, presumably with Lois Lane and his son, than Ant-Man's. This is identified by dropping from the tangency of his utility curve and ability constraint, the black dot, down to the "Hours of personal time" axis, which lands at SM_{PT}. This is to the right of Ant-Man's optimal hours of personal time, AM_{PT}, found by dropping down from the white dot. Supes' ability to discern true emergencies might play a role here. Also, the original Ant-Man had a lot of issues, including being an abusive husband (Shooter and Hall, 1981).

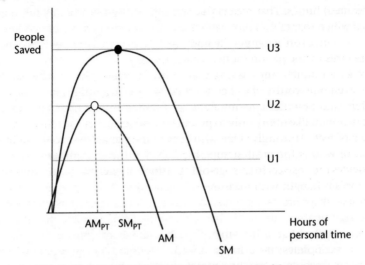

Figure 10.2. Optimal Hero Work for Ant-Man and Superman.

Perhaps Hank Pym, Ant-Man's alter ego, never destined to be a great hero, is also so troubled that he would never achieve a great personal life.

And the Winner Is???

So, who is it? Which hero is the greatest of all? Well, it probably isn't Ant-Man. But that isn't the real question, is it? Why was Ant-Man involved in the first place? Shouldn't the comparison have been between Superman and Thor or Wonder Woman? Here's the problem. There is one significant shortcoming with the utility analysis. Like comics, utility is a fabrication. It is a figment of an economist's imagination. Let me explain. Economists are fond of saying you cannot make interpersonal utility comparisons. In other words, there isn't a universally accepted scale for how many utility points you get from eating an ice cream, or reading a comic book, or saving someone from a burning building. The concept of trying to measure such a thing is almost as preposterous as Spider-Man's *Clone Saga*. How you measure happiness won't ever compare to how I measure it. The only real thing we can say when comparing utility is that something makes you happier or less happy, not by how much or how that change in happiness improves your life relative to mine. Regardless of how economists have tried to measure utility, there is no firm and fast rule on how much joy each util (remember, this is the way utility is measured) brings. That means that while this is certainly a helpful tool with which to establish motivations and whether to increase or decrease the amount of an activity—like how much hero work to do—we have to apply this to one person (or hero) at a time.

Wait a minute! Am I saying that utility curves are just a ruse—and not even one worthy of a cheesy 1960s villain? This sounds like a ploy. What kind of writer puts his audience through the idiosyncrasies of a crazy notion like utility only to pull the rug out from beneath their loyal readers' feet? Truthfully? One who doesn't have an answer to the question of who is the greatest superhero. Do I think that utility analysis provides the answers to this age-old question? Actually, I do. Sure, utility analysis is fraught with measurement issues, but it does provide a valid framework for breaching such a debate, and it is at least as legitimate as the arguments made at the bar, although I would suggest you don't actually talk about utility when debating superhero greatness at a bar. While economics has a lot to offer in terms of understanding what motivates people, even when those people are wearing capes and spandex, it isn't always well-received.

Nevertheless, as we have seen in the preceding nine chapters, many of the curious questions that arise in comics have an ancillary in economics. But economics is not perfect, just as our comic heroes are not perfect. In the case of heroes, the flaws they exhibit make them more human. Understanding the flaws in economic analysis might make economists more human as well. As social scientists, economists try to understand the choices that people make, the career paths they follow, why they fight, or what causes them to don the masks they hide behind. While this is a noble effort, it should not be undertaken lightly. In the real world, economists are often thought of as possessing considerable powers, yet, as in the comics, those powers can be used for good or for evil. By pulling on a cape and exploring fictional worlds, we may begin to see far more similarities between what is imaginary and what is real, and that can lead us to a more complete understanding of what makes our world tick, which might just help us wield those economic powers with considerably more responsibility.

Endnotes

1. At least this is the presumption. Kenneth Arrow (guess what? That's right. He's a Nobel Prize winner, and sadly he will be the last one mentioned in this book), among others, has championed the competitive market, casting monopolies as he who should not be named. Others aren't so sure monopoly is the great evil. Most famously, Joseph Schumpeter (1942) said that non-regulated

monopolies would result in at least as much innovation as a competitive market, if for no other reason than they wanted to maintain their monopolies. The debate goes on regarding the validity of these positions, and alas, the empirical evidence is not clear for either position. Blundell, Griffith, and van Reenen (1999) and Etro (2004) provide interesting analyses of this question.

2. Although if you're crazy you may not know the truth, or even comprehend the meaning of the question Wonder Woman is asking you, in which case your insanity plea not only holds up in a court of law but it makes the lasso moot.

3. Yes, this is a line from a movie, but it makes the point.

4. If you remember the movie *Ghostbusters* (1984), the idea of never crossing the streams emanating from their ghost-busting proton packs is a regular shtick. Why not? According to Egon, to understand what would happen if you crossed the streams "Try to imagine all life as you know it stopping instantaneously and every molecule in your body exploding at the speed of light." That isn't going to happen if you cross utility curves, at least we don't think so.

5. The constraint could also be their willingness to dominate.

References

Aaron, J. and Kubert, A. (2012). *Avengers vs. X-Men*, #9. Marvel Comics.

Blundell, R., Griffith, R., and van Reenen, J. (1999). Market Share, Market Value and Innovation in a Panel of British Manufacturing Firms. *Review of Economic Studies*, 66(3), pp. 529–54.

Brenzel, J. (2008). Why Are Superheroes Good? Comics and the Ring of Gyges. In: T. Morris and M. Morris (Eds.), *Superheroes and Philosophy: Truth, Justice, and the Socratic Way*. 1st ed. Chicago: Open Court, pp. 147–60.

Dini, P. and Ross, A. (1998). *Peace on Earth*. New York: DC Comics.

Etro, F. (2004). Innovation by Leaders. *The Economic Journal*, 114(495), pp. 281–303.

Ghostbusters. (1984). [Film]. New York: Ivan Reitman.

Hazlitt, H. (1979). *Economics in One Lesson*. New York: Three Rivers Press (Originally published in 1946).

Knauf, D., Knauf, C., and Zircher, P. (2007). *Iron Man*, #14. Marvel Comics.

Layman, C. (2008). Why be a superhero? Why be moral? In: T. Morris and M. Morris (Eds.), *Superheroes and Philosophy: Truth, Justice, and the Socratic Way*. 1st ed. Chicago, IL: Open Court, pp. 194–206.

Lee, S. and Kirby, J. (1968). *Thor*, #159. Marvel Comics.

Loeb, J. and Sale, T. (1999). *Superman: For All Seasons*. DC Comics.

Mackie, H. and Byrne, J. (1999). *The Amazing Spider-Man*, #12. Marvel Comics.

Millar, M. and McNiven, S. (2007). *Civil War*. Marvel Comics.

Moulton, C. and Peter, H. (1942). *Wonder Woman*, #1. DC Comics.

Percy, B. and Ferreyra, J. (2017). *Green Arrow*, #28. DC Comics.

Schumpeter, J. (1942). *Capitalism, Socialism and Democracy*. New York: Harper Row.

Shooter, J. and Hall, B. (1981). *The Avengers*, #213. Marvel Comics.

Smith, A. (1994). *An Inquiry into the Nature and Causes of the Wealth of Nations.* New York: Random House (Originally published in 1776).

Spider-Man 2. (2002). [Film]. New York: Sam Raimi.

Waid, M. (2008). The real truth about Superman: And the rest of us too. In: T. Morris and M. Morris (Eds.), *Superheroes and Philosophy: Truth, Justice, and the Socratic Way.* 1st ed. Chicago, IL: Open Court, pp. 3–10.

Glossary

Absolute advantage: the ability of one producer to make a greater quantity of output than another producer given the same inputs.

Assumptions: limitations placed on models in order to make the model more useful.

Asymmetric information: a disparity of information between parties engaged in an exchange.

Black market: a type of market where either illegal goods and services are sold, goods and services are sold at illegal prices, or sales are designed to avoid government notice.

Capital: the input that represents man-made inputs such as tools and machinery.

Capitalism system: an economic system that relies upon markets to answer questions about what to produce, how to produce, and for whom to produce.

Catallactics: the study of how we get what we want.

Classical production function: a production function that only requires the inputs of labor and capital.

Command system: an economic system that relies upon government to answer questions about what to produce, how to produce, and for whom to produce.

Comparative advantage: the situation that occurs when one economic actor can produce output at a lower opportunity cost than another.

Competitive market: a market that is characterized by many sellers and buyers each facing a price determined outside of their control. Firms in this market structure cannot earn long-term profit due to easy entry into the market by other firms.

Consumer sovereignty: the idea that producers must provide consumers what they want, otherwise consumers will shop elsewhere and the producer will fail.

Consumption bundle: the combination of goods a consumer can acquire.

Costs: what is given up when a choice must be made; the dollar amount paid by a firm to produce an output.

Dead weight loss: the reduction in well-being that occurs in a market that does not produce the amount of goods or services that are generated in a competitive market.

Demand: the combinations of prices and quantities buyers are willing and able to buy at different prices.

Direct incentives: an incentive where the reward or penalty for engaging in a particular action is obvious.

Dominant strategy: a strategy that yields the highest payoff for a player regardless of what the other player or players do.

Economic growth: the increase in the productive capacities of an economic agent. This is usually considered in terms of the output of a nation as measured by an increase in gross domestic product.

Economic systems: the way economies are set up to answer what to produce, how to produce, and for whom to produce.

Elastic demand: when a change in price results in a percentage change in the quantity demanded that is greater than the percentage change in price.

Entrepreneurship: the risk-taking, organizing talent that coordinates inputs into a final product.

Free market economy: an economy characterized by minimal government involvement, in which prices are set by the interaction of willing buyers and sellers.

Free-rider problem: when a consumer receives a benefit without having to pay for it. Because of the nature of the good or service, it is difficult to force the free-rider to pay.

Game theory matrix: a grid that provides the potential payouts for the players in all possible strategy combinations.

Game theory: a mathematical application to economic decision-making where strategic behaviors affect the outcome for those involved in the game.

Human capital: the skill, education, experience, or other non-tangible attributes a person brings to a task.

Incentives: forces that motivate people to act in a particular way.

Indirect incentives: the unintended result of an incentive.

Inelastic demand: when a change in price results in a percentage change in the quantity demanded that is less than the percentage change in price.

Infinite monkey theorem: the idea that given enough monkeys, enough keyboards, and an unlimited amount of time, monkeys could randomly reconstruct great works of literature.

Institutions: the social, political, and economic rules that govern society.

Interdependent: when the outcome of a game or other situation depends on not only your choices, but the choices of other actors.

Internalizing the externality: when an economic actor considers the costs they impose on others (or the benefits they generate to others) in their decision-making.

Invisible hand: a theory that suggests buyers and sellers are brought together and prices set, not by a conscious guiding mechanism, but by forces that work for the best interest of both parties.

Labor: the input that represents the human component of production.

Land: the input that represents natural resources.

Law of demand: the rule that says if price goes up or down, the quantity demanded will move in the opposite direction. This forms an inverse relationship between the two variables.

Lemons problem: a circumstance where, due to asymmetric information, the quality of a good or service brought to market tends to decrease.

Macroeconomics: the division of economics which focuses on the overall workings of an economy.

Market structure: the way the firms in a market compare with each other.

Microeconomics: the division of economics which focuses on smaller decision-makers such as individuals or firms.

Models: the tools an economist uses to form predictions about economic outcomes or to illustrate the workings of economic actors.

Monopolist: someone who runs a monopoly. They are the only seller of a good in a market.

Moral hazard: a phenomenon that occurs when people change their behavior based on the amount of risk they are exposed to. When risk is removed, they act in very different ways than if they had to bear the full burden of the risk.

Multiple stage game: a game where players have the chance to react to the strategies adopted by the other players in a game.

Natural monopoly: a firm who gains a monopoly because of scale. The larger they are, the lower their average cost of production.

Negative externality: when a market activity causes harm to a third party.

Negative incentives: a penalty or punishment designed to make a choice unattractive.

No such thing as a free lunch: a saying that means even if you do not pay for something, it is not free because making any decision, even to go out to lunch when someone else buys, involves opportunity costs.

Non-excludability: when it is impossible to keep someone from using a good or service even if they do not pay for it.

Non-rival: when the enjoyment of a good or service is not impeded by others using the same good or service.

One-stage game: a game where players make their moves only once.

Opportunity cost: the next best option that must be given up when a choice is made.

Peltzman effect: the way people tend to behave in a riskier fashion when safety regulations are put in place.

Positive externality: when a market activity generates benefits for a third party.

Positive incentives: a payout or reward designed to make a choice attractive.

Price: the monetized amount paid for a final product by the buyer and received by the seller.

Price mechanism: the interaction of supply and demand that yields a market price. This price is used to allocate goods and services.

Prisoner's dilemma: a game where the players' strategies result in a suboptimal result for both players.

Production function: a mathematical relationship that indicates how inputs are combined to produce outputs.

Production possibilities curve: a curve that illustrates various output combinations an economic entity can produce.

Productivity: how effective an input is at producing output.

Public goods: goods that are both non-excludable and non-rival in consumption.

Randomization: a strategy whereby the player adopting it tries to move in an unpredictable manner.

Rational ignorance: when decision-makers do not collect all of the information they need to make a choice due to the high cost of becoming informed.

Reasonable care: a legal expectation that says people are negligent if they do not take the precautions that a reasonable person would take in a given situation.

Scarcity: the condition that exists when there is not enough of a good for all people to have as much as they would like.

Sequential game: a game where players take turns reacting to the strategies of the other players.

Simultaneous game: a game where all players apply their strategies at the same time.

Specialization: breaking down a task into small parts so that a particular input, usually labor, can perform that task proficiently. Usually linked to the division of labor.

Strategies: the course of action a player takes in a game.

Sunk cost: a cost that once paid cannot be recovered.

Sunk cost fallacy: the belief that sunk costs can be recovered. This leads to making inefficient decisions.

Supply: the combinations of prices and quantities sellers are willing and able to produce at different prices.

Third-party problem: a circumstance where an unrelated party either bears costs or receives benefits from the actions of others. As a result, they are burdened by such actions or receive benefits for which they do not pay.

Tournament theory: a way of explaining the large differences in wages in a winner-take-all situation, such as CEO pay or winning a contest.

Transaction cost: the costs involved in carrying out a transaction. These are above the dollar price paid for a good and include things such as the cost of negotiation or transportation.

Transitivity: a mathematical property that says that if a particular relationship holds between options A and B, and between options B and C, it necessarily must hold between options A and C.

Unintended consequences: when the results of a choice or policy are not what was expected or desired.

Util: the measure of a single unit of utility.

Utility: how much happiness or satisfaction a person gains from an activity.

Utility curves: lines that illustrate various consumption bundles that yield the same level of utility.

Winner-take-all game: a game where the winner captures the entire prize.

Index

Index